REVISING THE BLUEPRINT

REVISING THE
BLUEPRINT

*Ann Petry
and the
Literary Left*

EDITED BY ALEX LUBIN

UNIVERSITY PRESS OF MISSISSIPPI
Jackson

www.upress.state.ms.us

Margaret Walker Alexander Series in African American Studies

The University Press of Mississippi is a member of the
Association of American University Presses.

First edition 2007
∞
Library of Congress Cataloging-in-Publication

Revising the blueprint : Ann Petry and the literary left / edited by
Alex Lubin. — 1st ed.
  p. cm.—(Margaret Walker Alexander series in African American studies)
  Includes bibliographical references and index.
  ISBN-13: 978-1-57806-971-2 (alk. paper)
  ISBN-10: 1-57806-971-8 (alk. paper)
  1. Petry, Ann Lane, 1911– —Criticism and interpretation.   2. Petry,
Ann Lane, 1911– —Political and social views.   3. Right and left (Political
science) in literature.   4. Race in literature.   5. Class consciousness in
literature.   6. Sex role in literature.   7. African Americans in literature.
8. African American women in literature.   I. Lubin, Alex.
  PS3531.E933Z86 2007
  813'.54—dc22

                                                        2007001527

British Library Cataloging-in-Publication Data available

CONTENTS

ACKNOWLEDGMENTS

As the editor of a collection of new essays, my role has been as an organizer. All credit for the work in this collection goes to the authors who spent considerable time engaging this literary conversation about how Ann Petry relates to the literary Left. I want to thank each of them for their contribution and for their willingness to work within the time limits and scholarly frameworks I established.

The University Press of Mississippi was the obvious choice to publish this collection. Not only does the press have an interest in Petry, as evidenced by its publication of Petry's family letters, it is also dedicated to publishing the works of African American writers who, like Petry, often fall outside the cannon. I want to thank the Editor, Seetha Srinivasan, for her patience with this project and for her commitment to publishing important scholarship in African American literature and culture.

Many of the authors in this collection draw on the Ann Petry Manuscript collection at Boston University. I want to thank the archivists at the Howard Gotleib Memorial library for making the Petry papers available to me and to other Petry scholars.

Special thanks to Kara McCormack for her help with putting the manuscript together. Margie Montanez and Elizabeth Swift also helped compile research on Petry many semesters ago.

One of the reasons I'm drawn to Petry is because of her interest in interrogating the fragile and often constructed bonds of racial and familial kinship. Her recognition that families and belonging are what we make of them reminds me of the important bonds linking me to Kelly, Eyob, and Solomon.

REVISING THE BLUEPRINT

INTRODUCTION

Alex Lubin

While writing her third novel, *The Narrows*, Ann Lane Petry wrote the following in her notebook:

> ... *Recently a debutante married colored nightclub singer ... the resultant publicity ... Walter White marries a white woman ... distances his colored wife of long standing by whom he has had two children. Paul Robeson [Jr.] marries a white girl ... story carried by every newspaper in the country ... all the white folk ask their colored friends about it. That's more or less inevitable when the social barriers are down ... there will be marriage. Why the alarm, the hysteria, the interference ... the public open interference in the forms of photographs, reporters, radio, everybody must know ... white men can marry Chinese, Indians, Japanese, etc. Let a Negro marry a white woman and the pack is in full cry.*[1]

The Narrows is a novel featuring an interracial romance between an African American veteran of World War Two and the white daughter of a wealthy munitions fortune. Like many writers in the postwar years, Petry focused on themes of interracial intimacy in order to link contemporary postwar racial and sexual politics to historical legacies of racial and sexual violence.[2] Yet what may be less apparent in this passage is Petry's fascination with tabloid news and the ways various popular cultural forms represent interracial intimacy. She was interested in a variety of forms of "publicity," including, newspapers, photographs, radio; everyone, Petry understood, must "know."

In this brief example from her personal notebook, we can see Petry's understanding of America's double standard when it comes to interracial intimacy; Americans sanctioned some interracial relationships, while scorning others. More importantly for our purposes, however, is Petry's engagement with popular forms of spectatorship and what scholars today might call the "white gaze." This gaze refers to the ways dominant cultural forms represent non-white people in order to control and manage popular perceptions. Petry was keenly aware of the link between mass cultural representations of African Americans and the daily forms of racial abuse and terror felt by Black people; hence her fiction made frequent reference to popular culture, tabloid news, and visual culture. Moreover, Petry was interested in how popular representations shaped African Americans' self-perceptions and behavior toward each other.

In her focus on popular culture, her interest in the "white gaze," and her astute analysis of how dominant cultural representations shaped African American privacy, Ann Petry crafted a radical critique of early Cold War America during a time when pre-WWII artistic forms were undergoing important changes. *Revising the Blueprint: Ann Petry and the Literary Left* collects new essays that examine the novels, short-fiction, and political non-fiction of Ann Lane Petry in order to locate her in the postwar left while also posing new frameworks for identifying the left. Petry's use of literary tropes outside the framework of social realism—popular culture and noir, just to name two examples—suggest new frameworks for understanding what has come to be known as African American protest writing in the postwar years. *Revising the Blueprint* suggests an expanded understanding of the post-World War Two left by considering what Michael Denning has called, "the politics of form" and by examining the literary aesthetics that informed many post-war radical artists and writers.[3]

The title of this collection obviously draws on the "blueprint" for African American protest writing defined by Richard Wright. In 1938 Wright articulated a vision for Black protest literature in his seminal essay "Blueprint for Negro Writing."[4] Wright advocated a form of social realism that could shed light on the plight of the black proletariat through a Marxist analytical lens. "Blueprint" became paradigmatic and helped shape the cannon of African American protest writing and what some scholars would call the African American "literary Left."[5] The literary Left of which Wright was an early member constituted a loose network of Black writers who used a variety of literary tools in order to illuminate, as well as criticize, racial inequality in the U.S. Although there had been radical African American writers for as long as Blacks published, the African American literary Left formed some cohesive, if even imaginary, bonds in the cultural milieu of the 1920s and 1930s that helped sustain the Communist Party USA (CPUSA) as well as what would become the Popular Front. While the CPUSA articulated a critique of racism in the United States, a wide range of visual, literary, theatrical, and musical artists—some communist and some not—participated in Popular Front social activism that viewed artistic and literary production as indispensable components of social movements.

The Popular Front constituted a diverse group of cultural producers who saw artistic production as labor, or cultural work. Aesthetically, therefore, the Popular Front was dedicated to representing the lives and struggles of the working class, and in some cases, African American life in America. It is beyond the scope of this introduction to chart the multiple trajectories of the Popular Front; yet for our purposes, it is important to note that the movement benefited from and, indeed, was shaped by the ascendancy of the inclusive labor union, the Congress of Industrial Organizing, that sought to create a "culture of unity" among working Americans as well as political mobilization on the part of the Communist Party USA that took special interest in the problem of race in America. CPUSA was committed to the "problem of the color line" and saw African American civil rights as central to working class protest. Some CP leaders, such as the African American member, Harry Haywood, argued that blacks were an oppressed nation within the United States, and he advocated black statehood as one possible remedy. The CPUSA's "Black Belt Thesis" helped link the class-based Marxism of the Popular Front to African American concerns about racism. The convergence of political movements such as CPUSA and the CIO, institutions such as the Works Progress Administration's Federal Arts Projects, and vibrant African American social moments created a moment of radical possibility. Within this milieu, a milieu described in more detail in this collection by Rachel Rubin and James Smethurst, many African American writers found their work respected and admired.

World War Two and the early years of the Cold War radically transformed the culture of the Popular Front. The postwar ascendancy of anticommunism severely limited the ability of radical institutions like CPUSA and the CIO to function in the same ways it had prior to the war. For its part, the leaders of the CIO promised to support the wartime effort by agreeing to a non-strike pledge. After the war, the CIO purged many suspected communists from its ranks in order to conform to postwar norms. In addition, global events such as the 1939 Hitler/Stalin non-aggression pact undermined the CPUSA's ability to organize African Americans. In the postwar years, many African Americans who during the 1930s had supported the CPUSA abandoned the movement, forming a variety of other socialist organizations. Richard Wright, for example, left the CP, as did Chester Himes, who wrote a scathing critique of communist organizers in his novel, *Lonely Crusade*.[6] Himes's protagonist, Lee Gordon, is a labor organizer who feels abandoned by black and white CP organizers who just do not understand that the "Negro problem," for black workers, is inseparable from the class struggle.

He challenges the CP-led unionization drive by telling African American workers, "The union could be very wonderful for Negroes if it first took into consideration that you can not have equality in the plant and inequality on the street" (140).

While it would be a mistake to underestimate the profound impact the postwar culture of anti-communism had on a wide range of artistic workers, it would also be a mistake to overlook radical critique that endured through the McCarthy years. Although the Popular Front waned as a result of various dominant cultural strategies of ideological and political containment many artists shifted their artistic commitments and aesthetic forms in order to continue their commitment to radical possibilities, but they did so in a way that was less visible and perhaps even under the radar. As Stacy Morgan argues in his study of African Americans social realism, after WWII a number of African American writers turned to alternative genres and artistic forms such as murals. Moreover, as Paula Rabinowitz argues in this collection and in *Black & White & Noir*, left writers sometimes turned to popular cultural forms like noir and pulp fiction as a means to develop their political critique through a narrative form less regulated than overt "protest" literature. And finally, some radical culture workers left the United States and formed what Rebecca Schreiber calls, a "political culture of exile" in places like Europe and Mexico.[7]

Although the 1940s and 1950s were indeed "lean years" in terms of the sorts of radical literary and social movements that were allowed to develop, it is important to recognize that a vibrant radical culture of African American left writing flourished during these decades. Writers such as Ann Petry, Willard Motley, William Gardner Smith, Chester Himes, Alice Childress, Lorraine Hansberry and many others used diverse literary styles and generic conventions to wage radical politics. Smith wrote in a journalistic mode to critique the wartime prohibition on interracial intimacy. Himes wrote social realism, but also turned to mystery writing as a means to explore American racial attitudes. Himes's final novel, *Plan B*, is a futuristic narrative in which a race war destroys all white people.[8] Motley, in an unpublished novel, wrote a travel narrative.[9]

Each of these writers, while employing genres not usually associated with protest, provide a critical lens through which to understand how the vibrant culture of African American artistic production that would emerge in the 1960s Black Arts Movement was made possible. Indeed, all of the essays in this collection make a case in some way for reading Ann Petry as an important link between the Popular Front and the Black Arts Movement. The point here is not to show an endless progression of left politics, but instead to show how a variety of material and political realities made possible, or even required, a new literary aesthetic that maintained certain Popular Front commitments while also revising them. In Petry, we are able to see how Marxist social realism could be infused with an analysis of black nationalism and black feminism in order to lay the groundwork for writers like Gloria Naylor and Toni Morrison. Moreover, Petry illustrates Michael Denning's contention that in the postwar years, popular culture was the medium of Popular Front aesthetics. While Petry remained committed to literary production, her literary aesthetic employed popular culture genres and her novels are each structured by contemporary popular culture. In this way, Petry is an important link between the social movements of the 1930s and those of the 1960s.

Ann Lane was born in 1908, in Old Saybrook, Connecticut. She earned a degree in pharmacy in 1931 from the Connecticut College of Pharmacy and worked as a registered pharmacist in the drugstores owned by her family in Old Saybrook and Lyme. In 1938 she married George David Petry, and moved to New York City where she decided to turn her passion for writing into a career. That year, under the pseudonym, Arnold Petri, she published her first short story, "Marie of the Cabin Club," in the Baltimore *Afro American*. During her early years in Harlem Petry joined the American Negro Theater. In 1940 she played Tillie Petunia in *On Striver's Row*. Her first position as a writer was in 1939 in the advertising department of the Harlem *Amsterdam News*. In 1941, Petry joined the staff of Harlem *People's Voice* and edited the women's pages and wrote news stories. The *People's Voice* (PV) was one of the most radical newspapers; it was edited by Adam Clayton Powell, Jr., and was an epicenter of left activity.

As editor of the women's pages at PV, Petry was a perceptive journalist, offering readers an account of day-to-day life in Harlem, as well as a critical view of the plight of African American female workers. She focused her attention on the lives of domestics and children. Her interest in the drama led her to write plays and to act in amateur theatricals. In 1943 Petry published "On Saturday the Siren Sounds at Noon" in the NAACP's *Crisis*. On the basis of this essay, in 1945 she was awarded a Houghton Mifflin Fellowship of $2400 that helped her publish her first novel, *The Street*, in 1946. *The Street* was one of the most successful novels written by an African American woman, selling over two million copies. The book focuses on the plight of Lutie Johnson, a single African-American mother attempting to support her son amidst the hardships of poverty, racism, and sexism. *The Street* poses the impossibility of the "American dream" for African American families whose lives are determined by the unseen forces of white supremacy.

Just one year after publication of *The Street*, Petry published *Country Place*. *Country Place* seemed like a radical departure from her first novel in that it was set in a mostly white New England community and its protagonists were white. Moreover, the novel employed the generic conventions of pulp fiction and not the sociological approach employed in *The Street*. Because of this, literary critics attacked the novel because it did not fit the "protest" genre critics imposed on "Negro writing" and seemed overly melodramatic. Because of the critical reception of *Country Place*, the novel remains an understudied text among scholars of literary radicalism.

In 1949, Petry gave birth to her daughter, Elisabeth Ann Petry and published her first children's book, *The Drugstore Cat*. In 1953, Petry published her third, and final, novel, *The Narrows*. Arguably, Petry's masterpiece, *The Narrows* focuses on an illicit interracial sexual affair between a WWII veteran, Link Williams, and the heiress to a local munitions faculty, Camila Treadway. The interracial sex plot is a means for Petry to explore historical legacies of slavery, interracial violence, and postwar American popular representations of African Americans. Moreover, in *The Narrows* Petry began to develop a critic of U.S. empire by showing how the expansionist goals of the nation, beginning with the enslavement of Africans, structured the U.S. homefront and, literally, its homes. In this way, Petry would articulate an anticolonial and black feminist critique that writers in the Black Arts Movement would develop even further.

After *The Narrows*, Petry turned to writing juvenile fiction. In 1955, Petry published *Harriet Tubman: Conductor on the Underground Railroad*. In 1964 she published *Tituba of Salem Village* and in 1970, *Legends of the Saints*. In 1971, Petry became the first African American women to publish a collection of stories in *Miss Murial and Other Stories*. The collection included many stories written during her early career, but it also includes some new essays that show Petry's interest in Black nationalism and feminism.

Unlike many of the better know writers on the left, Petry wasn't a working class writer and didn't come of age in a black community. If one were to attempt to place Petry in the left merely by listing the groups she joined, she would be disappointed. Although she supported many left groups and organizations, Petry disliked being affiliated with groups merely because she was black and wrote radical fiction. Her manuscript collection thus reveals a complex person who was frequently wary of how her fame could be used to confine her. Her personal letters reveal an ambivalent radical, someone who was wary of ideological labels and radical organizations.

For example, in June 10, 1942, Petry was angered that her name appeared as a supporter of the Negro Labor Victory Committee's conference. The

Committee was a biracial group of trade union officials that was organized to encourage black workers in the wartime struggle for equality within the government, organized labor, and the armed forces. Although each of Petry's novels engaged the plight of Black GIs and workers during WWII, she was insulted that the Negro Labor Victory Committee had listed her as a supporter without first asking. In a letter to Edward G. Guinier, Petry wrote,

I was very much amazed to discover that you had placed my name on your list of endorsers of the Negro Labor Victory Committee's mass meeting and conference. This is a rather high-handed proceeding in view of the fact that I had not endorsed the Committee as an individual nor had the People's Voice *unit authorized me as its chairman to endorse your organization. . . . I urge that you immediately remove my name from the literature that is being put out by your Committee.[10]*

Petry disliked the presumption that she would support the Negro Labor Victory Committee on the basis of her affiliation with the *People's Voice* and her race.

She was similarly dismissive of the Harlem Writer's Guild, a writing community that helped spawn the Black Arts Movement, because of its presumption that Petry would naturally join the group. Writing to Samuel Thompson, Petry wrote,

I am sorry that I can not accept honorary membership in the Harlem Writers Guild. I have made it a principle never to become a member of any organization unless it can take an active part in its program, and I live too far from New York City to be able to participate in the program and activities of this group. I am sorry, too, that I can not serve on the Board of Judges for your Awards Program. I would appreciate your removing my name from the list of persons invited to become Honorary Members because I have now declined the invitation.[11]

Her manuscript collection also contains a stinging letter to a Trinity College professor who sought to include Petry's "white life" novel *Country Place* in a list of novels about race. Again, Petry seems to have disliked the presumption that, as an African American writer, all of her novels were primarily about race. Petry wrote to Kenneth Reeves,

The following novels by black authors do not deal with racism in the United States: Baldwin, James GIOVANNNI'S ROOM, Motley, Willard, KNOCK ON ANY DOOR, Petry, Ann, COUNTRY PLACE, Yerby, Frank, THE VIXENS, FOXES OF HARROW, etc. Yerby is a black author who has written at least

20 novels—they have nothing to do with the ghetto or with the black experience. I am enclosing reviews of 2 new books. Don't you think that Cleaver's POST-PRISON WRITINGS AND SPEECHES sounds as though it would be more stimulating and more thought-provoking than Yerby's JUDAS, MY BROTHER?[12]

Of course, each of the novels Petry cites as "not about race" could be said to be about whiteness; yet more to the point, Petry was challenging the hegemony of one blueprint for black writing, mocking whites' insistence on the ghetto and "black experience" as the main tropes of the African American literary Left.

Moreover, in a little known 1950 essay, "The Novel as Social Criticism," Petry, like many famous African American writers before her, discussed her vision of the possibility of literary arts in a way that suggests her disdain for generic labels. In particular, Petry attempted to undermine critics' assumption that in order to be political, the novel had to be sociological. According to Petry, all great fiction was about individuals overcoming obstacles, and in this way, whether sociological or not, good literature was inherently political. Petry sought to locate her writing in a universal human condition of struggle rather than in the particular struggles of "the race." She therefore argued that all great writing was concerned with the fundamental biblical story of Cane and Able, of how to become "your brother's keeper." Moreover, Petry recognized the importance of Marx on all social criticism, while also arguing that, "Not all of the concern about the shortcomings of society originated with Marx. . . . Though part of the cultural heritage of all of us derives from Marx, whether we subscribe to Marxist theory or not, a larger portion of it stems from the Bible."[13] Here Petry creates a space for protest fiction outside of Marxism, and in this way, undermines anti-communist arguments about the left's use of Marx. Given how so-called African American protest fiction came under attack during the Cold War, Petry's focus on more universal claims about social problems and humanitarian brotherhood claimed a space outside of generic formulas.

Thus, while her refusals to join some left organizations, and her insistence that her work was more than Marxist, might make it difficult for the critic to locate her left credentials, I want to argue that these facts beg for new ways of locating the "left" in the early Cold War years. As Michael Denning has argued in his seminal work, *The Cultural Front*, the left was not always the "core members" but also its "fellow travelers." More importantly, however, Denning defines the left not in terms of members and non-members, but instead, in terms of a commitment to various aesthetic forms which themselves suggest a political commitment. Following Denning's argument, I want to suggest that we could profit by looking less to group membership and circles of friends, and more to what Denning calls "the politics of form" when discussing Petry's art. While her affiliation with the *People's Voice*, her membership in the Harlem Negro Theater, her participation in the South Bronx Slave Market, and much more suggest a political commitment to the organized left, there are as many criticism of the left in Petry's manuscript collections that also beg for alternative ways of understanding Petry's political commitments.

One of the central claims of this anthology is that Petry helps us understand the critical years of the early Cold War when the social and political movements understood as the Popular Front were in decline and the nascent politics of Black nationalism that would flourish in the 1960s Black Arts Movement were slowly growing. Moreover, in spanning a period in history when overt radical writing was censored and scorned, Petry relied on aesthetic forms that, on their face, do not necessarily conform to blueprints for radical fiction. For example, Petry focused on popular culture, on interracial intimacy, and on domestic melodramas. The use of these genres made some critics skeptical that Petry was part of a literary Left; yet as this collection shows, Petry's use of these narrative forms allowed for a radical critique of postwar society, one that anticipated the nationalist radicalism that would become important to the Black Arts Movement. Locating Petry in postwar literary, political and social movements helps give nuance to this critical moment in left and African American history.

Revising the Blueprint begins with "Ann Petry's 'New Mirror'" in which Rachel Rubin and James Smethurst argue for a reevaluation of Petry's fiction as a bridge between the Popular Front and the Black Arts Movement. They suggest that Petry, like many other African American left writers during the 1940s and 1950s, took up the Communist left's proposition that question of race was both about class and nation. Moreover, especially in her short fiction, Petry anticipated a black feminist consciousness and a nascent black nationalism that became important to the Black Arts Movement of the 1960s.

Next, in "Object Lessons: Fetishization and Class Consciousness in Ann Petry's *The Street*." Bill Mullen advocates a Marxist reading of Petry's most popular novel, *The Street*. Here Mullen's focus is on the ways Petry's novel uncovers the social relations that have historically contributed to the exploitation of laboring Black female bodies. Mullen shows that Petry's "naturalism" actually participates in a Marxist literary project of demystifying the commodity, which in this case refers to black women's labor.

Paula Rabinowitz's essay, "Pulping Ann Petry: The Case of *Country Place*" advocates a new reading of Petry's often disregarded second novel. In particular, by locating *Country Place* within the postwar culture of pulp fiction and film noir, Rabinowitz argues that Petry used these generic conventions in order to claim a space where she could talk about racial and class issues in a way that was "under the radar." While *Country Place* might therefore be overlooked when attempting to locate Petry in the left, Rabinowitz instead shows that the novel's politics were enacted through literary form. Moreover, Rabinowitz shows that many aspects of Petry's personal angst in the postwar years were expressed through pulp genres.

Rachel Peterson's essay, "Invisible Hands at Work: Domestic Service and Meritocracy in Ann Petry's Novels" reveals Petry's political commitment to Black women's labor as a generative site for discussing postwar racial, gender and class politics. By looking at Petry's engagement with domestic labor issues in Harlem, as well as the presence of domestic workers throughout Petry's novels and short fiction, Peterson illustrates how Petry engaged the political commitments of the Popular Front while also anticipating the black feminism and black nationalism of 1960s radical movements.

John Charles's essay, "The Home and The Street: The Dialectics of Racial Privacy in Ann Petry's Early Career," locates Petry's writing in the context of postwar domestic containment. Charles argues that Petry's focus on the dialectics of racial privacy was a means for Petry to contest the racial politics of domesticity in the postwar years. In this way, Charles shows Petry's engagement with black feminist politics. Moreover, he is able to locate *Country Place*, a novel that's often regarded as anomalous, within Petry's literary project of exposing the social relations that enable white domestic privacy.

Melina Vizcaíno-Alemán's essay exposes the transnational imaginary that structures Petry's last novel, *The Narrows*, and her civil-rights era short fiction. By showing how Petry's writing invokes the trans-Atlantic slave trade as a formative history of post-WWII race relations, Vizcaíno-Alemán illustrates Petry's anticipation of the Black Arts Movement's interest in anti-colonial struggles. Moreover, Vizcaíno-Alemán illustrates Petry's concern with the ways intra-racial dynamics, themselves highly gendered, delimit black women's participation in their communities and in radical politics.

Finally, in "Hunting Communists and Negroes in Ann Petry's *the Narrows*" Griffin both stakes a claim for Petry in a literary tradition of black feminist writers while also showing how the Cold War context of anti-communism shaped Petry's final novel *The Narrows*. Griffin attempts to recuperate

The Narrows from a view of protest literature that pits "the political" versus "the literary." *The Narrows*, Griffin shows, was both. Moreover, attending to the political and literary forms of the novel helps suggest new ways of representing a writer who spanned the Popular Front and Black Arts Movement.

Taken together these essays make an important claim about how to locate Petry in the Cold War literary Left. Petry's literary form represents a bridge between the Popular Front and the Black Arts Movement. Rubin and Smethurst, as well as Rabinowitz and Griffin, show how Petry crafted a response to the anti-communist years of the early Cold War. In many ways, Petry was able to maintain a radical project during the Cold War by focusing on the legacies of slavery on American life. In this way, each of her novels return, in some way, to slavery and its legacy on all Americans' lives. Vizcaíno-Alemán makes the important point that the interracial intimacy so central to much of Petry's fiction enforces silence on Petry's female characters that go back to slave relations.

In showing how Petry worked during the Cold War, the essays in this collection illustrate her Marxist literary aesthetic. Mullen, for example, argues that *The Street* should be read as a novel about commodity fetishism. Mullen argues Petry's "naturalism" was meant to reveal and demystify a nexus of social relations between oppressed workers and the objects they produced. Similarly, Rachel Peterson argues that Petry's novels and short fiction sought to uncover "invisible hands at work." Peterson identifies the persistence of domestic workers throughout Petry's non-fiction and fiction. John Charles also suggests that Petry's politics focused on shattering the norms of "racial privacy" that help hide exploitative labor relations and to maintain white racial privilege.

Finally, a number of the essays focus on Petry's interest in the deployment of popular culture, both as a means to explore dominant culture and to engage radical possibilities. Petry's post-WWII writing often focused on mass culture in order to show how Blacks were represented in the national imaginary and how various forms of spectatorship such as photographs and radio made privacy illusive for African Americans. Thus, as Rubin and Smethurst, as well as Vizcaíno-Alemán show, when the protagonist of Petry sort story, "Mother Africa" finally inspects the statue he has been worshiping as African, he realizes she is white. In this way the statue, Mother Africa, like Junto's night club in *The Street*, illustrates how visual and popular culture are inevitably structured by racial capitalism and white supremacy. Moreover, anticipating a future cohort of black feminists, Petry recognized that black women suffered most in the American alchemy of race and sex.

It is hoped that this collection sparks new interested in a range of African American writers who, for a variety of reasons have been left out of the literary Left cannon. *Revising the Blueprint* makes the case for a different framework for identifying radical fiction during the Cold War. Moreover, the collection makes a case for Ann Petry, with her revised blueprint, as an architect of radical possibilities.

ANN PETRY'S "NEW MIRROR"

Rachel Rubin and James Smethurst

Ann Petry's short fiction has received considerably less critical attention than has her novels—bafflingly so, to the authors of this essay. Yet the window it provides onto the literary politics of two different periods of African American cultural activity—the cluster of publication and discussion during what might be thought of as the extended Popular Front period from the late 1930s until the early 1950s, and the new ideas about politics and aesthetics brought forth during the Black Power era of the 1960s and 1970s—is unique and instructive. Furthermore, Petry's short stories (written between 1939 and 1971) remind us that the two periods are perhaps not so discrete after all. In this essay, we aim to demonstrate that Petry's short stories should be reappraised as an important bridge between the "Old Left" of the 1930s, 1940s, and 1950s (to which she was materially connected) and the Black Arts Movement (the inseparable artistic twin of Black Power). These stories also anticipate the vital strain of African American feminism that to a significant extent emerged from the Left end of the Black Arts/Black Power spectrum.

Petry's short fiction engages, revises, and critiques the major ideological and aesthetic concerns of the African American Left milieu from which it issued. Like other black writers in the 1940s and 1950s, such as Margaret Walker, Frank Marshall Davis, Richard Wright, Lloyd Brown, Langston Hughes, Gwendolyn Brooks, and Alice Childress, Petry takes up the proposition of the Communist Left that the question of race is in fact both a class question *and* a national question (in the sense of African Americans as a nationality or people), a proposition that was seen as central to social progress in the United States. Her short stories investigate Left notions of the folk that link folk culture to a truly proletarian national "Negro" culture (often in opposition to popular culture), notions that arose in the late 1920s and early 1930s and continued to exert considerable influence in the decades that followed. Petry's work also reflects (and reflects upon) the new and largely—though not exclusively—positive engagement with popular culture that marked the work of black artists during the Popular Front era. This engagement not only forced many artists to rethink the meaning and place of "popular" culture, but also to question the very categories of "high" culture and "folk" culture. In some cases, as in much of the work of Hughes during the period, these different sorts of culture exist on a sort of continuum even as notions of cultural appropriation and cultural authenticity trouble any simplistic acceptance of that continuum. In other cases, perhaps most famously in Wright's 1940 *Native Son*, the folk culture seems to be completely irrelevant to the needs of the younger black residents of urban ghettoes in the industrial North—though the popular culture that has replaced the folk culture is also viewed with considerable ambivalence. In yet others, such as the poetry of Sterling Brown and Margaret Walker, there is a continued sense of the folk culture of the South as the bedrock of African American people, North and South.

Petry attends to all these complexities in her evocatively-named story "The New Mirror" (1965), which through its title immediately summons up questions of representation and self-presentation. The protagonist, who is the unnamed teenaged daughter in the only black family in a small New York town (or, to be perfectly accurate, the only "admittedly black family," as there is another black family claiming to be Mohawk Indians) draws the strength she needs to deal with the white establishment from a family tale that reads like folklore. In the family story, her father's ancestors arrived in New York State on a Hudson River boat. As the boat maneuvered into position at the dock, the family patriarch became worried that it was reversing its course and heading back to New Jersey

The old bearded man who was my great-grandfather gave a cry—a trumpeting kind of cry—and took a long running leap off the boat and landed on the dock, hitting it with his cane and bellowing, "You ain't takin' us back now, you know! Throw that baby down to me! Throw that baby down to me!" . . . One of the Layens threw the baby down to the old man and he caught it. He glared up at the scowling deckhands and the staring people and shouted, "Ain't going to take us back now you know! We paid to get here. Ain't going to take us back now. Jump!" he roared. "All of you, jump!" (76)

This handed-down story is clearly polished by many fond retellings and is designed to invoke the familiar folk tale or "toast" about Shine leaping off the sinking Titanic with the words, "Get your ass in the water and swim like me." Much later in "The New Mirror," this lore enters the narrator's mind as she steels herself to place a difficult call to the police station without embarrassing her family in front of the white officers: "I looked at my dark brown hand and thought, Throw that baby down to me, you ain't going to take us back now, you know; all of us people with this dark skin must help hold the black island inviolate" (88).

In the same story, popular or mass culture, as opposed to the potentially empowering folk culture, is pictured as having costs and limitations for African Americans—particularly African American artists who choose to engage with it. The father has caught sight of himself in a new mirror and been seized by worry over what white people will see when he opens his mouth to sing in church. Abruptly, he has left the family and gone off to buy false teeth; since he had resisted this remedy for years, his daughter wonders why. The answer, she ultimately concludes, has to do with the power of popular culture's images to oppress and misrepresent:

I thought, Well, now, perhaps the reason my father hadn't wanted to replace his teeth was that one of the images of the black man that the white man carries around with him is of white teeth flashing in a black and grinning face. So my father went toothless to destroy that image. But then there is toothless old Uncle Tom, and my old black mammy with her head rag is toothless, too, and without teeth my father fitted that image of the black man, didn't he? (87)

Here, we are also reminded of the contradictions and burdens that have historically characterized African American involvement in mass culture: both the grinning "darky" of the minstrel tradition and the toothless "faithful old soul" of plantation tradition are popular cultural images with which the father—who, since his role as a singer is emphasized, operates as a stand in for the African American artist—must contend. Too, by pointing up these contradictions and burdens, Petry engages and at least partially critiques the dominant political and aesthetic vision of the Popular Front era, which proposed popular culture as an arena of struggle against fascism and for social progress, as well as invoking long-standing black cultural criticism about the sense forced on African Americans that one is, in the words of W. E. B. Du Bois's 1903 *The Souls of Black Folk*, "always looking at one's self through the eyes of others."[1] However, there is no way to opt out, no place outside of popular culture—so the father chooses a course that his daughter sees allowing him the most agency as individual and as the member of an oppressed people.

The years when Petry began her career as a writer were turbulent ones for the African American Left—and for the Left in the United States generally. One might mark the era as beginning with the dislocations caused by the

Soviet-German Non-Aggression Pact in 1939 and ending with the onset of the high Cold War, particularly after the failure of the Henry Wallace presidential campaign of 1948 and the resulting expulsion a year later of most of the Left-led unions in the Congress of Industrial Organizations (CIO), ostensibly over the issue of their support of Wallace, as well as with the first Smith Act indictments of Communist Party of the United States of America (CPUSA) leaders in 1949. The decade also saw the brief jailing of CPUSA General Secretary Earl Browder in 1940, the dissolution of the CPUSA in the Communist Political Association in 1944 and its reconstitution a year later, and much turmoil among African American and trade union CPUSA activists caused by a new Communist concentration on winning World War II after the German invasion of the Soviet Union and the Japanese attack on Pearl Harbor, a focus that many saw as putting the Communist's longstanding emphases on militant trade unionism and "Negro Liberation" on a backburner. The rapidly shifting internal and external political landscape of the CPUSA and the world Communist movement caused many disconcerting ideological shifts, but also the rapid changes in the political scene of the United States occasioned by lingering economic depression, hot war (and alliance with the Soviet Union), and growing Cold War.

The non-Communist Left, or what many have called the anti-Stalinist Left, also suffered many ruptures during the 1940s, despite the increasing prominence of such "anti-Stalinist" (if often formerly Communist) groups as the "New York Intellectuals" and such journals as *Partisan Review*. The Socialist Party continued a long decline as an organized political force, and as the main Trotskyist organization, the Socialist Workers Party (SWP) splintered into the SWP and the Workers Party, which was led by Max Schactman and included the important "Johnson-Forest" tendency led by the Trinidadian intellectual C. L. R. James (aka Johnson) and Raya Dunayevskaya (aka "Forest") that in various configurations would come to exert considerable influence over radical African American political thought. The Johnson-Forest group, too, moved in and out of both the SWP and WP during the 1940s before completely breaking with both in the 1950s.

However, despite the turbulence, shifts, debates, breaks, and repression, the 1940s were in many respects the highpoint of Old Left influence among African American artists and intellectuals. Building on a base created largely during the Popular Front era of the mid- and late-1930s, more high profile black Left cultural institutions were created during the 1940s and early 1950s than anytime before the 1960s. In fact, the persistence of these institutions into the 1950s (and beyond in a few cases) as well as the creation of new African

American Left groups, journals, newspapers, theaters, and so on in the post-World War II era, did much to create a cadre of black cultural activists who would help shape the growing Black Arts and Black Power movements in the 1960s. Also, as such scholars as Bill Mullen and Alan Wald have noted, in addition to the creation of Left arts institutions, the 1940s also saw a greatly increased Left impact on "mainstream" African American institutions, especially the black press, that in turn greatly marked African-American literature (and politics) in the 1940s and the 1950s (and the 1960s). In particular, the vision and activities of the Communist Left, despite various ideological zigs and zags, that saw the struggle of African Americans as both a national question and a class question, as a fight for both equality and self-determination, continued to make the CPUSA and its circles attractive to a large portion of a black intelligentsia shaped by the Great Depression, the struggle against a hyper-racist Nazism and Jim Crow in both its Southern and Northern variants. It was in this matrix of Left institutions, Left-influenced "mainstream" institutions, and black radical activists that Ann Petry came of intellectual and artistic age.

As long as there has been something that might be termed a "literary Left," African Americans have been part of it. Fenton Johnson, Claude McKay, and Jean Toomer, among others, were active participants in the so-called "Lyrical Left" and the new bohemia of *The Masses, Others, The Little Review, Poetry,* and *The Liberator,* of Chicago's Towertown and New York's Greenwich Village in the early twentieth century. In fact, the comparatively free intermingling of black and white artists and activists during a time of increasing segregation in the South and the North might be said to be a defining characteristic of this new bohemia with a distinct Left cast—a characteristic that became even more pronounced during the post-Bolshevik Revolution, Harlem Renaissance era of the 1920s and early 1930s during which a considerable portion of the leading writers of the Renaissance, including McKay, Toomer, Langston Hughes, Countee Cullen, Eric Walrond, George Schuyler, Gwendolyn Bennett, Dorothy West, and Alain Locke, joined in the campaigns and organizations, and published in the journals of the new Communist Left.[2] Still, both the number of black artists and intellectuals taking active part in the institutions of the literary Left and the sense of the centrality (as the Communists would say) of African American artists to Left notions of progressive or radical arts movements increased enormously during the 1930s. The Left in turn did much practically and ideologically to promote the production of black art during the Great Depression.

A full account of all the ways in which African American artists and intellectuals influenced the literary Left of the 1930s and in which the Left helped shape the production of African American art is beyond the scope of this essay. However, it is worth outlining some institutional and ideological aspects of the so-called "Third Period" and Popular Front eras of the Communist Left that Petry encountered upon her arrival in Harlem in the late 1930s and that would be of great consequence to black literature in the 1940s. During the "Third Period" of the late 1920s and early 1930s, the Communist Party of the United States of America (CPUSA) and the Communist International (Comintern) advanced the notion that African Americans in the South, particularly in the largely rural "Black Belt" where black people constituted the overwhelming majority of the population, were an oppressed nationality entitled to self-determination. This notion of self-determination included the right to form some sort of independent, federated, or autonomous state following the model of the former Russian Empire after the October Revolution from which independent nations (e.g., Finland), the federated republics of the Soviet Union, and autonomous regions were formed following this principle of national self-determination (whether or not these republics and regions had any true self-governance). The "Black Belt Thesis," as the Communist position became known, also declared African Americans in the urban North to be a "national minority" that should be integrated into civil society on the basis of full social equality.

Though the distinction between the Southern black nation and the national minority status in the North was quite significant in terms of how the Communist Left saw the final adjudication of the destiny of different black communities, both categories carried with them at least the implication that African Americans, both North and South, city and country, had a common history and common culture with its roots in the slave South. It also noted that black people, regardless of class, suffered from a common national oppression—though the fact that the black community was overwhelmingly composed of workers and small farmers was held to be an extremely significant factor in determining the character of and black resistance to that oppression. As a result, though there was resistance to the idea of officially all-black Party units (or "clubs," as they later came to be known), the CPUSA initiated various sorts of organizations, journals, and so on, devoted to the struggle against Jim Crow and for "Negro Liberation," such as the League of Struggle for Negro Rights and *The Negro Liberator.*

The Comintern, and subsequently the CPUSA, also posited this struggle against segregation and for liberation as a central task of the Communist movement in the United States, one with a dramatic impact on virtually all political work. The CPUSA pursued "Negro Liberation" and black civil rights with such vigor that the advocacy of social equality for African Americans, especially on the part of a white American, came to be seen as a telltale sign by which one could recognize a Communist—at least until the 1960s. Communists paid a particular attention to challenging the legal infrastructure of Jim Crow in the South, especially the criminal justice system as it intersected with the racist vigilantism of the Ku Klux Klan and other manifestations of mob violence. The most famous example of such challenges in the 1930s is undoubtedly the Left-led campaign in defense of the nine young black men accused of rape in the Scottsboro case. This focus on racism in the legal system, or what came to be known as "legalized lynchings," gained new intensity in the late 1940s and early 1950s through the efforts of the Left-led Civil Rights Congress. The CPUSA also vigorously undertook to cleanse what it termed "white chauvinism" from its own ranks.

When Ann Petry arrived in Harlem in 1938, the notion of a "Black Belt Republic" was somewhat downplayed by the CPUSA—though it was not dropped as an official position of the Party until the 1950s (and, in fact, underwent something of a renewal within CPUSA circles after World War II). Nonetheless, the sense of African Americans as a nation or people with a distinct history and culture continued to be a powerful strain in Popular Front politics and art. In fact, if anything, the Communist Left initiated even more (and larger, more successful) black organizations and institutions during the Popular Front years of the 1930s, such as the National Negro Congress and the Southern Negro Youth Congress—anticipating the establishment of similar organizations in the 1940s and early 1950s.

The Communist Left also pushed hard, and to a considerable extent successfully, for the inclusion of African Americans and in the union organizing drives of the CIO (making its slogan "Black and White Unite and Fight" practically ubiquitous) and in the various WPA arts projects, including the Federal Writers Project (FWP), the Federal Theatre Project, and the Federal Artists Project. The number of black writers, visual artists, and theater workers who found support in the various arts projects of the WPA was enormous, especially in those cities where the Left was strong, such as New York, Chicago, Detroit, and Cleveland. Thanks to these projects, for the first time in the history of the United States, large numbers of black artists were able to support themselves through their art while gaining valuable skills. The arts projects not only gave support to black artists and made public art and art training broadly available in many African American neighborhoods (at least in areas where the Left was strong), but also emphasized the collection, preservation, and presentation of African American folklore (including urban folklore), history, and expressive culture, like the Popular Front generally see-ing these materials as articulating the identity of a "Negro" people while see-ing that people as an essential part of a larger multicultural, multiethnic, and multiracial "American" nation.

There was also a considerable intersection between the WPA arts proj-ects, especially the FWP, and another set of institutions that provided support for black artists, the African American press. By the late 1930 and early 1940s, there was a pronounced pro-Popular Front strain in quite a few of the most important African American newspapers, including the *Chicago Defender*, the *Baltimore Afro-American*, the *Michigan Chronicle*, the *Boston Chronicle*, and the *California Eagle*. These papers brought together a pro-labor, anti-colonial Left internationalism and the black press's traditional focus on com-munity events (and even neighborhood gossip) and civil rights issues. Many black writers, such as Petry, Langston Hughes, Frank Marshall Davis, Robert Hayden, Melvin Tolson, and Richard Wright, gained much of their income from work in the African American or leftwing press in the late 1930s and early 1940s.

There is still a tendency to emphasize the disruptions to such Popular Front organizations as the League of American Writers, the National Negro Congress, and the Southern Negro Youth Congress caused by the Hitler-Stalin pact and the subsequent CPUSA ideological oscillations between an antiwar stance after the pact and a position of total support for war against the Axis powers after the Nazi invasion of the Soviet Union in June 1941 and the Japanese attack on Pearl Harbor less than three months later. Unquestionably, these shifts caused considerable disruption in the CPUSA and various Popular Front organizations, alienating some former support-ers and limiting the ability of the Communist Left to work with some non-Communist progressives, such as A. Phillip Randolph. However, though the pact caused uneasiness among some close black participants in the Popular Front, such as Langston Hughes and Frank Marshall Davis, relatively few actually dropped out of the CPUSA and its circles. In fact, one can argue that after an initial disruption, the influence of the Left on the African American community actually increased. One important marker of this new influ-ence was the successful strike and recognition of the CIO's United Automo-bile Workers (UAW) Local 600 at the Ford Rouge plant, which contained the largest number of black industrial workers of any work site in the United States (and perhaps the world) in the Spring of 1941. The UAW victory at the Rouge plant was unquestionably a result of the efforts of what might thought of as the extended Popular Front, making Local 600 a center of interracial

Left leadership (and ultimately opposition) within the UAW at least until the mid-1950s.

Once the United States directly entered World War II, this renewed Popular Front took on an even higher, if somewhat contradictory profile. It was contradictory because the Communist Left downplayed even more the Black Belt thesis and put the defeat of Fascism as the first order of political business. The CPUSA officially opposed the "Double V" campaign (victory over Jim Crow at home and victory over Fascism abroad) proposed by the *Pittsburgh Courier* in early 1942 because it did not designate winning the war against the Axis as the main task of the moment. It also had a critical relationship to the March on Washington for black civil rights and against racist discrimination proposed by A. Phillip Randolph later that year. Of course, part of the troubled relationship of the Communists to the March on Washington Movement (MOWM) did not simply come from a sense that such a march would undermine the war effort, but also Randolph's public comments that Communist support was not welcome—though he did not rule out the participation of individual Communists in MOWM (and, in fact, many black Communists did participate on one level or another). Certainly, some notable black artists and activists who had been CPUSA members or supporters, such as Richard Wright, Chester Himes, and Ralph Ellison, were alienated by what they perceived as the party's retreat on the "national question" and its willingness to sacrifice the interests of black people to the imperatives of Soviet foreign policy—though, as Barbara Foley has shown, Ellison's break with the CPUSA during the mid- and late-1940s was far more gradual than that of Wright.[3]

At the same time, the war and the fight against the extreme racism of the Nazis allowed the Communist Left to at least some extent revitalize older Popular Front organizations and to increase its ability to recruit African Americans and to build new Popular Front-style coalitions. Petry's Harlem was a particular center of such efforts, as older Popular Front organizations, such as the National Negro Congress, joined new groups spawned in the war years, such as the People's Committee, the Negro Labor Victory Committee, the American Negro Theatre (ANT), and Negro Women, Inc. Benjamin Davis, a well-known black CPUSA leader, was elected to the New York city council in 1943, replacing Adam Clayton Powell, Jr., who then worked closely with the Communists, after Powell moved on to run for the United States Congress. (Davis would be indicted under the Smith Act before he could finish his second term in 1949.) In the post-war years of the late 1940s and early 1950s, Left African American organizations and institutions, such as the Civil Rights Congress, the National Negro Labor Council, the Harlem Writers

Guild, *Freedom* newspaper, and Sojourners for Truth and Justice, continued to appear—though by the mid-1950s most of these groups and institutions had collapsed under the pressures of the Cold War.

Powell became the publisher of a new Harlem newspaper, *People's Voice*, at the beginning of 1942. Among the staff of the *People's Voice* were many black Communists or supporters of the CPUSA, most prominently the general manager Doxey Wilkerson and Marvel Cooke (a journalistic mentor to Petry whose title was "assistant managing editor," but who was in fact the paper's managing editor for its history). Though not a formal member of the staff, Benjamin Davis, too, had a great deal of influence on the editorial policies of the *People's Voice*.[4] In fact, one might say that the *People's Voice* became the newspaper of record for activities of the black Left in New York, covering not only the work of the Communist Left, but also the work of non- (and even anti-) Communist radicals, such as Randolph and MOWM. Black Left union leaders, of whom the National Maritime Union's (NMU) Ferdinand Smith was probably the most prominent in New York, became increasingly visible in this renewed Popular Front. Smith, an NMU vice president and open Communist who was deported to his native Jamaica in 1949, became a regular columnist in the *People's Voice*. While the Communist Left retreated in some respects from an emphasis on African Americans as a nation, African Americans were still seen as possessing a sort of double status, as a distinct "people" with a particular history and culture as an essential part of the "American people." This sort of balancing act between a black particularity and a participation in multi-racial, largely working class democratic formations that also had strong support in the intelligentsia was especially strong within the black Left and can been seen in the *People's Voice*'s statement of basic principles:

WE ARE MEN AND WOMEN OF THE PEOPLE. THE PEOPLE ARE OUR AND WE ARE THEIR. WE RESPECT NO AUTHORITY EXCEPT THEIR AUTHORITY. WE OBEY NO MANDATE EXCEPT THEIR MANDATE. WE LOOK TO NO ONE TO JUDGE US EXCEPT—THEY THE PEOPLE. We will at all times serve all people. Whether they be Jew or Gentile, black or white, Catholic or Protestant, theist or atheist, the people will be served. FOR OUR NEGRO PEOPLE WE SHALL AT ALL TIME GIVE NOT ONLY "THE LAST FULL MEASURE OF DEVOTION" BUT THE FIRST AS WELL.[5]

Here the paper draws a slippery, but significant distinction between an inclusive "people" and the particular, one might even say nationalist formulation of "OUR NEGRO PEOPLE," who will receive the paper's first and last devotion even as it attempts also to serve the broad democratic front against "Hitler abroad" and "Hitlerism at home" (a restatement of the "Double V" whatever the official "line" of the CPUSA). It also proclaims African Americans a "working class race," saying further that it will give its full support to the trade union movement (even as it will criticize that movement where it discriminates against black workers).

This period was the beginning the greatest public involvement of Paul Robeson with the Left in Harlem. Even local affiliates of organizations often thought of as anti-Communist, such as the Harlem NAACP and NAACP Youth Council, had strong Left currents within them and often joined with more openly Left organizations and individuals in campaigns against the Axis *and* racism during this period. Also, Socialists like Randolph and other activists of the non-Communist (and even "anti-Stalinist") Left in Harlem often maintained a public criticism of the CPUSA, but maintained a practical cooperation with groups and individuals associated with the Communist Left on many issues. In short, Harlem was a whirlwind of demonstrations, lectures, and meetings against racism in the armed forces, colonial oppression, lynching, police violence, segregation, racial discrimination in housing and employment, and poll taxes, and for a victorious war effort, including Soviet relief, in which liberals, such non-Communist leftists as the Amalgamated Clothing Workers' Dorothy (Dollie) Lowther Robinson, and such Communists or CPUSA supporters as Davis, Smith, Robeson, W. E. B. Du Bois, Vito Marcantonio, Audley ("Queen Mother") Moore, and Howard ("Stretch") Johnson joined. The neighborhood was also awash in concerts, poetry readings, plays, book parties, arts society gatherings, and so on, that were a part of this renewed Popular Front. Of course, separating arts events from political rallies and demonstrations is not really possible as attested by the June 1943 Negro Victory Rally at Madison Square Garden, where Robeson, the dancer Pearl Primus, the actor Canada Lee, and the musician and composer W. C. Handy performed in Langston Hughes's short play "For This We Fight."

Ann Petry placed herself in the center of this new Popular Front. She was among the founding staff of the *People's Voice*, following a stint at the *Amsterdam News* (where Marvel Cooke, too, had previously worked). There she performed a variety of tasks as columnist, reporter, editor, and so on. If the *People's Voice* was the paper of record of the new black Popular Front in Harlem, then Petry's column "The Lighter Side" was a whirlwind digest of how the political, cultural, and personal intersected in Harlem during the war that is essential reading for any scholar trying to understand that moment. Stylistically, it is a fascinating example of the engagement of Popular Front politics with mass culture. Petry adopts the style of a typical women-oriented "gossip column" familiar in both the black and "mainstream" press. However, among the births, birthdays, engagements, vacations, and breathless allusions to scandals, one finds a composite portrait of the rallies, art exhibits, fund-raising parties, plays, picket lines, conventions, meetings, electoral campaigns, and so on, going on in Harlem—and New York generally. Petry also demonstrated with Negro Women, Inc. (an organization she co-founded with Dorothy Lowther Robinson and Dunbar Apartments tenants leader Anna Moore) against discrimination in employment and racist portrayals of Harlem and African Americans in the "mainstream" press.[6] She studied art at the Harlem Community Art Center. She also acted in the ANT's "On Striver's Row," a play by one of the theater's founders and FTP veteran Abram Hill. She volunteered in the educational program of the Laundry Workers Joint Board (an affiliate of the Amalgamated Clothing Workers led by Dorothy Lowther Robinson).

Petry wrote much of her short fiction during this period; eight stories were written during the 1940s, with seven more following in the 1950s and 1960s, and two in 1971. This work shows the imprint of the cultural and political Left Harlem milieu that she tracked in her column. Indeed, sometimes concrete details or observations find their way into both Petry's reportage and her fiction. For instance, in 1949, Petry published a relatively lengthy piece in *Holiday* magazine called "Harlem."[7] In that article, she mentions in passing a calypso singer at a Trinidadian carnival, singing a song that goes "Always marry a woman uglier than you" (164). That tiny yet potent word-picture had already found its way into the short story "Olaf and His Girl Friend" (1945).

Petry's stories, which first appeared in magazines such as *Crisis, Phylon*, and *Opportunity*, were not collected until 1971, when they appeared under the title *Miss Muriel and Other Stories* (Boston, Houghton Mifflin Company)—and stood as the first collection of short stories to be published by an African American woman writer. But even after that publication, the collection spent considerable periods of time out of print (and is not in print as we write this essay). Furthermore, Petry's earliest published short stories, "Marie of the Cabin Club" (published under the name Arnold Petri in the Baltimore *Afro-American*, then perhaps the most consistently Left of the major black newspapers, in 1939) and "On Saturday the Siren Sounds at Noon" (published in the NAACP's journal *Crisis* in 1943) are not included in the collection and have not been in print since their original publication.

One remarkable aspect about Petry's short fiction is the range of characterization and settings of the stories. Her chief characters are black and white, male and female. Settings include Harlem, small-town Connecticut and New York, Massachusetts and the West Indies. Petry was, in fact, one of the very first writers to deal successfully with Harlem as a literary landscape after Wallace Thurman's *Infants of the Spring* marked the end of the optimism of the New Negro. She is one of the architects of the image of Harlem as the archetypal slum that also contains the sense of the earlier optimism and promise as a sort of index of the failure of the American Dream to include black Americans. Her story "Like a Winding Sheet" represents this dynamic. The story introduces a hard-working night-shift worker, who has worked the same job for two years and feels he has little to show for it: his body aches and his apartment is too small to sit down in. He is struggling through a particularly bad day on the job when the white forewoman calls him "nigger." Johnson resists hitting her because she is a woman, but his anger, humiliation, and sense of exclusion build in him all day, finally bursting out at home, where he finds himself beating his wife as though he could not control what his own hands are doing:

And he groped for a phrase, a word, something, to describe what this thing was like that was happening to him and he thought it was like being enmeshed in a winding sheet—that was it—like a winding sheet. And even as the thought formed in his mind, his hands reached for her face again and yet again. (210)

In terms of the ideology of the Communist outlined above, one might say that the dreams deferred, to use Langston Hughes's contemporary formulation, by the failure of the New Negro Renaissance and the emergence of Harlem in Petry's fiction as a sort of symbolic "everyghetto" are those of genuine black citizenship and of black self-determination; and that dreams particularly fail for the poorest (and largest) stratum of Harlem society—a theme that James Baldwin would take up in his great essays of the 1960s.

Petry's stories engage this longstanding Popular Front balance between African American particularity, or what one might call a black nation, with a class-conscious vision of an "American" identity. "In Darkness and Confusion" (1947), for instance, stands as an early example of what would become a familiar trope of African American fiction: the story of the World War II soldier, fighting for his country (and against Hitler's racial "solution") and facing institutionalized (and often legally codified) racism at home. The protagonist of Petry's story, Jones, is the soldier's father. He listens to scraps of neighborhood wisdom about the likelihood of genuine black citizenship as he waits for his turn in a Harlem barbershop:

"White folks got us by the balls—"
"Well, I dunno. It ain't just white folks. There's poor white folks gettin' their guts squeezed out, too—"

"Sure. But they're white. They can stand it better . . . "

"You're wrong, man. Ain't no two ways about it. This country's set up so that—"

"Only thing to do, if you ask me, is shoot all them crackers and start out new—" (266)

The story overlaps the narrative of the father, who has suddenly stopped hearing from his son Sam, stationed in Georgia, with a narrative of the 1943 Harlem riot that takes place after a white policeman shoots a black soldier. The two narratives, both engaging the long-time Left concern with both northern and southern versions of a racist and repressive criminal justice system, come together the day Jones learns why he hasn't heard any news from Sam: Sam's buddy tells him that he "got shot by a white MP. Because he wouldn't go to the nigger end of the bus. He had a bullet put through his guts. He took the MP's gun away from him and shot the bastard in the shoulder. . . . They court-martialed him. He got twenty years at hard labor" (268). Jones enters a bar to drink up the courage to tell this news to Sam's mother, and there he witnesses a white policeman shooting a black soldier. Overwhelmed by grief, Jones and his wife join the rioting and looting that ensue, and at the story's end, the wife drops dead from a combination of the grief and overexertion. The final line of the story is howled to the sky by Jones: "The sons of bitches," he shouted. "The sons of bitches" (295). Again anticipating Langston Hughes's treatment of the same issue in the 1951 *Montage of a Dream Deferred* with its famous line "Or does it explode?" Petry, like many on the black Left, proposes that the real instigator of the riots of 1943 in Harlem and Detroit are not "outside" agitators or foreign agents, but domestic racism, the true "Fifth Column" within the United States. She puts an even greater urgency on the pursuit of a "Double V" campaign (whether or not one uses the term proposed by the *Pittsburgh Courier*) and suggests prophetically that such riots are sure to happen again long after Hitler, Mussolini, and Tojo are gone.

Through scenes like the barbershop conversation in "In Darkness and Confusion," Petry presents in certain of her short stories a chorus of vernacular commentators, whose language and brand of wisdom are counterpoised (both story to story or even within certain stories) to those of "standard" or "educated" speakers. But Petry's use of folk figures or practices is not simple, and might more accurately be called a meta-commentary on uses of the folk. Petry is an astute "on-the-spot" chronicler of the complex relationships connecting intellectuals and "folk" and popular arts and artists. Petry consistently portrays folk "heritage" and practices—for instance, Afro-Caribbean dance and song, as well as conjuring, find their way into several of her stories and novels. (Oddly, at least one critic actually faults Petry for an absence of this concern, remarking that it is a pity that Petry could not have read novels by the likes of Alice Walker and Toni Morrison, who could have taught her to draw more strength from the folk tradition of her grandmother.[8]) The story "Olaf and His Girl Friend," about a dockworker from Barbados, is told with deliberate stilted-ness from the point of view of an American painter who first encounters Olaf in Bridgeport, then again in Harlem. "I liked to watch him," the painter admits, going on to describe him in a rather objectifying way:

When the sun shone on him it caught highlights in his skin, so that he looked liked an ebony man. I soon discovered that there was a native girl who found him even more interesting to watch than I did. I only wanted to paint him against the green water of Carlisle Bay. She wanted to marry him. (182)

The strains of fetishization in this passage come above the surface later in the story, when this same painter visits a nightclub in Harlem called "the Conga" every night to watch the girl, who has moved their with her aunt, dance:

[S]he looked liked some gorgeous tropical bird . . . she was barefooted. There was a good anklet around one ankle and a high gold collar around her neck that almost touched her ear lobes. The dress she wore was made of calico and it had a bustle in the back so that every time she moved the red calico flirted with the audience. . . . A towering red turban covered her hair completely. There were flowers and fruit and wheat stuck in the turban. (194)

The undertones in this scene, in which a white audience watches a young black woman wearing, among other evocative garments, a metal collar around her neck and exported products on her head, as she dances a sexualized dance Olaf's friends describe as "not a good dance," call into question the powerful economies of watching and gaze. In addition, this scene serves to remind the reader of the story's opening, and the narrator's admission that he "liked to watch" Olaf. Since the link between the two scenes is the artist sitting there watching, Petry's story becomes a commentary on those who "watch" (as well as describe) the "folk," what their motivations might be, and what effect on the actual persons who are, in fact, the "folk" this watching might have. In this case, the young couple disappears into the night, hand in hand, leaving the nightclub owner to fume, "That black baboon!" and the painter to muse that while the father of Olaf's beloved was a schoolteacher, her grandmother was an obeah woman; in other words, "folk" practices here both elude and trump intellectual and high-artistic ones.

Petry maintained this interest in the idea of the "folk," but she could be suspicious, even sharply critical, of the particular political uses to which it has been put. One problem raised in "Olaf and his Girl Friend" is that versions and visions of the black folk have been such a central feature of popular culture in the United States for so long that popular culture structures the idea of the folk, even for African Americans, in ways that have a particular impact on black women. The short story "Miss Muriel" (the title story of the 1971 collection, originally published in 1963), narrated by the same young black girl as "The New Mirror," introduces a character named Chink Johnson, a blues piano player. In Johnson, Petry slyly re-creates a recognizable stock character from the Harlem writers of the New Negro Renaissance, particularly Langston Hughes, with whom Petry occasionally shared publication space. He's not an unsympathetic character—at least, not at first—but the father of the narrator, the young daughter in a "respectable" black family in a small town in New York State, cannot stand him because he considers Johnson's profession, music, and his personal style to be vulgar and overly-sexualized. When the father, Samuel, contemptuously describes Chink Johnson, his sheer hatred leads him to start speaking almost in poetry, a kind of poetry that mocks the vernacular artist (whom Hughes sought to elevate) and also parodies the multitude of poetry Hughes wrote about piano players and other blues or jazz musicians:

> . . . he started talking very fast and in a very loud voice. "Lightfoot Jones," he said. "Shake Jones. Barrelhouse Jones." He started tapping on the glass case in front of him. I have never heard him do this before. . . . There he was with a pencil in his hand, tapping out the most peculiar rhythm on the glass of a showcase.
>
> "Shake Jones," he repeated. "Rhythm in his feet. Rhythm in his blood. Rhythm in his feet. Rhythm in his blood. Beats out his life, beats out his lungs, beats out his liver, on a piano," and he began a different and louder rhythm with his foot." "On a pi-an-o. On a pi-an-o. On a pi-" (21)

Samuel can't stand the nightlife scene the very sight of Johnson invokes for him:: "Every time I look at him I can hear him playing some rags and see a whole line of big-bosomed women done up in sequined dresses standin' over him, moanin' about wantin' somebody to turn their dampers down, and I can see poker games and crap games and—" (48). This is a scornful recitation of some of the subjects that make up Langston Hughes's *Montage of a Dream Deferred*—and, indeed, much of Hughes's poetry since the 1920s.

As it turns out, the real reason that Samuel hates Chink Johnson is that Johnson wishes to court his beautiful sister-in-law, in whose sexuality Samuel has a somewhat disturbing proprietary interest. Samuel has his own way of describing Sophronia's beauty: he says she looks like an Egyptian queen. Here, Petry collapses time in her story to set the "Old Left" point of view or interest (through Chink Johnson/Langston Hughes) directly against the emerging turn toward Black Power (and a long-established trope of the Garveyite nationalist tradition still powerful in the Harlem of the 1930s and 1940s, seen, for example, Marcus Garvey's 1927 poem, "The Black Woman"), as represented in Samuel's language about African queens. Petry establishes the figure of the woman as object of desire for two literary traditions. Both are always looking at her—Chink, tellingly, first spots her in a store window—and neither has her best interest at heart.

In this story, Petry works to establish a mode of reflexive social criticism that would serve as a crucial model for celebrated writers like Toni Cade Bambara, who made a "from-within," affirming and loving criticism of the Black Power and Black Arts movements that placed gender issues in the foreground. In Bambara's story, "My Man Bovanne," for instance, the narrator, a Southern born New York mother of three adult children, becomes fed up with her children. They have become political, to which she is not unsympathetic—but they talk about "grassroots" and "council of elders" without attending to the feelings of actual neighborhood people, and they are embarrassed by their mother's sexuality and lecture her about what she should wear and how she should dance. Petry's story "Mother Africa" (the only story original to the *Miss Muriel* collection) pre-dates this insider criticism of "Black Power," foregrounding the gender dimension even more than Bambara does. In this story, a junkman is given a statue to sell for scrap metal. His name is Emmanuel, which mostly people shorten to "Man," underscoring his generic importance and preparing him to stand in for his gender. The statue causes a minor scandal in the neighborhood because it depicts a naked woman. But although it makes his customers and neighbors uncomfortable and angry, the Man finds he cannot simply get rid of it as planned. Indeed, he embarks on a course to please the statue, to be worthy of it. He cleans the metal and finds that it "glows." He places it carefully in his yard, where his neighbors will be less likely to see it—but then tills the earth, plants grass in the yard, and buys a little bench to place near the statue. Looking at the beautiful metal woman, he is unaccountably moved:

He felt something stir within him, an emotion that he could not put a name to. It was like seeing something dark and beautiful beyond description for the first time and yet recognizing it, because in the deepest part of your mind you had

always known that the kind of dark glowing beauty existed. Mother Africa, he
thought. That's what she really is: Mother Africa. (139)

Man takes his nascent Afrocentrism, worked out through his personification of the statue as Mother Africa, very seriously. He not only cleans up his yard, he cleans up himself. For the first time in 25 years, he gets a shave and a haircut (allowing Petry humorously to depict a familiar "folk" scene in urban black writing: the barbershop setting). He bathes to get rid of a "goatish" smell that had previously caused people to cross the street when walking near him. He changes his greasy, odorous pants for new courderoys. He feels like singing, and his usual work cry, "I buy—buy—buy—ole clothes—ole rags—ole sewin' machines!" becomes a "paean of praise" (149) sung in the moonlight. The very idea of the dark beauty, of Mother Africa right there in his own yard, makes Man peaceful and happy for the first time in decades, and he completely transforms himself.

In short, the symbolic recognition of, and relationship with, Mother Africa lifts Man from a paralyzing depression he has suffered from since his wife died in childbirth 25 years earlier. At the core of the depression is racism, for Man believes that "if they hadn't been black and lived in Harlem, Mary Lou and the baby might have survived."

Petry gives a lot of credit here to the potential of cultural nationalism, as unsubtly as it may be represented here by a metal statute. But there's a problem: Man (whose name now appears just to represent gender) has been so preoccupied with the breasts and thighs of the statue that he hasn't looked at her face. One day, he is forced to do so, because someone has tied a bright red bandana on Mother Africa's head:

The dress that he held in his hands was made of cheap cotton. White mission-
aries had put dresses just like this on African women, covering them from neck
to ankles, even the arms, and Africa a tropical country. They had them wear
bandanas and head rags, so even their hair was concealed. They made Africans
ashamed of their good strong black bodies. (160)

Climbing up to remove the bandana, Man comes face to face with the statue for the first time and falls crashing off his ladder. He has noticed for the first time that Mother Africa, for whom he has transformed his yard, his body, and his psyche, is white. The story ends with Man painfully pulling himself up off the ground and calling the scrapyard to come and get the statue for melting. "Come right away," he shouts. "Hurry" (162).

Once again, Petry has offered a gentle criticism of the new forms of Black artistic and political empowerment. Man's history as an African American is concisely presented in the story: from racist Mississippi, to the segregated army, to Harlem where his wife and baby die because of their lack of access to medical care. A symbolic sense of himself as an African—the symbolic nature heightened by the fact that he thinks of Africa as a "country"—has the potential to stir him deeply. But Petry's gender-based criticism pulls the rug out. First, focusing on a woman's breasts and thighs and neglecting to look her in the face blinded him to reality. And perhaps more important, turning a woman, or Woman, into "Mother Africa"—a symbol and one based on old gender roles, at that—erases the needs and contributions of actual Black women. Besides, the fact that under the vision of "Mother Africa," the woman represented by the statue, is suddenly recognized as "white" once more questions the provenance of notions of the essential folk and folk spirit that has been shaped by mass cultural visions of Africa and African Americans that originate outside (or are at least not under the control) of black people. Petry's criticism here resembles that of Alice Childress (another figure bridging the Old Left and the Black Arts period) in her 1969 play "Wine in the Wilderness," in which a painter plans a triptych of Black women, one of whom he calls the "African Queen," or Wine in the Wilderness. The painter's conception of this idealized figure is at the expense of actual black women, whom he looks down on as degraded and "ruined" by racist American society.

Petry does not completely reject popular culture in her fiction. In fact, both in the way she utilized the venues of the African American and "mainstream" press for her work and in the ways she drew on the formal resources and generic conventions of popular culture in her work, she attempted, as did many Popular Front writers, to use these venues, resources, and conventions to make her radical fiction accessible to a mass audience. Indeed, the title of one of her stories, "Has Anybody Seen Miss Dora Dean," is taken from the lyrics of a hits song the New York stage and the tune, as Petry puts it, "suggested cakewalks, beautiful brown girls, and ragtime" (96). Her column "The Lighter Side" (see above) is also instructive in this regard. So, too, is her landmark, best-selling novel *The Street*, which combined the conventions of gothic literature and popular journalism to become the first novel by a black woman to sell more than a million copies.

As did many radical black writers of the 1940s, Petry seeks carefully to place her usages of "folk" and "mass" culture within a specific cultural and political moment. One might say that she anticipates Frederic Jameson's famous admonition to "always historicize" in this respect.[9] Petry particularly investigates the special impact of the intersection of visions of race, class, and nation, often structured or framed by mass culture (and, in turn, often a structuring element of mass culture), on black women. In this sense, Man in "Mother Africa," like the father in "The New Mirror" and Lutie Johnson in *The Street*, is neither completely free nor completely a victim of "false consciousness," but is caught in a web of cultural and ideological contradictions, requiring constant negotiation. In this fashion, Petry's stories reach back to interrogate the structuring concerns of Popular Front literature, while reaching ahead to foreshadow similar concerns by later black women writers, such as June Jordan, Toni Cade Bambara, and Ntozake Shange during the Black Power and immediate post-Black Power eras. Her stories, then, form a crucial bridge between the so-called Old Left radicalisms of the 1930s, 1940s, and 1950s and the new black radicalisms of the 1960s and 1970s.

OBJECT LESSONS

Fetishization and Class Consciousness in Ann Petry's *The Street*

Bill V. Mullen

It is as clear as noonday, that man, by his industry, changes the forms of the materials furnished by nature, in such a way as to make them useful to him. The form of wood, for instance, is altered, by making a table out of it. Yet, for all that the table continues to be that common, every-day thing, wood. But, as soon as it steps forth as a commodity, it is changed into something transcendent. It not only stands with its feet on the ground, but, in relation to all other commodities, it stands on its head, and evolves out of its wooden brain grotesque ideas, far more wonderful than "table-turning" ever was.
—Karl Marx, *Das Kapital* (50)

No pictures, no rugs, no newspapers, no magazines, nothing to suggest anyone had ever tried to make it look homelike. Not quite true, for there was a canary huddled in an ornate birdcage in the corner. Looking at it, she thought, Everything in the room shrinks: the dog, the woman, even the canary, for it had only one eye open as it perched on one leg. Opposite the sofa an over-ornate table shone with varnish. It was a very large table with intricately carved claw feet and looking at it she thought, That's the kind of big ugly furniture white women love to give to their maids. She turned to look at the shapeless little woman because she was almost certain the table was hers.

The woman must have been looking at her, for when Lutie turned the woman smiled; a toothless smile that lingered while she looked from Lutie to the table.
—Ann Petry, *The Street* (24)

In these two remarkable passages, the literary technique of personification conveys both the extinction of social relations and the objectification of the human under capital. In Marx, commodity's capacity to both disguise and conceal productive labor and produce surplus value is playfully disclosed as a table's consciousness of its own commodity allure. In Petry, former domestic Lutie Johnson's precarious relationship to private property is symbolized by disfigured furniture, a hand-me-down accessory and index to the exploitation of the laboring Black female body. Indeed though worlds apart—nineteenth-century Europe, twentieth-century Harlem—Marx and Petry use personification to signify one of capitalism's most fundamental processes: fetishization. In *Capital*, Volume 1, Marx and Engels describe fetishization as the mystification of labor necessary to capital's romance with the commodity form. "A commodity is ... a mysterious thing, simply because in it the social characters of men's labour appears to them as an objective character stamped upon the product of that labour" (446). What is sacrificed, they write, is not simply labor's value in the production of the commodity, but a whole chain of social relationships of the human. Put coarsely and abruptly by Marx, "There it is a definite social relation between men, that assumes, in their eyes, the fantastic form of a relation between things" (447).

It is this complex process, I argue, rendered as apartment hunting in the scene described above, in which protagonist Lutie Johnson is engaged in Ann Petry's 1946 novel *The Street*. Lutie's search for commodified *space* both discloses and erases the human behind the surface of its objects: "after bowing to her," she writes of Lutie's introduction to the toothless tenant we met a moment ago, "Lutie completely forgot the woman was in the room, while she went on studying its furnishings." Confronted with the world of real estate, Lutie literally and figuratively weighs her own value as a working-class woman against the market value of the apartment. What she will learn, appropriately, is the price of her exploitation. She will rent this piece of private property (owned by a exploitative white man named Junto), live under the gaze of a superintendent (named Jones) who will attempt to rape her, and will eventually be separated from the one *human* object she most desperately seeks the apartment for: her eight-year old son Bub. Thus despite her ability to read the interior and material designs that precede her, Lutie enters "blind" into a dangerous set of unseen social relationships particular to her status as a working-class African-American woman of the 1930s and 1940s when she enters into a rental agreement in *The Street*.

This anecdotal analysis suggests a broad number of ways in which commodities, fetish and value resonate in Ann Petry's book. Indeed the life of Lutie Johnson may be used as a kind of critical hermeneutic to disclose not only the general law of Marxian festishization, but the historical fetishization of African American women under capitalism. Lutie's own "transcendent" commodity value, what Marx calls the commodity's "enigmatic character," obtains in the novel in the public and private expropriation of her sexuality, her labor and the material value of African American women, particularly as mothers, in sustaining capital accumulation and reproduction. Lutie's internal struggle to think her way out of her own commodification through, ironically, the pursuit of Benjamin Franklin's wisdom on the accumulation of wealth, might be understood a la Marx as the "grotesque idea" evolving out of her wooden brain. Likewise, as Marx did with the "raw material" of wood, *The Street* deploys a variety of "natural" images and tropes which underscore commodification as the process of material transubstantiation, expropriation and change. Beginning and ending with images of stormy weather itself personified as predatory, starved and consumptive—"It even took time to rush into doorways and areaways and find chicken bones and pork-chop bones and pushed them along the curb" (2)—these tropes of the natural complicate conventional (and predominant) critical readings of *The Street* as a "naturalistic" novel. Specifically, emphasizing the role and treatment of the commodity form in the novel helps demonstrate how "naturalism" itself may perform the generic work of mystification.

This reading of *The Street*, I hope to argue, is important for expanding the narrow parameters in which Petry's career has been considered. Seldom discussed for example except elsewhere in this collection is her work for the progressive and Communist-influenced *People's Voice* newspaper in Harlem during the period of her writing of *The Street*; her participation as an actress in the American Negro Theater in Harlem at a time when Left influence in Harlem was at its peak; and her public written awareness (though often critical and veiled) of the role of Marxism in creating literary movements she explicitly considered herself a part of. While I will only begin to offer an outline of this contextual history for reading *The Street* in this paper, my goal in a larger sense is to suggest the necessity of recovering Marxist critical tools, and Marxian categories of analysis, to understand more firmly Petry's place in relationship to broader literary movements that pre-dated her (like the proletarian literary movement of the 1930s) as well as to individual writers with whom she has been repeatedly but at times diminutively compared, especially Richard Wright. At the very least, I want to argue, *The Street* offers readers of twentieth-century American literature a rigorous test case for the influences of Marxist cultural production, while challenging Marxist cultural production to see its influences in places it has heretofore hesitated to look.

CAPITAL, GENRE, AND *THE STREET*

*The characters that stamp products as commodities, and whose establishment is a neces-
sary preliminary to the circulation of commodities, have already acquired the stability of
natural, self-understood forms of social life, before man seeks to decipher, not their historical character, for in his eyes they are immutable, but their meaning.*
—Karl Marx, *Kapital* (451)

In a seldom-discussed essay in *The Writer's Book* in 1950, "The Novel as
Social Criticism," Ann Petry produced one of her few published works of self-
evaluation and literary analysis. Published four years after the widespread critical and commercial success of *The Street*, the essay was a reaction to critical
designation of her work as "social criticism." She begins the essay by arguing that the category of "social criticism" was unbeknownst to her prior to
writing the book, but positions the book as broadly as possible so that it may
encompass a wide variety of traditions of social protest. Stories, she writes,
that "point a moral, convey a message" are as old as Greek tragedies or the
Bible, and newer ones—like Wright's *Native Son*, Mailer's *The Naked and the
Dead*, or Lillian Smith's *Strange Fruit*—are merely reiterations of classical
themes: "And the Lord said unto Cain, Where is Abel they brother: And he
said, I know not: Am I my brother's keeper?" (33). Yet hard after that assessment, Petry offers a more secular argument that points to a critical tension,
or contradiction, in her own attempted definition of social criticism:

*Being a product of the twentieth century (Hitler, atomic energy, Hiroshima,
Buchenwald, Mussolini, USSR) I find it difficult to subscribe to the idea that art
exists for art's sake. It seems to me that all truly great art is propaganda, whether
it be the Sistine Chapel, or La Gioconda, Madame Bovary, or War and Peace.
The novel, like all other forms of art, will always reflect the political, economic,
and social structure of the period in which it was created (33).*

Petry's inclusion of the Soviet Union in a list of twentieth-century "atroci-
ties" would seem to mark her as a recognizable type in post-World War II
culture, namely a Cold War liberal and anti-Stalinist. Indeed, Petry complains
that too much social protest literature is ascribed to Marxist influence, and
describes socialism and communism as "corruptions" of Old Testament ideas
about fraternal responsibility. Yet elsewhere in the essay she avers that "part of
the cultural heritage of all of us derives from Marx, whether we subscribe to
the Marxist theory or not" (35). She also singles out for praise of all the books

cited in her essay Alan Paton's *Cry the Beloved Country*, for it "tells the reader in no uncertain terms that society is responsible for the tragedy of the native African" (37). Yet it is in a brief critical overview of the differences between "naturalism" and "realism" that Petry comes closest, I think, to providing us a cogent and self-conscious description of *The Street* that lends itself to and requires a Marxist set of reading tools. I quote here at length:

A professional patter has been developed to describe the awareness of social prob-lems which has crept into creative writing. It is a confused patter. Naturalism and realism are terms that are used almost interchangeably. Studs Lonigan *and* USA *are called naturalist novels; but* The Grapes of Wrath *is cited as an exam-ple of realism. So is* Tom Jones. *Time, that enemy of labels, makes this ridicu-lous. Dickens, George Sand, Mrs. Gaskell, George Eliot, Harriet Beecher Stowe wrote books in which they advocated the rights of labor, condemned slums, slav-ery and anti-Semitism, roughly a hundred years ago. They are know as "the humanitarian novelists of the nineteenth century." Yet the novels produced in the thirties which made a similar comment on society are lumped together as proletarian literature and their origin attributed to the perfidious influence of Karl Marx.*

This particular label has been used so extensively in recent years that the ghost of Marx seems even livelier than that of Hamlet's father's ghost—or at least he, Marx, appears to have done his haunting over more of the world's surface. (34)

Two points require underscoring here. First, Petry offers something like a critique of the "liberal imagination" in her considering of social protest fic-tion. Refusing to choose between realism and naturalism, she builds a literary category—"social protest"—capacious enough to include any serious atten-tion to two issues: political economy or racism. It is also worth noting that these two categories are, if not interchangeable, directly interlinked or at least continuous: "rights of labor, condemned slums, slavery and anti-Semitism." Secondly, the trope of Marx's ghost here, while meant to be a witty ironic gloss on critical confusion over generic categorization, in fact functions to cohere or "materialize" the amorphous and diffuse body of thought and writing classifiable as "social protest." Like the Old Testament God, as Frank Lentricchia has said of Foucault's conception of power, Marx's ghost is both "everywhere and nowhere" in twentieth-century thought and letters, a dan-gerous and "haunting" specter of that century's long woes.

This particular form of Marxist allusion, I want to argue, is important to understanding both Petry's strategic position as Cold War critic, and as a way of reading productive tensions in the novel's own representations of material processes. I will address this point first by considering the cultural and political context in which *The Street* was produced. Petry's most tangible link to the American Left in the time immediately prior to publication of *The Street* was undoubtedly her tenure on the Harlem progressive weekly *People's Voice*. As Martha Biondi has noted, *People's Voice* was a centerpiece of what might be called the Black Popular Front in Harlem in the years between the end of the depression and the end of World War II (10, 15). The *Voice* provided coverage and support for the election of Communist Party member Benjamin Davis to the New York City Council in 1943 and again in 1945. During the war, the paper was the most aggressive advocate for coalitions between Harlemites and Left political parties. It was unflagging in its support for numerous Black labor struggles, including the struggles of Black women domestic workers. *People's Voice* in fact was to the Left of the war-time politics of African American papers like the *Chicago Defender* and *Amsterdam News*, openly employing a progressive editorial rhetoric to signal the influence of Communist Party thought and influence on Harlem.

As such, as Biondi has argued, Harlem in the years of Petry's tenure at *People's Voice* represented more than twenty years of African American efforts in literature and journalism to establish a broad "cultural front" for the expression of Black progressive and radical thought. Indeed, while Petry was writing for *People's Voice* Richard Wright, having fled Chicago, was using Harlem as his home for the composition of *Native Son*, and writing occasional pieces for the *Daily Worker*. Likewise, during the war years Harlem resident Ralph Ellison published both reviews and journalistic pieces in *New Masses*. While I will discuss the impact of Wright's novel on Petry's book in a moment, it is important to consider what might be called the political and cultural milieu of its production as an index to what might be called its cultural value. This seems especially important to a project like Petry criticism for two reasons: first, it allows us a social and political frame that has commonly been used by some of Petry's more famous (and mostly male) contemporaries. Second, it places Petry's first novel squarely in a tradition of African American cultural politics that has heretofore been elided in discussion of her work. Indeed as Bill Maxwell, James Smethurst, Robin D. G. Kelley, Barbara Foley and others have shown in recent years, African American appropriation, engagement and most importantly re-making of Socialist and Communist thought and practice is one of the prevailing stories of early to mid-twentieth-century African American literature. Symptomatic of many of these engagements is a coded, covert or indirect process of borrowing in which ideas and tactics of the organized Left or Marxist thought are mutated or borrowed for application to Black political and cultural struggles.[1]

It is this process of appropriation and borrowing that I think it is at work in Petry's novel. It is rendered in at least three ways in the book: in Petry's conscious response to and revision of Wright's proto-Marxist novel *Native Son*; in Lutie's inchoate development of "consciousness" about the objective conditions of her life; in the book's symbolic order, which tends to use material objects precisely to symbolize Lutie's enigmatic alienation in the novel. Indeed in Marxist terms, Lutie's *alienation*—the distance from her self as a laborer, as a woman, as a worker—is rendered through the book's representation of the value of commodity forms. "It is value, rather," writes Marx, "that converts every product into a social hieroglyphic. Later on, we try to decipher the hieroglyphic, to get behind the secret of our own social products; for to stamp an object of utility as a value is just as much a social product as language" (449). Repeatedly in *The Street*, Lutie is faced with physical objects whose meanings are deeply embedded with the meaning of her own life. Her ability or inability to recognize these meanings is the ontological and political problematic of the novel, finally "solved" through the violent attachment and association of *all* possible meanings on to one object—Boots Smith. Thus the social logic and "plot" of the novel may be said to be a gradual coding and decoding of value as social hieroglyphic, and the attendant struggle for class consciousness that logically follows from it.

READING VALUE IN *THE STREET*

As many critics have noted, Petry's novel bears the influence of Richard Wright's *Native Son*, a book she read and admired. References, parallels and allusions to Wright's novel abound. Like Bigger Thomas, Lutie is an isolated working-class urbanite forced by racism and economic violence into an act of retaliatory violence and flight. Like Bigger, Lutie's fate is largely controlled by a white man—Mr. Dalton in *Native Son*, Junto in *The Street*. Real estate plays a prominent role in both books: Bigger's family apartment is controlled by the Dalton family; Junto owns the building in which Lutie and Bub rent. Yet the material history *The Street* reclaims more specifically derives from African-American women's experiences of slavery and exploitation, recuperated and revised by Petry as an allegory or blueprint of Black women's historical relationship to capitalism. This difference is significant. From the beginning of the novel, Lutie's dependence upon and sexual objectification by men is the primary determinant of her decision-making and desires, each of which is specifically linked to material conditions and needs. Racism and economic disability force Lutie out of the domestic sphere of her father (Pap) and an unemployed ex-husband (Jim) into the role of domestic to a white family, the Chandlers, at the start of the novel. There her striking good looks (beauty, as Harriet Jacobs reminds us, was in white women a blessing, in black women a curse) enhance and enigmatize her commodity value in the white household. This is revealed by white women who view her as both domestic servant and sexual competitor: "'Sure, she's a wonderful cook.' offers one of the women visiting the Chandler residence, 'But I wouldn't have any good-looking colored wench in my house. Not with John. You know they're always making passes at men. Especially white men'" (40–41). As in the slave narrative, the white Chandler family is also scarred by its participation in chattel control: a family member commits suicide, probably to mask an illicit sexual relationship in the home, and the local media camouflage its causes in order to preserve the family's (and by extension America's) ruling class hegemony. The suicide also precipitates Lutie's leaving the Chandler's for Harlem. On her journey, Lutie carries forward the wisdom and social aspirations of upward mobility symbolized by two "lessons" she draws from the Chandler experience which, I will argue, manifest as the problematic of commodity fetishization throughout the novel. The first is that the Chandler's wealth is tangible proof of the good faith return of industry and thrift as symbolized by her infatuation with the writings of Benjamin Franklin. Petry writes, "These people had wanted only one thing—more and more money—and so they got it. Some of this new philosophy crept into her letters to Jim" (43). The second is the impact on Lutie of the suicide of John Chandler. Lutie's response to this event, or more specifically her *interpretation* of the event, denotes an important thematic in *The Street*:

After Mr. Chandler's brother killed himself in the living room, she didn't lose her belief in the desirability of having money, though she saw that mere possession of it wouldn't necessarily guarantee happiness. What was more important, she learned that when one had money there were certain unpleasant things one could avoid—even things like a suicide in the family.

She never found out what had prompted Jonathan Chandler to kill himself. She wasn't too interested. But she was interested in the way in which money transformed a suicide she has seen committed from start to finish in front of her very eyes into an "accident with a gun." (49)

Lutie here enacts an initiation into the laws of the commodity fetish necessary to her continued participation in what Marx calls capitalism's mystifications: the object lesson of the scene, literally and figuratively, is that capital obscures social relationships even as its enacts the terrible violence capitalism produces. This contradiction is the "unpleasant" epistemic weight of the suicide. In order to render this contradiction as a constant *class* systemic in *The Street*, Petry reiterates the keyword "unpleasant" in a later moment of interior monologue voicing Lutie's increasing frustrations about *her own* objective conditions. After complaining that her poverty and frustrations could be found in "any city where they set up a line and say black folks stay on this wide and white folks on this side," and "any place where the women had to work to support the families because the men couldn't get jobs," Lutie concludes thusly: "It all added up to the same thing, she decided—white people. She hated them. She would always hate them. She forced herself to stop that train of thought. It led nowhere. It was unpleasant" (206).

The weight of misrecognition here is crucial: Petry deploys euphemism—literally linguistic substitution—as a metonymy for not seeing, not saying, not knowing. Euphemism also returns us to Marx's insistence that "to stamp an object of utility as a value is just as much a social product as language." What then is the "object of utility as a value" that is actually being *represented* in this scene of euphemism? It is, crucially, Lutie herself, or more specifically, the value of Lutie's *labor* in the political economy of capitalism. This is registered, significantly, as a semiotic articulation in the form of an advertisement Lutie sees on the subway. Indeed the advertisement deliberately returns us to the primal scene of her initial misreading, reiterated, like the word "unpleasant," as a hieroglyph of her social existence. I quote at length to underscore Petry's attention to the process of value and value-making as they relate to social consciousness and social relationships:

Like some of the other passengers, she was staring at the advertisement directly in front of her and as she stared at it she became absorbed in her own thoughts. So that she, too, entered a small private world which shut out the people tightly packed around her.

For the advertisement she was looking at pictured a girl with incredible blond hair. The girl leaned close to a dark-haired, smiling man in a navy uniform. They were standing in front of a kitchen sink—a sink whose white porcelain surface gleamed under the train lights. The faucets looked like silver. The linoleum floor of the kitchen was a crisp black-and-white pattern that pointed up the sparkle of the room. Casement windows. Red geraniums in yellow pots.

It was, she thought, a miracle of a kitchen. Completely different from the kitchen of the 116th Street apartment she had moved into just two weeks ago. But almost exactly like the one she has worked in in Connecticut.

So like it that it might have been the same kitchen where she had washed dishes, scrubbed the linoleum floor and waxed it afterward. Then gone to sit on the small porch outside the kitchen, waiting for the floor to dry and wondering how much longer she would have to stay there. (28)

The advertisement might be understood as an objective correlative in *The Street*'s rendering of commodity fetish. To recall T. S. Eliot's famous definition of that term, in 1919, Eliot wrote, "The only way of expressing emotion in the form of art is by finding an 'objective correlative'; in other words, a set of objects, a situation, a chain of events which shall be the formula of that particular emotion; such that when external facts, which must terminate in sensory experience, are given, the emotional is immediately evoked" (48). Yet here, as in Marx, the advertisement renders the effects of commodification as a complex of social processes that begin and end with the alienation of labor itself. Lutie's isolated inability to *see* herself in the advertisement is the keynote of this.[2] The advertisement depends upon both the appropriation of her labor and its erasure to establish the "miracle" of the commodity as hieroglyphic form. "The object which labor produces—the product of labor" writes Marx, "confront it as an *alien being*, as a power independent of the producer": "The product of labor is labor embodied and made material in a thing; it is the *objectification* of labor. The realization of labor is its objectification. Within political economy, this realization of labor appears as the *loss of reality* of the worker, objectification appears as the *loss of the object* and bondage to it; appropriation appears as *alienation [Entfremdung]*, as *externalization [Entausserung]*" (133).

The advertisement thus emblematizes the social contradiction of *The Street*: in this case, for Lutie Johnson, the challenge is to see through the commodity as hieroglyph to the social relationships beneath it, to see as it were the "reality" of her life. In terms of plot, this contradiction manifests itself as Lutie's perennial pursuit of the gleaming kitchen simultaneous with and against recognition of the social processes of capital that produce it. The book, in other words, is about the production of a form of political consciousness. Making this process of reading difficult is that Lutie is herself constantly rendered as the *object* of capital and thus is alienated from recognizing this self-same social process. In Harlem, for example, Lutie meets Boots Smith. A former Pullman Porter, he now works for Lutie's landlord

Junto. Boots perceives Lutie primarily as a sexual conquest. She perceives him as facilitating her desire to develop a career as a club singer. In a provocative symbolic passage from the novel, Boots contemplates the parallel trajectories of their lives—one might call it their social relations—and the potential benefit to each of them of collaborating:

Balance Lutie Johnson. Weigh Lutie Johnson. Long legs and warm mouth. Soft skin and pointed breasts. Straight slim back and small waist. Mouth That curves over white, white teeth. Not enough. She didn't weigh enough when she was balanced against a life of saying "yes sir" to every white bastard who has the price of a Pullman ticket. Lutie Johnson at the end of a pullman run. Not enough. One hundred Lutie Johnsons didn't weigh enough.

He tried to regret the fact that she didn't weigh enough, even tried to work up a feeling of contempt for himself. You'd sell your old grandmother if you had one, he told himself. Yes. I'd sell anything. (265)

Boot's own commodity logic is rendered as the legacy of the auction block, which might justly be called the marketplace shorn of euphemism—capitalism with its clothes off. Here historical context for reading *The Street* also helps to underscore sources for the novel's quite obvious critique of capitalist social processes. By the time of Petry's writing of *The Street* both the Domestic Workers Union in New York City and the Brotherhood of Sleeping Car Porters were two of the strongest collectives representing the labor interests of the respective classes of African American servants represented by Lutie and Boots. Those unions and their labor are each literally outside of the scope of "interest" for Lutie and Boots as *workers* in *The Street*. The characters stand in naked relation to each in a music industry that is itself a racist monopoly in the text controlled by Junto, literally the book's invisible hand. Boots's physical evaluation of Lutie likewise echoes the novel's motif of the scrutiny of the black female body as a marker of commodity value, a practice familiar to Petry, at least in one possible source, via the history of the Bronx Slave Market. In 1935, three years before she moved to Harlem and eventually began her own observation and writing for *People's Voice* on the conditions of African American women there, the Bronx Slave Market opened on 167th street in New York City. The Black communist journalist Marvel Cooke and her collaborator Ella Baker would tell the story in the *Daily Compass* starting in 1950 of black women, many of them migrants from the South, lining 167th street every morning hoping to be selected for a day's domestic labor in white homes. Wages averaged 30 cents an hour. By all accounts slave market days began with white housewives canvassing the street. "If they had crust on their knees, they'd hired them," recalls Harlem Communist and one-time Garveyite Queen Mother Moore (Erickson). This method of reading the black female body for its potential transformation from use to exchange value (i.e. from raw material, or wood, to table) is replicated in the novel in Mrs. Hedges's surveillance of black girls on 116th street as she measures their potential as prostitutes:

Looking out of the window was good for her business, too. Here were always lonesome, sad-looking girls just up from the South, or little girls who were tired of going to high school, and who had seen too many movies and didn't have the money to buy all the things they wanted.

She could pick them out easily as they walked past. They wore bright-colored, short-skirted dresses and gold hoop earrings in their ears. Their mouths were a brilliant scarlet against the brown of their faces. They wobbled a little on the exaggerated high-heeled shoes they wore. They wore their hair combed in high, slick pompadours. (252)

Again as in Marx, the commodity's "grotesque" aspect is rendered as an index to fetishization. The iconography of prostitution is, to return to Petry's description of the hand-me-down table, the "overornate" objectification of the African American female's deeply estranged relationship to capital. Symmetrically, Lutie's often-underscored physical beauty embodies the contradiction of fetishization which drives the plot towards its ironic climax. In an effort to avoid Mrs. Hedges's inducements to turn tricks by pursuing a singing career, Lutie is nearly raped by Boots Smith who "weighs" her in his mind as his single means of competing with and avenging his racial subordination to Junto. Junto in turn controls the high-scale prostitution trade in the novel. Thus, Lutie is by book's end the fetishized object of two slave markets: the Sugar Hill joints for white men operated by Junto, and the 116th street shop of Ms. Hedges. Boots is the overseer on this triangular sexual plantation. His assault on her triggers this description of her violent response, which significantly returns us both to the initial problematic of the fetish as well as to the relationship between the object and its symbolic or "fetish" value:

A lifetime of pent-up resentment went into the blows. Even after he lay motionless, she kept striking him, not thinking about him, not even seeing him. First she was venting her rage against the dirty, crowded street. She saw the rows of dilapidated old houses; the small dark rooms; the long steep flights of stairs; the narrow

dingy hallways; the little lost girls in Mrs. Hedges's apartment; the smashed homes
where the women did drudgery because their men had deserted them. She saw all
of these things and struck them.

. . . Finally, and the blows were heavier, faster, now, she was striking at the
white world which thrust black people into a walled enclosure from which there
was no escape. (430)

In keeping with Marx's and Petry's use of "personification" to describe
the object's capacity to render fetish consciousness, Boots *embodies* the social
relations of her entire life as they are disclosed and revealed by Lutie's violent awakening. That is, Boots is both "objectified" and "personified" as the
cumulative weight of capitalist social process. Lutie "turns the tables" on him
in this scene, repulsing his violence with violence, while disclosing to readers
the social logic which has caused them to expropriate each other. Her violent
response likewise reveals what Marx calls both the "enigma" or mystery of the
fetish object as well as its brute and brutal materiality:

She backed away from the sight of him, thinking that if she took one slow step at
a time, just one slow step at a time, she could get out of here, walking backward,
step by step. She was afraid to turn her back on that still figure on the sofa. It
became a thing. It was no longer Boots Smith, but a thing on the sofa.

She stumbled against a chair and sat down in it, shivering. She would never
get out of this room. She would never, never get out of here. For the rest of her life
she would be here with this awful faceless thing on the sofa. (431)

The enclosed or sealed off room in this scene is the literal and figurative
coffin Lutie begins to build for herself when she signs the rental agreement
upon entering Harlem. It is the black room of the dead. It is the room of
what might be called the commodity grotesque. Lutie flees this room at the
end of *The Street* and boards a train to Chicago where she hopes to become
anonymous, particularly to her son, in her crime. Like Harriet Jacobs, and
Sethe in Morrison's *Beloved*, she abandons her hope of home in order to find
one; like each of them, she severs her maternal bond with her child in order
to preserve one. "And as the train roared into the darkness, Lutie tried to figure out by what twists and turns of fate she had landed on this train. Her
mind balked at the task. All she could think was, It was that street. It was that
god-damned street" (436). Lutie's both seeing and not seeing, recognizing and
not recognizing the object of her own objectivity is consistent with Marx's
suggestion that it is the nature of that objectivity to enigmatize itself.

The final paragraph of *The Street*, a coda to its own social processes, interestingly turns to the "natural" to suggest this veiling process: "The snow fell softly on the street. It muffled sound. It sent people scurrying homeward, so that the street was soon deserted, empty, quiet. And it could have been any street in the city, for the snow laid a delicate film over the sidewalk, over the brick of the tired, old buildings; gently obscuring the grime and the garbage and the ugliness" (436).

The naturalism that opens the novel—the predatory and molesting wind that fingers and blows everything on *The Street*—here configures a more deeply considered lesson in false consciousness and festishization. This is not the same snow that turns the landscape "white" in *Native Son* to signify Bigger's isolation and aloneness. Rather, the snow is a "natural" symbol of concealment. Here we need only recall the subway advertisement for a "miraculous" modern kitchen Lutie ponders not long before on her way to Harlem: its "whiteness" too functions to mask or erase black labor. Nature is then a mirror up to production in *The Street*. The blinding and manufactured whiteness in the advertisement's enigmatized representation of capitalism must necessarily be read in dialectical relationship to the natural whiteness of "snow" at the end of *The Street*. The ad allows us to read *that* whiteness as a literary symbol denaturalized to convey the process of commodity fetish. Likewise, the "naturalistic" ending of *The Street*, as novel, both reveals, and conceals, the mystery of the object. Readers are thus challenged to look past what might be called naturalism's "surface" aspect for a "totalizing" interpretation of a life and a tragedy enigmatically unfolded. It is by returning to Marx, dialectics and commodity festish, I contend, that we come closer to a fuller consciousness of Petry's object lessons, lessons which considered fully may turn the tables on the same world that turns on Lutie Johnson.

PULPING ANN PETRY

The Case of *Country Place*

Paula Rabinowitz

In 1947, Ann Petry's second novel, *Country Place*, appeared to generally scathing reviews. José Ygelsias, writing in the Communist Party-affiliated journal *New Masses*, summed up responses by noting it was more suitable to "movies" "woman's magazine" or "lending library fare" so full of "formulas" "banalities" and "idiocy" that "even Ethel Barrymore could not quite come off" in the part of the rich old lady. In fact he noted "the one diversion the book offers" would be "to cast the book for the movies" (18). The *New York Times* noted, "Gossip, malice, calculation, infidelity, adultery, murder, sudden death, and a set of surprise bequests . . . are some of the dominant matters treated in *Country Place*" (Sullivan 12). Just the year before, Petry had been featured in the newly launched black mass publication (an African-American version of *Life*) *Ebony* as a celebrity author sharing cocktails with New York's literati following the fantastic success of her debut novel, *The Street*. [This spread, entitled "First Novel" opens with a full-page portrait of Petry as something of a stereotype out of 1940s movies—the prim but eager librarian poised at her typewriter cigarette in one hand, ready to rip off her spectacles, loosen her bun, and pull a bottle of bourbon from her desk as had Carole Douglas when Humphrey Bogart enters her used bookstore in *The Big Sleep*.] Twenty years later, when *Country Place* was mentioned at all, comments such as those by David Littlejohn in his screed, *Black on White*, were typical. Despite her "intelligence" and "female wisdom," he finds she writes "sordid plots," "Peyton-Place plots." He advised "reading the novel, skipping the plot" (154–56). This sounds paradoxical at best, damning at worst. But what if this obscure critic were on to something? What if, like the dozens of film noirs Hollywood was churning out while Ann Petry wrote her major works, her novels are best read as one views any example of B-movie genres—skipping the predictable plot and watching the film instead, noting the atmospheric lighting, catching the scraps of snappy dialogue, tracking the moody interiors?

For a writer who only produced three major adult novels—her bestselling (1.5 million copies and paperbacked three times) 1946 first novel, *The Street*, *Country Place*, and her sensational 1953 chronicle of an interracial adulterous love affair, *The Narrows*—it is curious how little attention the second novel has gleaned. This, despite it being paperbacked as one of the first New American Library Signet editions with a cover by the highly-prized illustrator—the "Rembrandt of paperback illustrators," James Avati (Server 67)—and chosen as a British Book-of-the-Month-Club selection. Even as Oxford University Press, Beacon Press, Houghton-Mifflin (Petry's original publisher), Rutgers University Press, Northeastern University Press among others have highlighted Black women's literary history through extensive reprint series, that include her first and third novel, *Country Place* remains hidden.[1] O'Brien considers her, in part because of *Country Place*, "outside" the black literary tradition (vii). How to account for this dismissive attention?

Ann Petry's *Country Place* (set, like James Thurber's "Secret Life of Walter Mitty" (1941), in a small-sized town on the Connecticut shore), limned the outlines of America's bucolic New England as a claustrophobic, dark and sinister zone of social disarray—Grace Metalious's Peyton Place meets Nathaniel Hawthorne's Salem. Where social chaos appeared openly visible on the teeming city streets, rural America, with its drowsy small towns and its mid-sized cities built around a single industry—like *The Narrows*'s powerful Treadway Munitions, based on Bridgeport's Remington Works—masked class and ethnic and racial tensions within mostly impenetrable homes and isolated landscapes. It was not the sidewalks that seethed but the lone merchant or house wife trapped by four walls which, in Petry's version, burst wide open with the returning veterans of mid-century's second world war.

Despite standard contract language prohibiting authors from publishing "scandalous" materials with New American Library, *Country Place* has something of the scandalous about it, even more melodramatic than what Petry's critics have noted is her penchant for plots with "scandalous doings"—"secret affairs, family skeletons revealed, brutal crimes, whispered evil adulterous intrigue;" or her "chewy" recourse to "melodrama," and "sordidness," a constant refrain in the reviews of all of her fiction (Littlejohn 154). It's the scandal, the melodrama, the sordidness, of racial cross-dressing, of passing, of refusing racial biography even as she announces its sociological effect. "Some people in Connecticut," writes Rochelle Girson in the *Hartford Times* review of *The Narrows*, "thought grimly that the characters in her second novel, *Country Place* were easily identifiable." As a melodrama, *Country Place* relies on a set of stock characters—good and bad, rich and poor, insiders and outsiders—to stage its social critique. *Country Place*—lacking definite or even indefinite article—takes on the whole damned mess of the country, the nation; its manifest focus is white people—their relentlessly small-minded pursuits of base desires for sex and money. Paradoxically, I want to argue, its staginess, its seeming remove from the racial and social protest of her other works, masked Petry's intimate memories and experiences, her own autobiography. Unlike her other two novels, purposely based on her investment in the novel as a form of sociology, this pulpy and largely forgotten work reveals traumas operating latently on a micrological level—written as they are through vast tropes of natural and human devastation in the wake of maelstroms and war. "In *The Street* I wanted to achieve a swift-moving, almost passionate style in order to heighten the story of Lutie Johnson and her small son, Bub," Petry recalled. In *Country Place*, I tried to *under*write. . . . I tried to get into the style something of the surface quiet of a small country town—a slowness of tempo . . . absorb[ed] almost unconsciously" ("Great Secret" 217). Julien D. McKee of Houghton Mifflin noted in a letter accompanying the signed contract to NAL, that its publisher, Victor Weybright considered it "a good novel and perhaps a more mature novel than THE STREET . . . it lacks the sensationalism of THE STREET" (McKee).

Briefly, *Country Place* follows a few days in late summer hurricane season in a small town, Lennox, Connecticut, as returning WWII vet, Johnnie Roane, discovers his beautiful blond wife has been having an affair with the town grease monkey, Ed Barrell—55 years old lecher, complete with hunting cabin (*the* country place), and wife stashed in a TB sanatorium. In addition, it compresses a subplot involving murder by chocolate overdose, interracial romance, and a struggle over a will into its slim binding. (NAL books were required to be less than 190 pages, so that the first paperback edition of *The Street* was an abridged edition, condensed by over 70,000 words.) Narrated by the town druggist "Doc," who begins his retrospective tale in typical hard-boiled fashion, with a first-person introduction of his own limitations—"a prejudice against women" (5)—as a narrative frame, the plot moves along through a series of revelations provided and sometimes provoked by the local cabbie, known as The Weasel. As The Weasel picks up and drops off customers, fills up his gas tank, and hovers around the train station and Doc's soda fountain, various characters fill in the gossip that substitutes for action. An interconnecting stream of locals: Johnnie, his parents, his wife Gloria, Glory's mother Lil, golddigging wife of Mearns Gramby, wealthy and cowed scion of the town's upper crust Mrs. Gramby, are all regular riders—the rich to and from their imposing house which sits above the town; the others from their modest bungalows, even the Gramby's servants move in and out of narrative range via the taxi's rear-view mirror and the drugstore's plate-glass window. Viewed in Weasel's mirror, the town is on reverse display, narrated after the fact much as Orson Welles, initiating this film noir convention, recounted *Citizen Kane*. Whatever happens, the Weasel's been there first: He utters Johnnie's thoughts "sticking his mouth into [Johnnie's] mind" as he peruses Lennox after four years overseas (17). Similarly, "I find you everywhere," remarks Mrs. Gramby to the Weasel. "Even in my thoughts. You reach them before I do" (182). Doc's storefront is not like those in the noir city featured in tough-guy fiction of the 1930s and film noirs of the 1940s "all wiggling neon lights and cosmetic bars and aluminum cooking ware" beckoning passersby from the grimy pavement. His store, instead, faces the "town green . . . where cows and sheep once grazed." Born in this village "surrounded by water and . . . filled with the salt smell of the sea and with the yammering sound of gulls," he possesses, as its sole druggist, an "intimate, detailed knowledge of its inhabitants." Like the Weasel, who "speaks for Lennox" (17), Doc's is the voice of a country place—insular, intimate. As the Big Storm brews so too do the murderous rages of Johnnie and Lil, the seething desires of Ed and Glory, the passionate interracial romance between the Gramby's servants, Neola and Portalucca, the machinations of the Iago-like Weasel, and the storytelling panache of Doc. In its wake, a new set of arrangements—domestic, environmental, social and economic—still cannot unsettle the "surface quiet" of this country place.

Based on Petry's experience of the devastating Hurricane of 1938—which left hundreds dead in Long Island and coastal Connecticut and Rhode Island, spurring floods as far inland as Hartford, destroying entire fishing fleets and railroad tracks in its path—the novel suggests Petry's effort to take T. S. Eliot's concept of the objective correlative and run wild with it. Marrying the environmental destruction of the weather to the social and psychological upheavals of WWII, Petry found the "perfect storm" to work through her training as a novelist, herself dealing with a husband home from the war. In her notebooks of the period, she constantly tallies the attributes of great fiction—its ability to take a bloody crime for instance, as in *Passage to India* or *Native Son*—and push outward, or inward, from sensationalism to art. She used her immersion in small-town life and her work as social worker and journalist during the war to explore the seamy side of an American pastoral, inadvertently finding a vehicle to express and explore some of her own ambivalences about marriage and art. Pulp about trashy white women provided, I want to argue, a safe space to unveil and even complain about her own situation.

761 A Revealing Novel of Marital Infidelity by the Author of The Street

...Good Reading for the Millions

COUNTRY PLACE

ANN PETRY

Johnny Comes Marching Home

He groped his way along, seeking the road. He felt as though some part of him; some vital part, had died there in the cabin. Well, Ed and Glory could hold a wake over whatever it was; they could sit up with the body, Gloria in her nakedness, and Ed puffing smoke from his obscene cigar . . .

When young Johnny Roane came back from the war in Europe he found the little town of Lennox, Conn., changed considerably. On the surface it was the same, the buildings were a little more weathered, the people older. But inside things had changed so much he almost didn't recognize the place. Especially his beautiful wife Glory . . .

In Country Place, Ann Petry has employed the same scalpel she used in The Street—to open the festering wound of Harlem—on a typical small town. Although in theme it's a vastly different book, the technique (and the mastery of it) are the same. Miss Petry shows the hidden sores and pollution which are masked by the cheerful facade of any Country Place . . .

Ann Petry

grew up in Old Saybrook, Connecticut, where her family has owned a drugstore for fifty years. As a result, the New England milieu of her new novel is entirely familiar to her. Her first novel, The Street, won international critical success and continues to be a best seller in its 25c Signet edition.

SIGNET BOOKS
Complete and Unabridged

Published by the New American Library

Ann Petry, *Country Place* (NAL Signet, 1950). Cover by James Avati.

In *Country Place*, as the back cover blurb of the 1950 NAL edition proclaims, "Ann Petry has employed the same scalpel she used in *The Street*—to open the festering wound of Harlem—on a typical small town. . . . Miss Petry shows the hidden sores and pollution which are masked by the cheerful façade of any Country Place. . . . " "Johnny Comes Marching Home" declares the first bold-faced line of the blurb, and Johnnie Roane's reentry into small-town USA sets the plot in motion.

Like so many works of popular culture during and immediately after WWII, *Country Place* ponders the "problem of the vet," which, along with the "disease hazards" of "sex delinquency" (as Elliot Ness pathologized interracial sex and unfaithful wives during wartime) was a growing concern among the military, law enforcement, journalists, social workers and educators, not to mention pulp fiction writers and Hollywood B-moviemakers, during the immediately after the war.[2]

Vets were seen in the words of Glory, referencing Dickens, as having "gone queer in the head" (149). She defiantly declares she "slept with Ed [because] he's a man and you're not" (142). By the mid-1930s, queer had come to mean both odd or crazy and homosexual or effeminate in American slang; Christopher Isherwood's 1945 *Goodbye to Berlin* (another NAL book with a James Avati cover) put queerness into literary circulation; so Petry, like so many other pulp and noir writers is linking the war to changes in masculinity and emerging sexualities: Johnnie wants to move to New York and become a painter, while Ed runs a gas station. And even if the New York School will emerge as a hypermacho construct with Jackson Pollock and the rest drinking in the Cedar Bar, there is no mistaking that in America artists possess suspect sexuality; guys who work on cars do not. The 1947 film of Dorothy P. Hughes's 1946 novel, *Ride the Pink Horse* refers to the anti-hero Gagin as "another one of those haywire vets."

In turn, the returned vet often finds his wife changed: Glory appears to Johnny as "a shadow of a woman," "a cheat" (142). Johnnie's dreams can't compete with his wife's beauty—represented by her blond hair—as "a gleaming net," a "fetish" drawing him back to his old life (87). Glory likes her job as a cashier in the local grocery store, where she knows she's the best-looking woman in town and can flirt with her customers. She's not so sure she can compete on Fifth Avenue. She refuses sex with her husband upon his return; he rapes her, almost strangling her, and later pursues her to the cabin where she and Ed tryst together to kill them both. But he cannot bring himself to murder, running instead from the scene feeling a "wreck," only now can he declare himself "a veteran" (143). War was not enough; rather, the true vet experience comes after the war—with his wife's desertion. [It is quite possible, that despite a long tour of duty, Johnnie never fired a rifle in combat, as the "kill ratio" during WWII was less than 25% and Johnnie's rank was as "Technical Sergeant." Which meant he'd spent four years "grubbing around the insides of airplane engines" (25).]

Houghton Mifflin seems to have rushed *Country Place* into print following the 1946 Paramount film, *The Blue Dahlia*, with an Oscar-wining screenplay by Raymond Chandler starring Veronica Lake and Alan Ladd, who, as another Johnnie, returned from "one bomber mission too many" discovers not only his wife's affair with a nightclub owner/gangster but his kid dead from a car smashup when she was drunk. When she turns up dead, he's pinned with murder although he insists on his innocence and must rely on his mentally and physically damaged war buddies to clear his name. Perhaps his amnesic war buddy did it, but Chandler's investigation into wartime guilt and violence was rewritten at the request of the U.S. Navy, laying the blame on a disgruntled night watchman.

In this typical post-war movie and fiction plot, the domestic front appears almost as violent and unstable as the combat zone. Elizabeth Sanxay Holding's novella, *The Blank Wall* (made into the film noir *The Reckless Moment* by Max Ophuls) suggests that because upstanding family men are away at war, criminals and gangsters have free access to middle-class women, who find their attentions strangely comforting, even as they involve naïve housewives in murder, extortion and blackmail.[3] This plot was not confined to the United States, either. For instance, in Yasugiro Ozu's 1948 *Hen in the Wind* the repatriated prisoner of war is immediately returned to work at Tokyo's Time/Life building, sliding back into his job in publishing even though his city is a wreck, its streets in rubble, its offices converted to dancehalls; but his homecoming is more troubled. He beats and rapes his wife after she admits she has prostituted herself to get money to pay for their son's hospitalization. But, this story of sexual betrayal was already circulating at home and abroad during the war. Novelist Josephine Herbst recounts her work in the Office of the Coordinator of Information in D.C. [OCI] as a propagandist using both her past experiences as a reader for pulps and a bohemian writer in Weimar Berlin, sending: "paper bullets for the fighting men, who were to be twitched by their erotic roots and reminded that their home fire pullulated. Beware the horde of war prisoners and displaced persons—foreign types leaking in through crevices, who might be useful on the home front to spade the wife's garden, to plow, to feed the pigs, but many of whom were strong physical specimens. Could a woman's honor prevail over stark loneliness, dark winters, frost, the cries of the flesh? Did they want to come back from the gory front to find a stranger's chick hatched in their next?" (104).

Petry connects this grim vision of post-war marriage as a site of betrayal, violence and greed to a dissection of small-town white America. Each theme grows logically from *The Street*, though, as the outlines of the novel appear to suggest, parts of *Country Place* preceded her first novel. In *The Street*, which, like *The Narrows* (1953), also features many aspects of film noir's plots, Lutie Johnson, the maid-turned-nightclub-singer, murders her bandleader when he suggests she sleep with the white racketeer to get money to pay a lawyer to spring her son from reformatory for stealing mail. She flees to Chicago on the train, revisiting the same station where she used to commute to her maid's job in Lyme, Connecticut. I have argued in *Black & White & Noir*, that the figure of the white femme fatale (Camilo Sheffield in *The Narrows*, for instance) traffics across more than sexual borders; she moves through a dark city, city populated by racial and ethnic Others who have access to a mirror world of corruption.

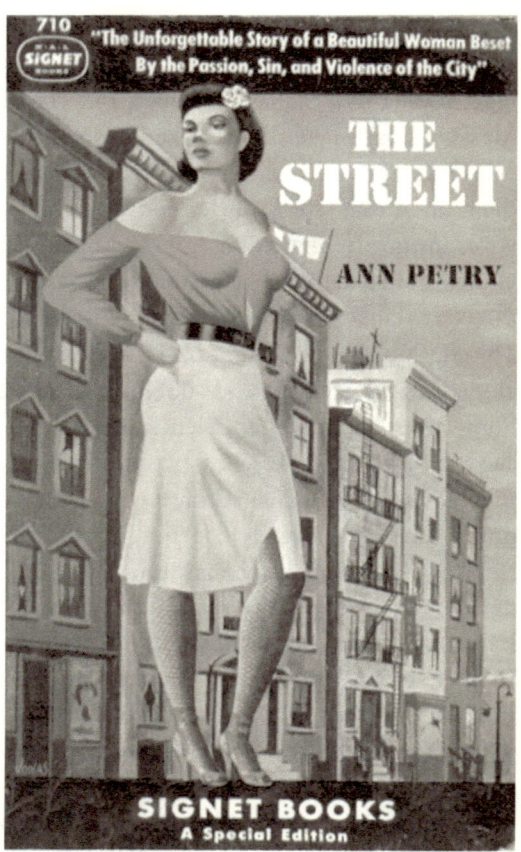

Ann Petry, *The Street* (NAL Signet abridged edition, 1949). Cover by Robert Jonas, an artist known for his abstractions. Lutie as Billie Holliday.

This boundary crossing, I suggest, ties the femme fatale to her (often) black maid, who like Lutie travels from chaotic urban zone to a seemingly benign suburbia. Petry astutely used these iconic venues. As a live-in maid at the Chandler's white-picket fenced house, Lutie witnessed first hand the corruption and deceit at the heart of white middle-class suburban marriage.

In *Ebony*, shortly after *The Street* was published, Petry claimed her next novel was also "about Negroes and other minorities as well" ("First" 36). In fact, she *had* been working on the sketches for characters that would populate *The Narrows* since 1944. Her notebooks are full of descriptions of Abbie Crunch and Mamie Powther as well as variations on the many plot twists—including rape, murder, pedophilia, bribery, gambling and so forth, piling on details over the public outrage Paul Robeson's son's interracial marriage generated in photographs and reports in the local newspapers and radio broadcasts. "This is Enfield, Connecticut—a state which believes it is a modern

The Unforgettable Story of a Woman Beset by the Sin and Violence of the City

THE STREET

Ann Petry

A SIGNET GIANT
Complete and Unabridged

Ann Petry, *The Street* (NAL Giant unabridged edition, 1954). Cover by James Meese. Lutie as Dorothy Dandridge.

state," she comments in her journals (Notebooks). However, this novel, like Richard Wright's 1953 *Outsider*, which also touches on an interracial affair situated within a bizarre noir plot, took, also like Wright's, almost a decade for Petry to complete. In the meantime, likely begun before the war, *Country Place* responds in part to Petry's own feelings about her WWII vet husband's return. [While he was in the army, she lived on his stipend and the $2,400 Houghton-Mifflin prize money thus quitting her job to write fulltime.] In a notebook from 1949, while she was reworking *The Narrows*, [though Petry never followed notebooks chronologically writing over old pages so dating them is difficult,] after her daughter Elizabeth was born, Petry bemoans her loss of time for writing. This triggers a memory from the past: "I was writing *Country Place* when he came out of the army and he was annoyed on something, at least he was always complaining[,] that time it was about Brandford, [sic] he was working on the docks, and before that at a hotel—then afterwards

Ann Petry, *The Street* (Pyramid edition, 1961). Cover by Dick Kohfield. Lutie as Lena Horne.

at the [*People's*] *Voice*—but never satisfied, never able to stick with anything, always irritable and fussing—some quality neurotic or infantile."[4] Clearly, Petry's own experiences, as an eyewitness to the 1938 Hurricane and to her own returned vet husband "gone queer," fed what became her second novel. Despite her insistence that her next novel was to be about race relations, *Country Place* only touches on "Negroes and other minorities," tangentially, through the prejudices of many of the townspeople, who recoil at the Jewish lawyer and find the interracial romance of the Gramby's servant Neola [perhaps a play on the passing daughter, Peola, in Fannie Hurst's 1934 *Imitation of Life*] and their Portegee, as he's called, gardener an abomination.

It seems the novel's central focus on class *ressentiment* and combat-ruined vets required white characters: Petry had asked herself, in another notebook with materials for what would become *The Narrows* with dates ranging from 1946–1951 [that is, while she was finishing *Country Place*], "why is it not possible to do with Negroes in America—that endless fascinating many-faceted subject, what has been done with earlier phases of life by the French—and by Dickens[?]—You have a middle-class society represented by Mrs. Abigail Crunch and Miss Abigail Jackson which has felt the impact of wars, has seen vast changes inside its lifetime ... " (Notebook).[5] Dissecting layers of bourgeois society could not occur in fictions of black Americans—they were not recognized as inhabiting it. Furthermore, for the most part, African-American GIs did not face combat directly; they were proscribed from fighting and served in more auxiliary roles. Their return home was thus not staged as a betrayal by disloyal women. Instead, it was portrayed (in such novels as Gwendolyn Brooks's *Maud Martha* or Petry's *The Narrows*, or Wright's *The Outsider*, all 1953) as a larger betrayal by white racist America, not the home but the country was the place of treachery, after experiencing relative freedom overseas. *Maud Martha* closes with the *Chicago Defender* reporting on lynchings in Georgia and Mississippi in the same issue that it covers a victory march of returning vets through the Southside.[6]

Like film noir, *Country Place* required a convoluted plot of murder and greed which, had she not made her characters white, might have been deflected onto the "social criticism" novel of race and its pathologies (Hull). Her two novels focusing on the black community—of Harlem or Monmouth, Connecticut—expressly link contemporary racial tensions to the long reach of slavery and racism into Northern urban spaces. *Country Place*, by contrast, suggests another trajectory of outrage—the traditions of New England's pilgrims that carries "a vein of violence running under the surface quiet" (7). It is only one among many by black authors written during the 1940s and 1950s where whiteness codes black rage and alienation through ethnic or queer characters; or, in which writers, stung by the sobriquet of "Negro writers" and trying to get out from under the shadow of Richard Wright—and many reviews of *The Street* called it "Black Girl" or "Native Daughter"—sought to broaden, which in publishing meant whiten, their perceived subject matter: Willard Motley's *Knock on Any Door*; James Baldwin's *Giovanni's Room*; Zora Neale Hurston's *Seraph on the Sewanee*; Wright himself followed suit with *Savage Holiday*. At the same time, white and black novelists, such as Worth Tuttle Hedden (*The Other Room*) and Lillian Smith (*Strange Fruit*) and William Gardner Smith (*Last of the Conquerors*) were anatomizing racism through explorations of interracial sex and its attendant violence; marketed as salacious with crossover potential, they became appropriate for pulp paperbacks, which assumed a minimum of 150,000 copies in sales.

Victor Weybright, publisher of New American Library, began his publishing career at *Survey Graphic*; he was a contributor to the Urban League and

NAACP and pushed for paperback distribution in African-American neighborhoods cultivating new audiences. His reprints of black authors, such as Alain Locke, as well as his commitment to publishing James T. Farrell, Gore Vidal and Norman Mailer established NAL as a progressive press—interested in combating racial prejudice. As Weybright noted in his 1952 bid for *Satchmo* Louis Armstrong's autobiography: "We have one other unique asset . . . our outstanding position in the field of literature by Negroes and about the Negro in America. Five years ago, with the publication of James Weldon Johnson's *Autobiography of an Ex-colored Man*, we launched a special effort to distribute our books, and especially those of racial interest, in the Negro communities of American cities. . . . We publish such books as *The Street*, books by Richard Wright, Willard Motley, Chester Himes, and such books as *Strange Fruit*, and encourage major wholesalers to add book specialists to their staff for Harlem, South Chicago and the colored sections of scores of cities, North and South" (Bonn 31).

But the big money-making author for NAL was Mickey Spillane, whose popular quasi-fascist lurid and misogynist detective stories supported the other literary aspirations of the press. Because crime plots enable violence to enter the narrative space of domestic fiction, they reveal how social relations were altered in the immediate post-war era. By linking leftist and black authors to Spillane through standardized formats and similar cover art, NAL's works anticipate a new post-war civil rights landscape, in some ways helping make *Brown v Board of Ed.*, Montgomery bus boycott and their aftermath legible to a largely white working-class readership through detailed chartings of cross-race intimacy. They bring civil rights into popular cultural sites, much as film noir coded changing racial and class relations through diabolical women, or as Truman Capote's *Other Voices, Other Rooms* and Gore Vidal's *City and the Pillar* popularized male homosexual desire through pulp. Always repressed within American popular forms, trauma is deflected—from race to class and from both onto gender and sex. Domesticity serves as the one sanctioned site in which political tensions, renamed private life, can be expressed and fought out—often with murderous ends.

Furthermore, following the 1934 release by Bennett Cerf of the first American edition of James Joyce's *Ulysses*, authors, such as Petry who listed Joyce as one of her three most admired writers, democratized the episodic, interiorized mode of narration, swerving from inside one character's stream-of-consciousness to another's diary entries, for a mass audience. Making accessible a popular high modernism through the mechanisms of pulp, these works further shrink the already demotic Bloom to fit into the American pocket. Thus

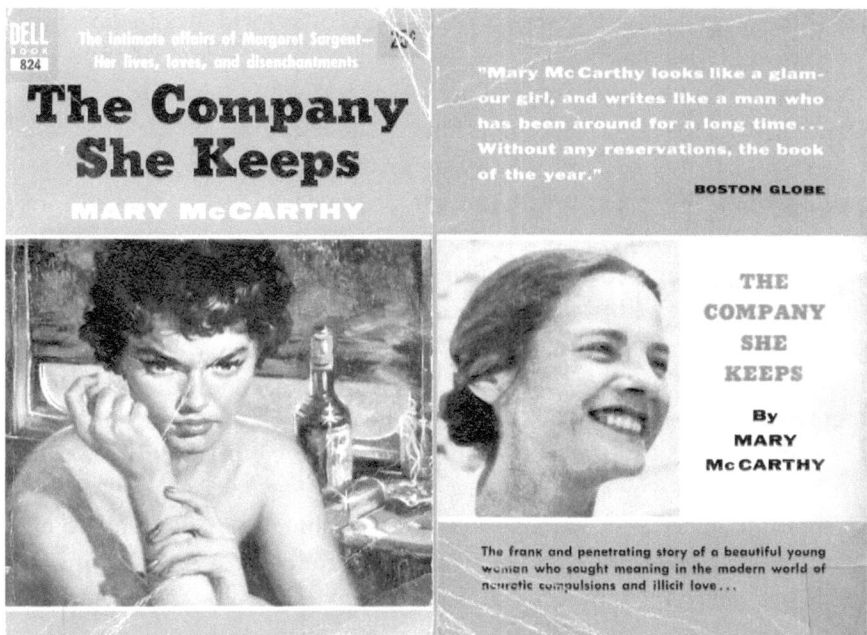

Mary McCarthy, *The Company She Keeps* (Dell, 1942). Cover by Robert Maguire.

the crime and sex novels of pulp not only glimpsed a political space where racial and class antagonisms could be expressed, they sought to do so as modernist literature—a pedagogic project that was formal as well a thematic. As Raymond Chandler put it: "All I wanted to do when I began writing was to play with a fascinating new language, to see what it could do as a means of expression which might remain on the level of unintellectual thinking and yet acquire the power to say things which are usually only said with a literary air" (Ruhm 172).

Works such as Vera Caspary's *Laura* (1942) proceeds to uncover the heroine's murder through chapters written in varying styles by a number of characters—her patron Waldo Lydecker's columns and journals, the investigating detective Mark McPherson's police report, Laura's diaries, her maid's recollections. In Kenneth Fearing's *The Big Clock*, each chapter recounts a different character's point of view. The fragmentary radio broadcasts, trial transcripts, magazine articles offer fragmentary memories of the many survivors of the revolution in his earlier 1942 novel, *Clark Gifford's Body*. Edmund Wilson's 1946 *Memoirs of Hecate County* and Mary McCarthy's *The Company She Keeps* (1942) interlink stories from a single consciousness: Wilson's "I" and McCarthy's "Margaret Sargent" are both participants and observers of the many others with whom they drink, have sex, marry, argue, and divorce. These skillful moves from high modernist style to pulp vernacular appeared more successful than Petry's efforts, however. One British reviewer of *The Narrows* found it "rather as though Dickens should try to write as Virginia Woolf" (New Statesman).

Like the shifting narrative technique of Michael Curtiz's *Mildred Pierce* (1945), or the multiple narrative and visual frames of classic film noirs like *Out of the Past* (1947), these popular works investigate desire and destruction through fragments and repetition, using corny devices such as reporters following stories or detectives filing reports or cabbies picking up fares. In her notes for *The Narrows*, Petry plays with having Camilo study photography with photojournalist Jubine—who "believed that he could record the history of man in the 20th century just by taking pictures of the River Pye"—to explain why she too is covering the waterfront. Petry's reliance on a cabbie and a druggist—snoops, (as she calls Jubine, the tabloid photojournalist of *The Narrows* modeled on *PM*'s Wee Gee[7]), ever-present in film noir as ciphers who can move through the city (taxi drivers and journalists) or dispense illegal substances—echo clichés from cinema: "While I stood there a car went by; its headlights made the black macadam road gleam . . . totally dark [except for the houselights] pinpricks obscured by driving rain" (*CP* 74).

Country Place relies on the visual and narrative device of the frame: life viewed through mirrors and window panes. Doc frames himself as a "medium kind of man" (5)—he's middling in height, weight, age, intelligence, but he is also a medium—through him we learn the "truth," but, warning of "his prejudice against women," he reminds "truth has many sides" (7). Later he reframes "Weasel's words [which] had evoked a picture of raw hurt and pain and secret furtive love. Now he was putting a frame around it—a frame of laughter" (69). Like the obsessive return and replication of desires and crimes in film noir framed so often through rain-soaked windshields, bevel-edged mirrors, and the slats of partially-drawn Venetian blinds overheard or observed through optical and sonic recording devices, the Weasel watches his fares through his mirror, as Doc watches the town commons through his store window, each recounting others' words, thoughts, deeds: Watching and repetition—essential to the process of gossip—and to the labor of fiction writing. Critic Hilary Holladay notes that in *Country Place* the "narrators and characters repeatedly encircle and encroach on each other's territory . . . telling and retelling . . . expanding circles of narrative" (66, 69).

Petry's Houghton-Mifflin Literary Fellowship-winning novel, *The Street*, had elicited some consternation among some African-American critics, such as *The Crisis*'s James W. Ivey, for its brutal portrayal of Harlem's 116th Street, as a "seething cesspool of sluts, pimps, juvenile delinquents, and clucks ... worthless as a picture of Harlem though interesting as a revelation of Mrs. Petry" (154). [Though one might note that Lyme, with its adultery, racism, suicide, extortions hardly fares any better.] Almost a decade later, the reviewer for *The Sign*, asks: "Why does she concentrate all of our attention on the sex life of the people?" (Clippings) Petry's ten-years of experiences as a reporter for the *Amsterdam News* and the *People's Voice* and *PM* and as a social worker in the public school system, working in a school on the corner of 116th St and Knickerbocker Avenue led to her vision of the constrictions of racism as spatialized: the modern lynch mob was the ghetto. Married to a purported pulp mystery story writer, George D. Petry, her first publication (under the pseudonym Arnold Petri [and her clues send us to her pharmacy and chemistry classes]) was the mystery story "Marie of the Cabin Club," published in Baltimore's *Afro-American*.[8] An avid movie fan and admirer of Richard Wright, Theodore Dreiser and James Joyce, the former pharmacist from Old Saybrook, daughter of the town druggist to whom the book was also dedicated: [MRTEK: He was "Doc." PETRY: Yes. Except that my father was black. "Doc" of *Country Place* was white" (Visit 79)] and fourth generation New Englander, Petry's vision was shaped by her "definite progressive" politics as she noted to *Ebony* (36), her work exposure, and her "planned reading in psychology and psychiatry" (Green 79). Like Wright, she got the idea for her first novel from a newspaper clipping, "a brief item about a janitor in a Harlem tenement who had been arrested for teaching as eight-year-old boy to steal" ("Great Secret," 216) and her third from an item about an elderly white woman killing a black man (Notebooks). With her long-standing attention to tabloid news, a husband away in the army, and an acute knowledge of the discordance between the façade of American pastoralism and the brutality of its urban jungle, it isn't surprising that Petry choose to foreground the "faintly cheap horrors and contrivances" reminiscent of "the great Victorians or the tawdry moderns" (Littlejohn 154).

Nineteen forty-six to nineteen forty-seven, after all, were the same years Hollywood produced such noirs as: *The Big Sleep, Black Angel, The Blue Dahlia, Fallen Angel, The Killers* (1946) and *Born to Kill, Dead Reckoning, Fall Guy, Framed, Kiss of Death, Nightmare Alley, Out of the Past* (1947). The exploding post-war publishing world brought out suspense novels such as Elizabeth Sanxay Holding's *The Blank Wall*, Kenneth Fearing's *The Big Clock*, Dorothy B. Hughes's *In a Lonely Place*, and hundreds more. Bantam alone, one of dozens of paperback publishers churning out millions of books during

United States government poster promoting women's war work, WWII War Manpower Commission.

the immediate post-war boom ended paper shortages, published eight titles a month in the mid-1940s. How could she not go for cheap and tawdry?

Initially imagining herself a short story writer, Petry wrote three "adult" novels during the heyday of film noir and paperbacks, Hollywood's B-movies featuring the three D's: death, depravity and determinism; pulp novels spreading the three S's: sex, sin, and smoking guns. In many ways, her novels retranslated cinematic trash—already a translation of literary pulp—into narrative form. Like film noir, they encode an underworld geography of what I call pulp modernism: They dwell on murder, violence, adultery and prostitution, the entire gamut of post-war anxieties about nuclear war, anti-colonialism, holocaust and racism deflected mechanistically onto the streets of American cities and from there retreating into the bedrooms of the American home. Women on the move—WOW—trafficking back and forth across racial and class borders before settling into a testy motherhood. But could these homebodies be trusted?

By the mid-1940s, the labor of pulp fiction writers, editors and readers, was already a stock trope for the degradation of literature and triumph of the culture industry—and more broadly for the rise of "White Collar," the "Man in the Gray Flannel Suit," and other clichés of middle management. The pulp world was one of frustrated women and emasculated men, who like James Thurber's Walter Mitty, suffer henpecked lives of dull repetitiveness, escaped only by recourse to fantasizing pulp adventure plots. Rollo (Holly) Martins, in Graham Greene's screenplay for *The Third Man*, is a feminized writer of pulp Westerns. Asked to lecture on modern novels at the British Cultural Reeducation Section, he's interrogated about "the stream of consciousness" and what he thinks of James Joyce and *Ulysses*. (He replies that he doesn't read Greek and he's only influenced by Zane Gray [71–73].) Describing her job "reading for a pulp-magazine outfit," Herbst explained the links forging the new American modernism she sees already formed in 1927, "A Year of Disgrace," an industrial production line of "prim" writers, editors "reeking with gin" and a "soap opera" voiced Katherine Mansfield wannabe who read manuscripts:

There were a dozen magazines going full blast, a dozen editors, a dozen desks, a dozen bottles of bootleg gin concealed in a lower drawer. You had to have the stuff to wade through the day. Our publisher liked to remind his employees, some of whom were bright boys out of Yale and Princeton, that there were advantages to be had beyond the stipend, and with the air of a big foundation establishing a fellowship, held up Dreiser and other "big names" who had made a start in similar enterprises. When the visiting authors, curiously prim, elderly bodies, who wrote with lubricity about chorus girls and Rotarians on the loose, complained that the editors interviewed them "reeking with gin," we were scolded by our publisher and forced to add peppermint drops and cloves to the bottom-drawer arsenal.

Cooped up in a small office with a meek woman in black who read for a true-confession magazine, I might mix up her monologue with the manuscript I was trying to read and suddenly feel that I had fallen into a bear trap where the stinging bottle flies of words, written or spoken, were the real menace. Nothing could stop her; her voice was the voice of an endless soap opera that now and then disengaged itself from a recount of her love life with a Japanese "poet" to sing of the virtues of Katherine Mansfield, whom she was studying seriously, so she said, for that day of days when she would ditch all this for her "own work." And as if to prove her claim that she could write, she might drift into a descriptive passage, filled with periods and semicolons, dashes and pauses, and in which

she offered herself as a crucified relic of love with the flourish of Brutus extolling
the death of Caesar (Herbst 77–78).[9]

This image of the pulp machine destroying men and art took comically
sinister form in Kenneth Fearing's spoof *roman noir*—made into the classic
Ray Milland film, *The Big Clock*. Based on his years working at *Time, Inc.*,
Fearing savaged the machinery of pulp as editor George, married to Georgette
and father of Georgia, literally lives and works inside the Big Clock, Janoth
Enterprises' repetitive mechanics of reproduction of time and life.[10]

Newsways, Commerce, Crimeways, Personalities, The Sexes, Fashions, Future-
ways, *the whole organization was full and over-running with frustrated ex-
artists, scientists, farmers, writers, explorers, poets, lawyers, doctors, musicians,
all of whom spent their lives conforming, instead. And conforming to what? To a
sort of overgrown, aimless, haphazard stenciling apparatus that kept them running to psychoanalysts, sent them to insane asylums, gave them high blood pres-
sure, stomach ulcers, killed them off with cerebral hemorrhages and heart failure,
sometimes suicide. Why should I pay still more tribute to this fatal machine? It
would be easier and simpler to get squashed stripping its gears then to be crushed
helping it along (Fearing 114)*[11]

In the films based on these novels and stories, Hollywood had used the
expanding pulp industry to deride its own studio system, collapsing after tele-
vision replaced both pulp fiction and the movies as popular mass entertainment. Connecting pulp with suburban claustrophobia, these films find in pulps'
architects a desire to escape the clock into a bohemian world of either avant-
garde art (*Big Clock*) a lost era of swash-buckling romance (*Walter Mitty*). But
if pulp writers appear as exemplars of the clockwork regimentation of capitalist
productivity, the clock stood for escape—from social work and other jobs—for
Petry, who went on, in the late 1950s, to become "the first woman [by which I
think is meant black woman] scriptwriter on the West Coast for Columbia Pictures" according to the Baltimore *Afro-American* (Garrett).

Petry wrote by the clock, recalling that while her husband was away at war,
she survived modestly on his allotment and her prize money, thus she wanted
to "maintain a more or less constant rate of production." With the "clock as a
taskmaster, . . . the hands of the clock shamed me into writing," she remembered ("Great Secret" 217). The culture industry generating an industry of
culture: If Fearing imagined the Big Clock superintending the spaces of rou-
tinized labor, Petry needed one to keep up her "rate of production": having

finished her first novel, she immediately set to work on the second one, *Country Place*, she remarks, "like the shoemaker at work on his next pair of shoes" ("Great Secret" 217). With her meager allowance, she understood literary production as labor, as production—as a job—war work. Her accounts of expenses and earnings for Friday October 1942, for instance, read as follows:

Guild dues $1.75
New republic (3 mo) $1.00
Tin .15
Get wellcards .20
Rent 18.00
Ink .10
Notebook .10
Picture frame .30
Apples .14
Melon .15
Celery .10
Shopping bag .02
Carfare .05

These coincide with her detailed notes drawn from a handbook on writing on trimming "half the ands" and gaining a "general increase in sensitiveness" by "reading aloud of noble prose and poetry" and "writing of verse," as well as her lists of books on economics, psychology and culture to be studied, notes for characterizations, lists of titles, lyric of racist nursery rhymes, lists of signs glimpsed in shop windows, a description of a cat fight observed on Riverside Drive, the smells of Central Park zoo and snippets of conversation overheard on the bus.[12]

This slippage between her investment in literary craft, gleaned from Trollope and Dreiser and Wright and Joyce, and her sense that fiction must be churned out, by the clock, on a deadline, is also part of the "scandalous" nature of her work. Work she gave up, it appears, shortly after the birth of her only child in 1949 when she turned to writing children's and young adult books and returned to "a handsome white house with green shutters on the old Boston Post Road in Old Saybrook, Connecticut," where she was still working away like clockwork, it seems, but with less apparent rage: "She polishes words and she polishes silver: her collection of old silver is full of beautiful things, but they all require polishing!" says her biography at the end of *Harriet Tubman: Conductor on the Underground Railroad* (1955). These young adult

The white woman as Marilyn Monroe: Ann Petry, *The Narrows* (NAL edition, 1955), cover by Clark Hulings; Fletcher Flora, *Leave Her to Hell* (Avon edition, 1958), cover artist unknown. Inside disclaimer of *Leave Her to Hell* claims that a "professional model" was used for the illustration.

biographies—on Tubman and *Tituba of Salem Village* (1964), strong, brave, rebellious, even scandalous, and, in mid-1950s and 1960s America, unknown black women—may have developed out of her frustration as a "novelist" and as the family breadwinner who must still do housework: "A thousand-page book wins in MCM prize, B. O. M selection—and probably makes the author a half a million dollars—nothing happens to *Country Place*—in fact the boys let you off lightly with that one—would like beds made" (Notebooks). Her children's biographies may be seen as a defiance of the celebration of the mid-1950s white woman embodied by platinum blond Marilyn Monroe, whose image infected even Petry's own books—at least its cover.[13]

Polishing that silver may have been just a ploy; she's seething with righteous anger. Despite front page coverage in Houghton-Mifflin's 1947 catalogue and wide reviews—some calling it a "razor sharp" slice of life about a GI and

She went too far—too often

Leave Her to Hell!

FLETCHER FLORA

An Avon Original

AVON
25¢

A Dirty Rotten Trail To Murder!

It was a case that spelled trouble from the first come-on to the last bullet. I'm Percy Hand, not-so-private eye. You meet a lot of gals on the make in my business, but this case had too many dames.

It all started on the secluded patio of a blonde who liked nude sun-bathing. Before the case was over, one dame was dead, another missing, and The Mob was getting ready to write my epitaph in hot lead!

Printed in the U.S.A.

his faithless wife—she was still supposed to make the beds for the "infantile" guy. It's as if, now a suburban mother herself, she were embarrassed by her sympathy for the outrageous white and black women she creates in her novels. (In a journal entry from 1946, she writes herself notes on the difficulty of finding a place to breastfeed in the U.S. and wonders what would happened if a woman nursed a baby on the subway (Notebooks).)[14]

While both Lil and Glory—the one frigid, the other hot, according to Ed—cheat on their husbands, looking for passion, escaping boredom, seeking money or a name, Petry does not really condemn them, nor does she condemn Lutie as a murderer or her escape, abandoning her son. Her actions are perfectly logical within the sexual and racial codes of *The Street*. Even Camilo's slumming comes to be seen as true passion; the narrative turns against her only after her sensational accusation of rape against Link and her exposure as a drunk driver through Jubine's tabloid photographs. Glory and Lil's stories, narrated by an avowed misogynist and his ferret-like sidekick, might be viewed differently had they been able to assert some narrative control as Lutie or even Mamie Powther in *The Narrows* has. And this, of course, is part of Petry's strategy as a student of pulp conventions: blonds are dumb. At least Glory might have had something to say for herself; she, who never gets the mother-love she deserves from Lil, "hard-boiled" Lil, only to be abandoned by her new husband with the war, left living with in-laws (190). She—a "Lana Turner wasted in this town" (56)—is looking for love in all the wrong places. Like Lutie, smitten by the lyrics of "Darlin'" and taken in by Boots, she might be excused for responding to Ed's sexual obsessions; he keeps nude pictures of her and her mother hidden in his wallet. She's been home with him watching "Ingrid Bergmann and Cary Grant in that last picture—or was it Jennifer Jones?" (59). This Gloria—and she's one of many: Gloria Grahame of the smashed face in too many 1940s and 50s film noirs, the damaged 1930s Glorias of *Butterfield 8* and *They Shoot Horses Don't They?* Gloria—G-L-O-R-I-A!!! straight down to Patti Smith channeling a history of pissed off Madonnas—is both siren and victim. Johnnie never challenges her gossiped reports of his wife beating; after all he *had* raped her his first night back. So he never discloses what he knows of her and Ed, preferring to slip away from her "net," drawn away from watching *his* Lana Turner in *this* country place to the art and action of city streets.

Reversing Johnnie's path to the noir city, Petry returned with her husband to her natal town, buying an eighteenth-century captain's house with a view of the Long Island Sound and a white picket fence to raise a daughter in a town in which she grew up feeling isolated. Cloaking her autobiography in the clichés of 1940s popular culture—haywire vets, small town Lana Turners, village gossips—Petry literally whitewashed her dark places. Fascinated by the reticence of New Englanders—especially middle-class New England Blacks, such as herself—Petry found she could reveal some of her own troubles with her country, her place, her life as a black woman writing in the mid-twentieth century, through a far-fetched plot derived from various mass-media sources.

Nineteen seventies exploitation film director Stephanie Rothman claims that because her cheap B-movies were "under the radar, yet widely popular" and spoke to an audience far more intelligent than big studios assumed, could insert any content she liked as long as she included plenty of scenes of beautiful women (and men) taking off their clothes, in the first reel.[15] From then on, she was relatively free to shape the story anyway she liked. B-movies and pulp fiction, as popular forms floating under the radar, provide a covert opening for writers to broach socially taboo topics—interracial sex, homosexuality, abortion—often through unconventional narrative forms. Petry repeatedly claimed that "the weather" was the inspiration for *Country Place* because, shortly before decamping to Connecticut for New York to marry George Petry, she observed the devastation the hurricane caused Old Saybrook. She cobbled her plots ". . . from items in newspapers, from the weather, from conversations, from gossip" (Ervin 102). Her list resonates with Gertrude

Stein's 1936 inquiry into American writing: "And so we come to what is really what we write what we write is really a crime story" (79). Stein distinguished between "human mind" which excites immigrants to America to write letters home full of "the weather and money" and "human nature" which is all about "sex and jealousy" (95). Like old newspapers, full of yesterday's "events" and so passé the next day, nobody can write home about sex, jealousy, crime or the news; that is the province of "writing." Petry's almost forgotten second novel melded "the weather" with "sex and jealousy," allowing this "private person" a form (Ervin 102), in its borrowings from "what is really what we write . . . a crime story," to write (about) home—the public space of her father's country pharmacy and the private place of her husband's unsettled return. She kept it well hidden, like a purloined letter, in plain sight, like the mirror Doc left unsold on his counter "because the customers, male and female alike, enjoy admiring their faces in it" (190).

INVISIBLE HANDS AT WORK

Domestic Service and Meritocracy in Ann Petry's Novels

Rachel Peterson

Frequently compared to Richard Wright in terms of her naturalistic style and representations of alienated figures, Ann Petry adheres to a "Blueprint for Negro Writing" mandate that "in whatever social voice [the writer] chooses to speak, whether positive or negative, there should be always heard or *over-heard* his faith, his necessity, and his judgment" (36). Petry consistently assumes the voice of domestics who articulate grave judgments on their employers and, in showing the enervating isolation of domestic service, Petry illustrates the necessity of participation in social movements and networks. Amidst the neutralization of unions dominant in World War II and the early Cold War, Petry depicts workers who have always been particularly alienated and thus typify the labor conditions of many in this period.[1] Further, most of Petry's domestics are, as Claudia Jones argued, "thrice oppressed," and develop individualized adaptive strategies to their exploitation, necessitated by their general dislocation from larger unions, and their segregation within private homes. At the same time, these domestics perform reportage that publicizes the degeneracy of the wealthy. In placing Petry's fictional representations of domestics in dialog with the social, artistic, and political analyses in her essays and journalism, this essay explores Petry's commitment to exposing fallacies of class mobility, meritocracy and racial superiority, and her belief in the necessity of social movements to resist exploitation. Thus while not explicitly advocating Marxism, Petry's novels realized her political and aesthetic agenda in that each served as an "emotional arouser" that would "move [readers] to action," an ambition that aligns her with the left.[2]

While the manufacture of order and cleanliness is essential to elites, domestics' relegation to the private sphere prohibits the wide-scale class formation envisioned by Marx, one "disciplined, united, and organized by the very mechanism of the process of capitalist production itself."[3] However, the very intimate and dehumanizing conditions of domestic labor do shape their consciousness, often creating identification with the beliefs of their employers, or developing into resentment that only rarely leads to active resistance to their exploitation. Like Adam Smith's worker who is dominated by "an invisible hand to promote an end which was no part of his intention," Petry's domestics become vital features of the social order that subjugates them.

As producers of hygiene, food, health and child care, service workers' labor is so quickly and unthinkingly consumed that it suffers an erasure that extends to the worker herself. However, while these characters work just beneath the surface, overshadowed by more socially and narratively prominent characters, their own invisible hands sometimes determine the novels' plots. Petry's narratives probe the marginality of domestics who beneath the central conflicts of the novels create the conditions for some of the most climactic and revelatory scenes. It is through employees' interactions with maids, and domestics' attitudes towards their work and employers, that Petry enacts dialectic of invisibility and indispensability. These workers are not only essential to their employers, but their intimate knowledge of the lives of their employers facilitates Petry's vivid, complex portrayals of elite classes.

While Petry's fiction delineates clear class struggle, some of her more extensive literary comment disavows a Marxist influence on her literature. In her 1950 essay, "The Novel as Social Criticism," Petry observes that George Sand's "problem novels" primarily explored "bourgeois emotions: love and passion," and chastises those who will not "recognize and admit the fact that not all of the concern about the shortcomings of society originated with Marx. Many a socially conscious novelist is merely a man or woman with a conscience" (37). At the same time Petry's "conscience" issues condemnation on bourgeois employers of domestics, and uses the voices of highly conscientious domestics to expose the elite's conspicuous consumption and criminality via the disclosures of highly conscientious domestics. Petry's denunciation of the "perfidious influence of Karl Marx," recurs throughout her non-fiction during the early Cold War, and makes categorization of her commitment to leftist politics difficult.[4] Petry, at times, fails to make her "faith overheard," however, by listening to the accounts of typically silenced domestics, Petry's convictions can perhaps be amplified. In her repeated and trenchant dramatizations one of the most intimately unequal relationships, that of an African American servant and her white employer, Petry's place as one of several "Old

Left writers of color of the 1950s who helped forge cultural conditions for a New Left sensibility" is staked (Wald 118).

Other left-affiliated writers in the 1940s and 1950s depicted black domestics as representative of racialized labor at its most oppressed, including Brooks, Ellison, Hansberry, Hughes, Killens and Wright, and most famously, Childress in *Like One of the Family*.[5] While Childress's novel centers on a more defiant domestic than most of Petry's characters, the everyday conflicts that Mildred Johnson negotiates with her employers occur in Petry's novels as well. However, for Childress, the indignities and exploitation Mildred faces serve as often humorous, instructive accounts of a domestics' self-assertion and her employer's ignorance and reform, Petry's domestics' work experiences primarily register tragedy, entrapment and disconnectedness. While Mildred Johnson had a sounding board for her trials at work in her friend Marge and participated in a range of social institutions like the church and clubs, Petry's domestics are generally without friends or social networks to alleviate or politicize the domestics' experiences. Despite Mildred's apparent access to resources and connections that elude Petry's domestics, Mildred's keen sense of her own exploitation and isolation leads her to assert the need for a labor movement for domestics: "we need a union. Why shouldn't we have set hours and set pay just like bus drivers and other folks.... Well, I guess it would be awful hard to get houseworkers together on account of them all workin' off separate like in different homes, but it sure would be a big help" (Childress 140). Without such a movement, Mildred Jones vacillates between ire, bemusement and affection in her interactions with her employers, and each conflict she encounters is resolved on a personal, situational level, usually with surprisingly frequent epiphanies among white employers regarding their own racism, and thus Mildred somewhat implausibly reforms her employers.

Richard Wright's 1957 radio play, "Man of All Work" addresses many of the issues of domestic service that concern Petry but are absent from *Like One of the Family*, such as sexual assault, violence, and alcoholism shape the experience of a man who must impersonate a female in order to get a job. When veteran Carl Owens's wife is too weak to work after delivering their second child, and they are only two payments away from home ownership (thus realization of the post-war promise), Carl can find no jobs available for African American men, a dilemma faced by many of Petry's male characters. After searching the newspaper, Carl observes that "there're plenty of ads for domestic workers, it's always like that" (121), and decides, against his wife's objections, to don her clothes and use his experience as an Army cook and an active father to acquire a job with the Fairchild family, under his wife's name,

Lucy. His belief that his identity will not be discovered because "Who looks close at us colored people anyhow? We all look alike to white people" (124) is substantiated when he is hired immediately.

Carl discovers that the Fairchilds have gone through numerous domestics because of Mr. Fairchild's alcoholism and uncontrolled sexuality, which manifests itself in part by his drunken "wrestling," or physical attacks on African American female domestics when he comes home for lunch. On his first and only day at the Fairchilds, he is subjected to unsought personal disclosures, physical intimacy with Mrs. Fairchild (particularly unnerving because he is forced, as "Lucy" to bathe a white woman), alcoholic outbursts, sexual assault, and eventually being shot. In another theme that recurs in Petry's work, the Fairchild's daughter, Lily, is ignored by parents and, like Henry Chandler in Petry's *The Street*, eventually witnesses a shooting because of her family's violent inability to control their sexual urges or their alcohol consumption. At the conclusion of the radio play, Carl tells Lucy that "I was a woman for only six hours and it almost killed me. Two hours after I put that dress on I thought I was goin crazy. . . . Gosh, Lucy, how do you women learn it?" She replies, simply, "It's instinct" (162). Lucy's answer underscores the centrality of sexualized abuse of labor, and suggests that, as Petry's domestics also find, surviving these circumstances intact requires a complicated reflex mixing self-defense and deference. Thus while Carl's injury is the most dramatic aspect of his the play, his entire experience shows that, as Trudier Harris observes in *From Mammies to Militants*, "maids are looked at as sponges . . . [who] had to soak up the intimate slime of their employer's personal lives" (78).

Petry attends both the variegated forms of racism domestics encountered in the private home that Childress and Wright describe while also emphasizing themes of loyalty, the limitations of post-war racial liberalism, the difficulties of maintaining a marriage, and the particularly disadvantaged position of those domestics separated from urban centers by their work in rural areas and small towns. Thus while these are generally secondary characters, they allow Petry to delve the extremes of racialized labor, marginality and invisibility, inverting the class and race dynamics of triple oppression through the domestics' relationship to her white and wealthy "madam" (*The Street*, 136). In this, they also show how those most marginalized (within a text or in a society) can generate otherwise obscured insights into the most intimate dynamics of capitalism.

While the racialized and gendered abuse of domestics reproduces the paternalistic and debasing conditions of slavery, each of Petry's representations hinge on the specific context of World War II and the early Cold War.

If New Deal reforms failed to regulate and protect the domestics that popu-
late Petry's novels, WWII altered irrevocably the lives of male protagonists
(Boots in *The Street*, Johnny in *Country Place* and Link in *The Narrows*).[6]
As many scholars have noted, the 1940s and 1950s challenged racial boundaries, with the mediated gains made during the war complicated by Cold
War imperial and domestic imperatives. In *Romance and Rights: The Politics
of Interracial Intimacy, 1945–1954*, Alex Lubin shows how in the post-war era
African Americans were systemically denied the right to a private sphere, and,
in Petry's novels, white elites control a public sphere that shields their private
crimes and weaknesses, often through manipulation of the media. Petry's
domestics provide incisive exposés that challenge "definitions of publicness
and privacy as a way to reveal how black women's labor is rendered visible
and invisible" (Lubin 128–29).

If Petry's domestics do not perform the traditional Marxist version of class
consciousness through externalizing their individual oppression through collective efforts, they still contribute information about the private sphere that
is generally shielded from public view as one of the many privileges of wealth.
Thus Petry's domestics make interventions into our understanding of class
struggle via their unique access to the private sphere. Such crucial insights
serve a central function in Petry's project, one that strives to demystify racial
hierarchies and provide a counternarrative to the sensationalist, racist stereo-
typing of African Americans in the popular media and mindset that she so
vociferously deplored as a writer for *People's Voice*. In so doing, Petry brings
the experiences and knowledge of workers who are frequently overlooked to
the foreground.

In her work to reverse the invisibility of domestics through exposé, Petry
anticipates Ralph Ellison, an author she admired. While both authors' exhib-
ited distinctly different ambivalences regarding Marxism, they shared an
attention to the grave effects of racialized effacement. Domestics' unsought
intimacy with their employers' disorder and dissolution afford them a specialized knowledge and accordingly "invisibility has taught [their] nose to
classify the stenches of death" (Ellison 567). Judith Rollins, an African American scholar who worked as a domestic for research, found this invisibility
"one of the strongest affronts to my dignity as a human being" (209), and
confirms historian David M. Katzman's earlier finding that "only blacks could
be invisible people in white homes" (188). One employer's belief that her
domestic did not have "more than ten minutes worth of information" reveals
how white supremacist attitudes effaced the possibility of critical subjectivities among the employers' closest intimates (qtd. in Hamburger xiii). Petry's

novels show the wealth of knowledge contained in such discounted observers. The particular insight of domestics over laden with employers' dirty laundry is affirmed by life long domestic Mabel John's insistence that "I know them. Filth is to them just what water is to fish or air to a bird" (Gwaltney, 167).

As Petry's domestic workers witness, record and editorialize on their employers' vices, including, alcoholism, infidelity, pedophilia, and attempted murder, they perform a sort of reportage through which they acquire agency. Given voice by a former journalist who often took her plots from news stories, these "inside sources" articulate acutely felt understandings of racialized capitalism, and thus Petry's domestics answer Michael Gold's call for "revelations by rebel chambermaids."[7] In their inner thoughts and occasionally in conversation with other household staff, Petry's domestics reveal confidential details about their employers, and the passages describing the wealthy demonstrate a key strategy of reportage, the use of "a specific case to sabotage the general claims, the proud boasts, of those in power" (Stott 172).[8] Thus the content and form of these domestics' narratives is closely linked to Petry's experience as a journalist.[9]

After a short period in the *Amsterdam News* office, Petry worked as a regular columnist and occasional reporter for *People's Voice* from 1942–1944, and many of the newspaper's philosophies emerge in Petry's fiction. *People's Voice* in some ways followed the principles Bill Mullen attributes to the 1940s magazine *Negro Story* in that its "'integrationist' policies tacitly affirmed 1940s black nationalist, socialist, and Communist articulations on the need for progressive interracial solidarity—without formalizing any of these positions in its pages" (10).[10] Petry's years at *People's Voice* ended prior to Max Yergan's anti-communist crusade to purge the staff of CPUSA members, including Marvel Cooke and Doxey Wilkerson. Yergan led this effort between 1947–48 when the newspaper folded, after adopting policies which conflicted with its five year history, a trajectory not unlike Petry's own. Given these connections and the 1953 Army-McCarthy hearings regarding *People's Voice* which called several former employees to testify, Petry's abnegation of communism and Marxism perhaps seemed a prudent and prescient choice.[11] As Mary Helen Washington succinctly states, "(w)hether on the Left or the Right, African American were, by nature of their blackness, subversives during the Cold War," and accordingly Petry must have felt particularly vulnerable, even before infamous congressional hearings and blacklists. In situating her sharpest social critiques in the observations and experiences of domestics, Petry is able to voice her own anti-capitalist sympathies through the seemingly powerless, socially and politically negated figure of the servant. After her

1946 return to Old Saybrook, Connecticut removed her from the cultural and political activism of New York leftists with whom she had associated and the repercussions of McCarthyism that more high profile figures faced, Petry's continued to produce novels that make sharp political statements through the bodies of the most often overlooked and thus, least threatening.

If Petry's alignment with the paper's early support of Communism is unclear, she vociferously shared *People's Voice*'s contempt for racist sensationalistic media representations, as well as its dedication to social activism. The *People's Voice*'s mission was well-expressed by Marvel Cooke, who was assistant managing editor during and after Petry's association with the paper:

People's Voice *was a social-minded paper, interested in the betterment of the community. Certainly they would not hesitate to present a story that was newsworthy because it was sensational, but the editorial policy was more to building the community, to building the unions, and to building churches. (Currie)*

Petry supported political activism "for the betterment of the community" through writing and community action. For example, in May of 1942 *People's Voice* reprinted her letter of condemnation to Mayor LaGuardia over the closing of the Savoy Ballroom. Her argument rests on the Savoy's importance as "a community affair . . . used for the benefit of Negroes." Listing the AWVS, the NAACP, the National Urban League, the United Seaman's Service and numerous social clubs, Petry argues that the Savoy provided services otherwise unavailable to African Americans (May 22, 1943, 4). In espousing the need for such social institutions, the absence of such structures in the lives of her fictional domestics assumes special significance.

While much of Petry's work for *People's Voice* concerned similar community issues as well as consumer advocacy and social events, in her article, "Harlem Women Wax Indignant Over Latest 'Crime Campaign'" (August 15, 1942, 3), Petry explicitly addresses the sensationalism of popular media. When the *Daily News*, which frequently featured racist stories, condemned Harlem as a "vice area" that white soldiers ought to avoid (reportedly in concert with U.S. military warnings) Petry recorded the outraged responses of Harlem residents. Petry further expressed her own indignation by walking a picket line with other members of Negro Women, Inc. outside of the *Daily News*. Such conviction permeates her fiction, and not surprisingly, each novel contains commentaries on sensationalistic journalism. In these novels, the accounts of domestics offer another challenge to the white supremacy dominating mainstream media representations. By providing narratives that reveal the sordidness and criminality of white elite employers, Petry's novels reject the dominant practices in which whites were "accorded the privilege keeping . . . intimate affairs private," (Lubin 151). In the absence of genuine engagement with issues of inequality and "betterment," Petry finds most news outlets guilty of obscuring real injustices with trumped up scandals, including her former employer, *Amsterdam News*, which "headlines the ripest scandals and goriest murders," while "its editorials are as sedately written and innocuous as those in the *New York Sun*" ("Harlem," 116). Thus if mainstream newspapers then, as now, mobilized racism to generate profits and fortify the basest racist assumptions, Petry contests these categorizations via activism, fiction and journalism.

Petry's sentiments on these maters were echoed by *Daily Worker* reporter and CPUSA leader John Pittman in a letter to then *People's Voice* editor Doxey Wilkerson. Pittman acknowledged the popularity of "so-called 'society' news, church news, comics, and a sensationalized, personalized treatment of serious news: We love the scandal columnists, the stories of crime and passion." He praised the efforts of *People Voice* to balance these preferences with enlightening analyses of the broader significance of these seemingly trivial subjects.[12] In language evocative of Wight's "Blueprint for Negro Writing," Pittman posits that "new kind of world is in its infancy—and we have to show its possibility for all of us. But we must also show the other world . . . in such a way as to explain its causes and point to the remedy" (2). Petry's coverage of fictional scandal directly links it to the avarice and ruthlessness capitalism requires, and shows the destructive effects of an absence of a social movement to contest exploitation. Aligning herself with a leftist rejection of racially motivated news coverage, Petry's fiction publicizes among whites the very kinds of criminality attributed to African Americans in mainstream presses, and thus uses domestics as reporters who can reveal what would otherwise be kept out of the papers. Hence in Petry's novels the explicit denunciations of racist presses and the representations of whites by domestics are closely tied, as both serve to undermine dominant ideas about race.

As part of this project, in her "Lighter Side" column, she represents a counter image to the exploitative focus on crime among African Americans—her focus on the charitable works and social events among Harlem activists and aristocrats allows a more complex, variegated rendering of African American society. Thus "The Lighter Side" counters the stereotypes in other papers, often depicting the "aristocracy" she would later describe in her photo-essay "Harlem." However, Petry sympathized with fellow *People's Voice* writers like John Harmon's critique of the "women's clubs" Petry covers as apolitical.

Petry's own ambivalence towards the "women's clubs" and society news she covered was expressed in one of a few columns that addressed more serious issues. Most dramatically, in a 1942 "Lighter Side" column, Petry declares that "there was no lighter side" that week, because Odell Walker, a sharecropper, was executed for the murder of his landlord. Petry states that "I would have no respect for myself if I wrote about the trivia that cropped up in this week's news and no respect for the persons who would want to read it" (20). Instead, she issues a strong condemnation of poverty and injustice in the South, and quotes Walker's final statement, which addresses key issues Petry's fiction engages: "You take big people as the president, governors, judge, their children never have to suffer. They has plenty money. Born in a mention (mansion) nothing ever to worry about. I am glad some people are that lucky."[13]

Petry's 1949 photo-essay "Harlem" for the high society magazine *Holiday* exposes the contrasts between the rich and poor, the fortunate and unlucky, yet more safely restricts her analysis to Harlem. Considering the generally white audience for the magazine, however, Petry's indictments should be read in relation to her fictional depictions of the wealthy in general. Petry asserts that "if you subscribe to the theory that class distinctions in America are based on wealth, then Harlem can be said to have an aristocracy" in the affluent suburb Sugar Hill, with its professionals and those who "display all the glittering trappings of the 20th century brand of conspicuous consumption," including jewelry, cars, servants, and "sensational divorces" (112). With the exception of Frances Jackson's employment of Miss Doris in *The Narrows*, Petry does not depict such intraracial domestic service, however, her antipathy toward Sugar Hill's aristocracy's habit of eating at exclusive restaurants "on the maid's night off," evokes her fictionalized representations of elites (112).

In "Harlem," Petry creates a fictional Harlem everyman in George Jackson, and her characterization could reveal much of her own Harlem experience and political perspectives: Jackson supported *People's Voice* publisher Adam Clayton Powell's run for city council and "twice helped elect Benjamin J. Davis, Jr., a Communist, this hardly means, however, that our Mr. Jackson had become a member of the Communist Party. It is likely he was pursuing his usual political course and voting for a man, not a political party. [He voted for Davis] because he felt Davis would never sell Harlem down the river" (164). Petry's exemplar, then, is an independent activist, which recalls Petry's self-representation to the *Daily Worker* in 1946: Petry states that she is "not affiliated with any party. This, she admits, is a mistake, declaring that she believes that the only way a responsible human being can be an effective one is to join the party of his choice and become involved in its activities."[14] These conflicting attitudes can be attributed to the different audiences of these two articles, however both agree on the necessity of political and social activism. Thus the inability of domestic workers isolated in rural and small-town Connecticut (like all of Petry's domestics) to protest their conditions shows through what Wright called a "negative" voice the damaging effect of the absence of such structures.[15]

For Petry herself, physical distance from New York insulated her from the demands of political engagement, particularly as the attacks on left-associated writers were beginning. Equally telling in "Harlem" are how Petry's Cold War efforts to exonerate Jackson from any ties to Communism while simultaneously endorsing Ben Davis reflect her own ambivalence, which challenges definitive characterization of her politics. Such equivocation prefigures the dismissal of Marxism in "The Novel as Social Criticism" and illuminates the rationale behind Petry's choice to imbed her censure of capitalist excess in the testimony of domestics who hold what has traditionally been considered the most demeaned and thus disempowered position in the social order.

The stylistic relationship of Petry's journalistic work to her novels rests in part in the political potential of reportage. Paula Rabinowitz argues that reportage was "a site of genre confusion that slides historical observation into fictional form" (78), and indeed, the preponderance of domestics in Petry's novels reflects both the high number of African Americans in domestic service in the 1940s and 1950s and Petry's effort to assert "social criticism" through the reportage of domestics. Petry's workers, then, accurately represent the particular restrictions and abuses of such labor in her historical moment, and these fictionalized accounts render such exploitation more visible and allow for the lodging of sharp criticisms through the seemingly innocuous figures of fictionalized domestics.

The two domestics represented in Petry's first novel, *The Street* (1946), Lutie Johnson and Min, witness the excesses of the wealthy, and for both, the conditions of their labor determines all of their other relationships. These features underscore Petry's alignment with those who believe that "class distinctions [are] based on wealth" ("Harlem," 112). When economic necessity forces Lutie, *The Street's* main character, to live with a rich white family in Connecticut, the Chandlers, she must leave her young son Bub and husband behind in Harlem. Upon acquiring the hard-sought job, Lutie's aspires to be "the perfect maid: Patient and good-tempered and hard-working and more than usually bright" (37). As Lutie moves invisibly serving the Chandlers, their friends and relatives, she is thus particularly susceptible to the meritocratic rhetoric rampant at the Chandlers.[16] For Lutie, this internalization of meritocracy, the exposure to the benefits of money, and the separation from her own family that accompanied work for the Chandlers ultimately lead her to conclude: "That kitchen in Connecticut had changed her whole life" (56).

Lutie's experience with the Chandlers exposes her to the contradictions between their material privileges and their psychological despair. It leads Lutie to an increased awareness of her own oppression and a painfully ingrained desire to advance through "hard work." The Chandlers themselves, however, disprove meritocracy. Mrs. Chandler is depicted as a neglectful mother, a compulsive shopper, an adulterer, and an alcoholic. Meanwhile, her husband is so weakened by alcohol and his wife's infidelity that he is nearly powerless, except for his money. Only "Little Henry," the Chandlers' son who is close to Bub in age, is rendered sympathetically. An attention to detail that comes with being "the perfect maid," and the intimacy that comes from living with the Chandlers yields numerous appalling insights into the families' destructive habits, ultimately demystifying whiteness for Lutie, and by extension, the book's contemporary reader.

Her employers' familial dysfunction, observed over her two-year tenure at the Chandlers teaches Lutie all about "Country Living" (50). A key component of her education is the "fat sleek magazines" (presumably like *Holiday*) and books that Mrs. Chandler gives her. The importance of media is further emphasized in Lutie's recollection of she and Mrs. Chandler's shared train rides to New York during which they often discussed "some story being played up in the newspapers" (51). In regular public humiliation after such train rides into New York, Mrs. Chandler reinforces what Wright, in *Twelve Million Black Voices*, called "America's paternalistic code toward her black maid, [a] code of casual cruelty, of brutal kindness, of genial despotism" (18) by imperiously dismissing Lutie at the station. This leads Lutie to wish that she could be spoken to as if the two "were friends," and finds that despite "arguing with herself, she was answering in a non-committal voice, 'Yes ma'am'" (51). This phrase, which comes so easily that it surprises Lutie, bespeaks the degree to which Lutie has imbibed the patterns of racism and deference that characterize domestics' relations with their employers. Like the Invisible Man, Lutie becomes sick of "saying 'yes' against the nay-saying of my stomach—not to mention my brain" (Ellison 560). Such degradation negates the potential for resistance, and underscores the limited strategies available to racialized, alienated workers. Within such confinements, the act of asserting one's identity through the unmasking of oppressors, or reportage, allows domestics' to have an oppositional voice.

In an early gesture towards the novel's dominant metaphor, Lutie compares her experience with the Chandlers to peering through a hole in a wall, but "the people on the other side of the wall knew less about her than she knew about them. . . . She decided it wasn't just because she was a maid, it was because she was colored" (41). Such realizations produce an increased, if inconsistent, consciousness of herself as the triply exploited figure politicized by Claudia Jones and others. Thus each of Petry's novels contains moments where the domestic overhears her employers denigrating her racially. For Lutie this occurs when she overhears the Chandlers' friends and relatives describe her as both invaluable and a threat: "she's a wonderful cook. But I wouldn't have any good looking colored woman in my house" (40). As Trudier Harris notes, the sexualization of African American women forces female domestics to be "reassuringly invisible and self-effacing" (20).

Lutie's awareness that her employers "looked at her but didn't see her" has a devastating affect that again makes her an early, female embodiment of the Invisible Man who was "invisible, understand, and simply because people refuse to see me" (Ellison 3). Instead, the Chandlers objectify her racially and sexually, which leads Lutie to compare her own indiscernability as a domestic to a picture she saw in the newspaper. The Chandlers are aligned with the reporter who "saw a dead Negro who had attempted to hold up a store, and so couldn't really see what the man lying on the sidewalk looked like. . . . He saw instead, the picture he already had in his mind: a huge brawny, blustering, ignorant, criminally disposed black man" (199). In this, Petry demonstrates the preponderance of stereotypes that reinforce each other, making the private home and the public media partners in the criminalization of African American bodies.[17]

Even so, Lutie is fascinated by the Chandlers' power, particularly one Christmas morning when Mr. Chandler's brother kills himself and she witnesses how "money transformed a suicide she had seen committed from start to finish in front of her eyes into an 'accident with a gun.'" The combination of indispensability and invisibility that characterizes domestics is particularly vivid in this event—Lutie is the first to discern Jonathan Chandler's intentions and tries to stop him, and she is the only one to notice and comfort Little Henry after he is traumatized by witnessing the suicide, all products of her vigilance. As the Chandlers endeavor to hide the suicide through exerting influence on the coroner, Lutie's silence in the matter is assumed, as is her attendance to Little Henry. In this, Lutie's role as domestic allows her to reveal the truth about the scandalous suicide, as her "labor enabled the Chandler's private life" (Lubin 130). This experience does not dissuade Lutie from her faith in meritocracy, but instead teaches her that "when one had money there were certain unpleasant things one could avoid" (49).

Lutie is forced to leave the Chandlers in an unsuccessful attempt to save her marriage, and like many other domestics, works at a laundry as a better alternative, and eventually becomes an office worker.[18] On her way home from work, she takes note of the many women in Harlem who had "been out all day working the white folks' kitchens . . . and then they come home and cook and clean for their own families half the night" (65). This dual burden ultimately destroys Lutie's family, and also undermines the tenuous stability of the Chandlers. Mrs. Chandler begs her to return because they miss her cooking and Little Henry longs for her "so much he's almost sick" (55), thus she is still expected to serve as a "bosom of humanity on which members of the white family lay their individual burdens of white children" (Wade-Gayles 97). The Chandlers never expressed concern or interest in Petry's own child; despite the fact that her care for Little Henry daily reminded her of her separation from Bub. In *No Crystal Stair*, Wade-Gayles points out that domestics "see the stark contrast between the world of have-nots and the world of the haves they labor in to alleviate their families' suffering" (98). This excruciating vision is evident when Lutie finds Bub shining shoes and becomes enraged by the knowledge that Little Henry was probably "doing his homework in that big warm library in front of the fireplace. And your kid is out in the street with a shoeshine box" (67).

In *The Nation*'s review, "Class and Color," Dianna Trilling declares that *The Street* is a "straight-forwardly middle class document," yet one that compels "a confrontation with our class realities" (11).[19] While perhaps unfairly aligning Petry with a middle-class mindset, Trilling also recognizes Petry's acute awareness of a range of subjectivities emergent from economic status. In contrast to more idealistic depictions of class-based solidarity found in proletarian literature, Lutie's conflict between her internalization of the Chandlers' racism and her nuanced critique of it, combined with her lack of options, indicates the depth of Petry's political analysis which emphasized the interplay of structural exploitation and individual volition. John Meldon's review of *The Street* for *Daily Worker* (March 20 1946, 11) acknowledges that "the progressive movement in Harlem has not become broad enough or sufficiently rooted to the extent that a Lutie Johnson, in fiction or real life, would know where to turn for help" (11).[20] This observation certainly extends to *The Street*'s other domestic, Min, who repeatedly searches for support and is rebuffed by those around her.[21]

Min lives with the predatory superintendent of Lutie's apartment building, Jones, whose obsession with Lutie largely propels the plot. Unlike Lutie's

Franklinesque aspirations, Min's only goals are to "not be put out" by Jones and to save enough money for a set of false teeth. Min is at first invisible to Lutie, due to "a shrinking withdrawal in her way of sitting as though she was trying to take up the least possible amount of space" (24), and Lutie elsewhere describes her as "a drab drudge so spineless and so limp she was like a soggy dishrag" (57). Min's "shabby" and "timid" (94) countenance reflects her denigrated status in all areas of her life (work, home and the church), causing Lutie to compare Min to Jones's abused dog Buddy: "the whispering woman seemed to be holding her breath; the dog was dying with the desire to growl or whine" (25).[22] This parallel narratologically aligns Lutie, Jones, and Min's employers in acts of erasure.

Min's work as a domestic servant is another sphere in which she is victimized without protest. As with Jones and the other abusive men in her life, Min is entirely passive in response to her own exploitation, "never raising any objection to the actions of cruelly indifferent employers" (126), who abase Min through the "degradation ritual of deference" required of most domestic servants, but especially black women who are often treated as house slaves as a legacy of slavery (Romero 74). Indeed, Min "pride[d]" herself in never quitting a domestic work job, despite families that multiply her workload and force her to take care of children, work on Sunday, despite her dedicated church attendance. These "madams" were frequently "openly contemptuous women who laughed in her face as they piled on more work . . . years and years like that" (126–27). Without union representation, domestics like Min, "were vulnerable to speed-ups within private homes" (Jones 342) and susceptible to constant insecurity.

The centrality of a home to Min, who holds her keys "tightly clutched in her palm as though they represented something precious" (94) suggests an arduous life of evictions, material loss, and abuse that combine to explain both her defeated appearance and desperation to stay with Jones, and explains how her transient existence may not have afforded the ability to protest unfair labor practices in the same way that Mildred manages in *Like One of the Family*, or to confront Jones. Thus Min cares for Jones "as dutifully and unquestionably as she serves her madams" (Wade-Gayle 104).

When she fears that Jones will evict her from their apartment as part of his plan to win Lutie, Min decides to go to "the Prophet," and thus makes her "first defiant gesture. . . . Up to now she had always accepted whatever happened to her without making any effort to avoid a situation or to change one" (126). In these actions, we can observe the "faint stirrings of emerging life" that Wright heralds. Unlike Lutie, Min reaches out to her local social networks like the church, neighbors, and David the Prophet.[23] Min trusts the Prophet because he listens attentively to her, unlike Min's employers who "issued orders to some point over her head . . . and the minute she started answering, they turned away" (136). The Prophet lacked the "derisive look she was accustomed to seeing in other people's eyes" (133), including her preacher, doctors and employers, and instead "had listened and been interested and all the time she talked he had never shifted his gaze" (137). For domestics typically erased and discounted, the Prophet's power rests in his ability to see the invisible, not the future. Poignantly, this brief exchange with the Prophet constitutes "the most satisfying experience she had ever known" (136).

Min's marginalized status as an impoverished black woman and her endurance of domestic and labor abuse seemingly render her powerless, especially when compared to Lutie. In this, though subordinate to Lutie both in terms of her role in the novel and her status as a maid compared to Lutie's clerical position, Min provides the one revelatory aspect of the novel. It is her secondary narrative that reveals an attempt to fight her alienation and exploitation through working with others and points up the vacuity of Lutie's individualist faith in meritocracy.[24] Accordingly, Min is often seen as Lutie's foil because she acts positively to change her situation, as in Carol E. Henderson's observation that Min's "movement from invisibility to visibility, submission to self-confidence, and finally voicelessness to voice, provides an unsettling story of triumph and determination as a counter to Lutie's failure" (858).[25] In this, it is possible to see Min's individualized solution as limited, leaving the reader still wanting for more substantial responses, and to question what alternatives actually exist for abused domestics. In particular, Min's mode of resistance and the potential transience of her improved situation calls into question the degree to which she can be said to have found a solution. The Prophet advises her to clean the apartment every day as one means to prevent being thrown out. Min chastises herself for dust she has allowed to gather and grease that has accumulated in the oven—in short, the Prophet's prescription suggests that if she works harder, performs her gender role more completely, she will be successful. Thus the "solution" that one might expect to see in a leftist text is painfully absent as Min does not forge solidarity with other domestic workers or abused women, instead it seem unlikely that her "first act of defiance" will inform her work relations as well.

In contrast to the unremitting exploitation of domestics in *The Street*, Petry's 1947 novel *Country Place* depicts a domestic whose loyalty to her liberal, comparatively enlightened employer is rewarded with the upward mobility that Lutie craves. While at the time the novel appeared to be mere "entertainment" ready for Hollywood translation rather than a complex analysis of multiple oppressions, Petry's middle novel follows the template of her more renowned works in deploying an African American servant and her white employer in order to explore the contradictions of meritocracy.[26] Interestingly, aside from the melodramatic aspects of the novel that have appealed to scholars of 1940s films and literature, this novel, with its preponderance of white characters, still remains slighted in recent constructions of the Petry canon.

Petry was characteristically equivocal about how her middle novel's engagement with race. In a 1946 correspondence with Alain Locke, Petry states that she will continue writing, "novels, of course. Not all of them will be about Negroes—though I think we, as a people, offer the richest most fertile field for creative writers."[27] While seemingly validating *Country Place*'s status as a potboiler, this contradicts her more public declaration to the *Daily Worker* that she planned to explore the issue of racism by "taking segments of this problem and dramatize them in a series of books . . . and each time I hope to present the public with something that will serve as emotional arouser and move them to action."[28] As both comments were presumably made while she was writing *Country Place*, the apparent discrepancy gives insight into her strategies within the novel, particularly the broadening of definitions of racism to include anti-Semitism and xenophobia and therein marks the postwar moment's reevaluation of its racial politics.

In interviews, Petry refused to discuss *Country Place* as "raceless" or comment on other writers who wrote fiction exploring whiteness, and instead demurred that *Country Place*'s Lennox was based on her hometown Old Saybrook, which experienced a storm that Petry reenacts in her novel.[29] The autobiographical influence in *Country Place* extends beyond the town's physical resemblance to Old Saybrook. Petry acknowledges that Lennox's narrator pharmacist, Doc Fraser is, in part based on her father, Peter Lane, to whom the book is dedicated.[30] Mrs. Bertha Gramby shares Petry's mother's first name, and exhibits Petry's penchant for quoting poets, philosophers, the bible, and politicians.[31] Despite her father's importance as town pharmacist and member of civic and church organizations (like *The Narrows'* Major), Petry divulges that she "will never be an insider" in her Old Saybrook community.[32] This racially based sense of exclusion, difference and alienation haunts all of Petry's domestics, particularly those like Lutie and Neola located in small white towns.

The town pharmacist, Doc Fraser, narrates the interconnected stories of a World War II soldier, Johnny, who returns home to discover his wife, Glory, has been unfaithful and Lil (Glory's mother) who attempts to kill her mother-in-law, Mrs. Gramby, in order to inherit the Gramby Mansion. Though Lil's attempt is thwarted by Neola's attentive care of Mrs. Gramby, Neola's essential role in the novel has often been overlooked.[33] While Neola's function to the plot is considerable, the absence of her interiority mimics the domestics' lived experience as an invisible and indispensable presence.[34] One of a few characters in *Country Place* whose inner thoughts are not revealed to the reader, instead, Neola subjectivity must be discerned through other's observations about her in an implicit challenge to the invisibility of domestics.[35] If Neola presents somewhat of an anomaly in the pattern of Petry's servant/employer relationship, where wealthy white, paternalistic and racist women not only regularly demean their workers but also expect them to become complicit in the family's intrigues, the novel's conclusion unsettles easy endorsements of meritocracy.

Mrs. Gramby's interracial staff expresses solidarity with Mrs. Gramby as much as to each other, and this fidelity enrages Lil and Glory, who fantasize about firing the staff upon Mrs. Gramby's death. Both are unnerved by what Trudier Harris describes as the mask that domestic servants often use, as is seen in Glory's racist observation that "If Neola were white and didn't have that dead-pan expression on her face, she wouldn't be bad looking" (47). In Mrs. Gramby's absence, Neola exerts an authority over the house, projecting Mrs. Gramby's distaste for Lil and Glory through cold treatment. Neola serves as a witness to the mother and daughter's scheming, when she silently comes to serve tea and overhears a conversation between Glory and Lil in which Glory states "You can pretend you don't want that old women to die. But I do . . . I want to be somebody here in Lennox. I want to live in this house some day and have parties and dances here—in the Gramby house—and be waited on" (50). To torment Neola as she exits, Lil states "Who ever heard of a nigger divorce?" upon which Neola "turned around slowly and stared at Lil, at Glory. Her face was expressionless, but her eyes blazed with contempt" (50). Neola's dignified gesture of defiance, in which she, like Petry's other domestics, passes judgment on those she must serve, is empowered by the secret knowledge she has acquired from her silent, incriminating interventions.

Comparing Neola to Lutie suggests the impact of Lutie's environment as well as the continuity in expectations of domestics. Lutie's marriage ends because of her separation from her husband as a live-in servant, and Neola is also divorcing her husband. These divorces suggest the difficulty domestics faced maintaining a relationship outside the workplace. That Neola's future husband, Portalucca, is part of the household staff indicates the difficulty of disentangling work in a private home from a domestic's private life. Neola's impending marriage to Portalucca represents a limited challenge to restrictions on post-war interracial intimacy as the "Portegee" (as he is called throughout the novel) is highly exoticized through recurrent references to his "swarthy" complexion, his turquoise earring, and accent. Thus Laura Dubrek observes that the marriage of Portalucca and Neola represents an "otherness" that "gives meaning and simultaneously mocks postwar ideologies of whiteness" (74–75).

The habits of deference Lil assumed she would receive because of her whiteness and status as Mearn's Gramby's wife are frustrated by the staff's refusal to recognize her as a superior.[36] Indeed, as a former seamstress, her new social position leads to an overzealous effort to distinguish herself through white privilege. Lil's vicious racism towards Neola confirms the ugliness of Lil's character (who as a working class woman aspiring to improve her economic status we might otherwise sympathize with), and thus, as Emily Bernard notes, "the depth of Lillian's moral degeneracy is in direct correlation to the extent of her white supremacist attitudes" (107).[37] Overall, in *Country Place*, the most overt expressions of racism emerge from members of the working class, the anti-Semitic cab driver, the Weasel, Lil, a former seamstress, and Glory, a clerk at the local grocery store. Conversely, the one upper class figure depicted in detail, Mrs. Gramby, decries anti-Semitism and the history of anti-Irish segregation in the town. Thus she appears to serve as a benevolent mistress whose tolerance and generosity seems to affirm the potential for meritocracy that has miserably failed Lutie, Min and, as we shall see, *The Narrows*' Malcolm Powther. This marked reversal of prior and later portrayals raises questions about Petry's intervention into the post-war racial moment particularly in conjunction with the trenchant insights into race and ethnicity-based oppression among the span of characters and issues addressed, therein embedding her comment on meritocracy and liberalism (personified in Mrs. Gramby).

Accordingly, though Neola's perspective is nearly absent, a significant portion of the book is devoted to Mrs. Gramby's internal monologues, in which she worries over her household staff. As Mrs. Gramby despairs over her son's failed marriage while compulsively consuming the chocolates (left by Lil, who has hidden Mrs. Gramby's insulin) that will send her into diabetic shock, she is roused to action by the thought of Lil's already "imperious" attitude towards the staff and fears that upon inheriting the house, Lil would fire the staff, "insulting them when she gave them notice" (154).[38] Mrs. Gramby's attachment to Neola, in particular, shows the utter dependence of elites on their domestics' devotion; as Mrs. Gramby considers her needs, "peace of mind and a quiet heart" she muses that "even Neola could not get those things for me, though she would certainly try. Aloud she said Bless You. Neola smiled at her and went out of the room" (108).[39]

As Gramby enters diabetic shock, Neola, on her day off, passes the home and notices that the curtains are awry. This vigilance enables Neola's heroic rescue of Mrs. Gramby, in which her own life is endangered when she drives a car for the first time at high speed in order to get Mrs. Gramby her insulin and recalls Lutie's effort to seize the gun Mr. Chandler's brother uses to kill himself—in both cases, these "perfect maid[s]" demonstrate sacrifice and courage that go unrecognized by those around them.[40] When her life is briefly prolonged with Neola's intervention, Mrs. Gramby pointedly chooses the Jewish lawyer, Rosenberg, victim of Lennox's anti-Semitism, to make out her will.

In reflecting on her first encounter with Rosenberg, Mrs. Gramby romanticizes her youth in which "a man was judged solely by his actions," not on his ethnicity.[41] This critique of racial borders, with both official and unofficial redlining taking place in suburbs, Mrs. Gramby's decision to bequest her home to an African American, a Portuguese, and an Irishman reflect her desire to restore her remembered moments of racial tolerance and counters Petry's characterizations of employers in *The Narrows* and *The Street*. More importantly, Petry's signature indictment of meritocracy and the self-destructive delusion of dedication to exploitative white employers undergoes a remarkable transformation as Neola, so like *The Narrows'* Powther in her self-sacrificing dedication and internalization of her employers needs and idiosyncrasies, is ultimately rewarded for her hard work and devotion when Mrs. Gramby bequeaths her mansion to Neola, her soon to be husband, Portalucca, and the Cook who all attended Mrs. Gramby so faithfully. Mrs. Gramby's entwined desire for vengeance against Lil and remuneration of her staff eventually becomes a project to flip the town's class and racial lines through the symbolic transfer of the town's mansion.[42]

The house's stature as a class marker, as noted by Lennox's less privileged inhabitants, raises questions about the degree to which the household staff's ownership of the house can "change" Lennox (184).[43] Given that the story ostensibly centers on a returning G.I. who finds Lennox limited and intolerant, the book's ending may reflect an optimism regarding the potential for changes in the racial order in the post-war moment. However, Lil's abuse of Neola complicates this, as does the persistence of anti-Semitism in Lennox. Instead, Neola's rise in status to homeowner is the product of a random turn of events that reflect capitalism's volatility. Similarly, the will fails to affirm the right to private intermarriage and property between Portalucca and Neola, through the installation of the Cook as co-owner, who can be seen as either an overseer of this interracial union or whose inclusion in the will can more generously be viewed as Mrs. Gramby's attempt to turn over the means and site of production to all of the household laborers.[44]

When Lil discovers that she is excluded from the will, she unlooses a racist tirade against African Americans, the Irish, Jewish and disabled, stunning those assembled for the will's reading. Mearns justifies leaving the house to the household staff on the grounds that Neola, Portalucca and the Cook "loved [Mrs. Gramby]. They love this house. They will enjoy living here" (189).[45] In contrast to Lutie who is given Mrs. Chandler's cast-offs and Min who cherishes the table that Lutie describes as "the kind of big ugly furniture white women love to give to their maids" (*The Street* 24), Mrs. Gramby's servants' hard work is compensated. Thus meritocracy is preserved and exemplified—the hard working servants gain the house, the persecuted lawyer is given a recognition that will challenge Lennox's anti-Semitism, and the Weasel is rewarded for his "chivalrous assistance."[46]

The Saturday Review of Literature warned that *Country Place* "seems to say ... that humanity is as degraded in Lennox as it is in Studs Lonigan's Chicago." That Lennox Avenue is also a key site in Harlem challenges racialized constructions of crime areas, recalling Petry's own protests against the *Daily News*. Petry's Lennox Connecticut centers on a number of criminal acts among whites, and also suggests the impact of Petry's own New York experience. Thus *Country Place* allows her to situate stories of "crime and passion" motivated by greed and want among white characters. Rather than asserting an apolitical universalism, this indicates Petry's desire to render visible the depravity of those whose privilege usually affords their privacy.[47] The ending of *Country Place* also recreates Petry's larger political project. Rather than affirming meritocratic myths via the transfer of property to household servants because they "loved the house. They loved her," demonstrates the actual vagaries of capitalism, as it follows the whims of a vengeful, mythologizing, wealthy and white woman on her deathbed.

Petry's positive, though hedged, conclusion of *Country Place*, stands in sharp contrast to Petry's next novel, ostensibly the third in her trilogy on race, *The Narrows* (1953). Though now considered of the same caliber as *The Street*, upon publication, the charges of sensationalism leveled against *Country Place* recurred though critics also point out that despite salacious plot lines; Petry's characters redeem the book.[48] *Time* magazine claimed that *The Narrows'* plot resembles a "sordid tabloid standby" recuperated only by Petry's poignantly drawn characters. Lauding "the rich parallel story of little Malcolm Powther, the dignified Treadway butler" argues that if Petry had "stuck strictly to Malcolm and Mamie Powther, *The Narrows* would be remembered longer" (96).[49] That Petry may have indulged in "tabloid" encounters in her novel suggests her continued dialogue with the debates around sensationalism during her work with *People's Voice*, and the significance of domestics in reporting the scandalous behaviors of their elite employers.

In *The Narrows*, there are several domestics, but Malcolm Powther's seemingly superior position as butler, concomitant with his gender, presents elucidating contrasts to Petry's previous construals of the injustices of domestic service. Though he is one of two supervisors at the Treadway mansion, his authority is undermined by the racism of the Treadway staff, and the personal conflicts he faces align his narrative to Lutie, Min and Neola in telling ways. Unlike these other domestics, however, Powther's loyalty to his employer makes him complicit with the fatal persecution of Link, the novel's protagonist, suggesting the peculiar Cold War dilemma of those whose race made them already suspect. Malcolm Powther's seeks employment in Treadway home because he quits a more prestigious butler position in response to his former employer's lust for Powther's wife, Mamie, which presents yet another example of the sexualization of African Americans by upper class whites which leads to the novel's tragic end (Link/Camilo, Lutie/Junto).[50] Like Lutie and Neola, Powther's marriage to Mamie is compromised due to the time he spends working at the Treadway mansion, reinforcing the way that domestic service dispersed households.

Throughout Powther's narrative, his repeated identification with his white employers and his inability to fashion the understanding of the intersections between class and race that Lutie learns at the Chandlers lead to a perfectionism, fastidiousness, and internalized racism that doom him. Harris's description of *The Bluest Eye*'s Pauline Breedlove also applies to Powther, who "revels in the primness and cleanliness of the white house in which she works. Her work for whites becomes an elaborate form of self-hatred; she attempts to escape herself and her culture by identifying with those who hate her and her kind" (17). Like Lutie, Powther internalizes his employers' belief in meritocracy and racism. Powther's admires Mrs. Treadway's work ethic (she is the only white female employer in these novels who works), despite the fact that she has increased profits through an ever-increasing exploitation of the munitions plant employees.[51] Hence her employees suffer the same conditions as unprotected domestic servants in the 1940s and 1950s, and that these workers are factory workers involved in national defense further underscores Petry's critique of labor exploitation in the early Cold War.

Powther's belief that his specialized labor elevates his social status is articulated with imagery laden with military references, significant both because the Treadway fortune was made by munitions production, and because of *The Narrows*' context of World War II and the Cold War. Powther, demoralized as he thinks of his wife's possible affair and lack of attention to her children, "reminded himself, as he always did whenever he felt a little low in his mind, that though he was constantly defeated at home, he was a conqueror, a victor at Treadway Hall" (163). Powther's identification with his employers leads him to be disturbed by the Treadway's staff's resentments towards their employers, and he pontificates "that if you didn't like the people you worked for, you shouldn't take their money" (161), indicating a failure to recognize the circumscribed job opportunities and venues of protest available for particular racial and ethnic groups, and therein implicitly aligning himself with meritocracy. When the explosive news item appears in the *Monmouth Chronicle* reporting Camilo Sheffield's false rape charges against Link, Powther is especially concerned that the staff not demean Camilo, despite his inside knowledge that undercuts Camilo's accusation. Powther frets when he realizes that while the general public did not yet know the real circumstances behind Camilo's rape charge, "the staff at the hall would know instantly.... All Monmouth would know it eventually" (341), thus demonstrating the power of domestics' secret knowledge as exposé.[52] Such reportage from domestics counters the *Monmouth Chronicles*' capitulation to the Treadways power, and thus challenges the elite's control of the media.

Powther, like Lutie, sees parallels between his own experience with racism and a news item that dehumanizes African Americans, and suffers moments of humiliation at the workplace.[53] Of his fellow employees, the chauffeur Al in particular resents Powther, causing Powther to refer to him "mentally, as the Nazi" (162), recalling, as does *Country Place*, the persistence of fascist racialism in the post World War II moment. Al comes to accept Powther when he, in an act of dedication similar to Neola's care for Mrs. Gramby, nurses Al through a life-threatening illness. Forced to justify his previous abuse of Powther, Al explains that Powther was the first African American person he had worked with, and worse, he "was the butler, and that meant that you was over me.... But you're just like a white man, Mal" (162). Despite this troubled attempt at reconciliation, Powther overhears Al, along with the other employees, express ingrained racism towards the Narrows' inhabitants. Having so thoroughly identified himself with his employer, often exhibiting the internalized racism of Abbie Crunch, such reminders of racism are particularly unsettling for Powther. Further, he thought through his hard work and dedication to Al, that his co-workers would have overcome their racism, thus affirming meritocracy.

While Powther displays a loyalty to his employers that replicates Neola's devotion to Mrs. Gramby, he is ruined rather than rewarded when he is forced to identify Link for the Treadway/Sheffield assassination of Link. This action led Bernard Bell to condemn Powther as "a black Judas, [a] pompous, worshipful servant to rich white people, whose values he embraces" (113). As Powther's agonizes over his impending betrayal he distances himself from other African Americans on the grounds of his individual merit, implicit in which is a demand that African Americans be seen as individuals:

I have to prove he wasn't my brother. Prove to these people . . . that all Negroes are not criminal, some of them are good, some of them are self-respecting, and some of them are first class butlers named Powther. (386)

This painful study of misplaced alignment, of the need for human recognition, and the Cold War infused willingness to "name names" so as to exonerate oneself enacts Petry's perspective of what truly socially conscious literature should do: "[i]n a book which is more political pamphlet or sermon than novel the characters do not battle with themselves to save their souls, so to speak. Their defeat or victory is not their own—they are pawns in the hands of a deaf, blind, stupid social system" ("Social Criticism," 36). Hence Powther is in the throes of a great internal struggle, complicated by his attempt to retain dignity amidst denigration at home and work, and his ultimate struggle over turning in Link indicates moments when his resentment over the affair he imagines between Link and Mamie combines with his internalized racism to constrain his volition.

The Narrows also contains the only depiction of a defiant domestic, in the form of Miss Doris, the only one of Petry's domestics employed by an African American, Frances Jackson, a successful African American funeral parlor owner.[54] Miss Doris and her husband, Sugar, worked for the Orwells, whose alcoholic exploits elicit reactions from Miss Doris that act as object lessons.[55] To an even greater extent than Petry's other domestics, Miss Doris resists white supremacist constructs in one of the forms of resistance Jennifer Bickham Mendez locates among domestics, the exercise of "intimate knowledge of the employer in order to reject employers' definitions of workers as inferior" (116). When Miss Doris overhears Mr. Orwell describe her as "black and evil" after eating her meringue pie before desert, she holds a carving knife to his throat and tells him "I been workin for multonmillionaires all my life and I were never insulted by any of them until right now" (239). Orwell responds crying out "Miss Doris what have I done, what have I said. . . . I will never go in your kitchen again" (240), a promise he keeps. Miss Doris's act of defiance and insistence that she control the place of her labor suggests a class consciousness that escapes Petry's other domestics.[56]

Interestingly, Miss Doris's character was rooted in an acquaintance of Petry who appeared "hewn out of rock" and whose tales in the novel appear as she told them to Petry, "with a little editing here and there" (Petry, 1988, 266). Miss Doris's shocking stories and her assertion of her rights and visibility aligns her tangentially with Childress's Mildred Johnson, who according to Mary Helen Washington, is "both insider and outsider, a working class woman with a low-paying job and a knowledgeable political actor who is intended to be a model of resistance" (188).[57] However, the power she appears to have over the Orwells should not obscure that her experiences reveal the ways that domestics performed multiple jobs for little pay under difficult conditions, as she is humiliated in their presence and acts as a personal nurse, cook and servant.

Stacey Morgan identifies Petry among African American social realists who worked to "fashion dynamic representations of the most pressing social issues of their day in a manner distinct from, but integrally related to, politically engaged photographs, journalistic reportage, and sociology" (244). *The Narrows* combines these elements through the exposés of domestics who report, via Petry, the sordidness of their employers supplemented by the work of a "communist" photographer, revealing Petry's commitment to the necessity for social change, and for the transformative power of words and art to compel one into action.[58] In this context, Bullock's decision to not publish the story of the heiresses' drunken car collision with an impoverished little girl recalls the Chandlers' ability to misrepresent a relative's suicide as an accident for the presses in *The Street*, and therein elucidates Petry's commitment to exposure—if white run papers can bury stories about elite criminality, Petry's novels can exhume them. Such exposure acts as a leveling device, challenging the alleged superiority of the rich and wealthy. As Powther notes, "Scandal in a wealthy, important family like the Treadways served to bring the Treadways right back down to the level of the trolley car operator, the bootblack. It showed they could be hurt, ruined, just like other people" (*The Narrows*, 381).

In revealing the depravity of employers and the internal conflicts of domestics, fears about aberrance that marked the McCarthy era become entwined in questions of loyalty that are so central to the quotidian interactions of the private home as a site of exploited labor. In narratives where employers demand a self-negating complicity, domestics struggle to balance multiple allegiances to family, fellow workers, and the necessities of their job. Marx argued that the worker has "only to take note of what is happening before their eyes and to become its mouthpiece" in order to make a political intervention (Marx, *Poverty*, 120). Petry, as a reporter, Old Saybrook inhabitant and Harlem resident recorded what she witnessed, and used her skills as a writer to work as a "mouthpiece." Marx's observation can be usefully applied to the many domestics in Petry's novels, who through gossip and internal narratives, witness and report the vices and exploitation before "their eyes." As Lutie and Malcolm Powthers temporarily come to adopt the values of employers through identification that seemingly supplants the solidity of their own families, they become witnesses or collaborators with the criminality and deviations of these families. Conversely, Miss Doris and the gossip of the Treadway and Gramby staff suggest the domestics' power as reporter, a role Petry assumes as she recounts the corruption and malice of her domestics' employers. In such representations, Petry adroitly portrays the complex variations of racism and exploitation in the North between domestic servants and their employers, and secures Petry's reputation as an acute observer of the triple oppression her contemporary, Claudia Jones, explored.

THE HOME AND THE STREET

The Dialectics of Racial Privacy in Ann Petry's
Early Career

John Charles

Arguably the most productive and significant period of Ann Petry's literary career was the four year stretch from 1943 to 1947 when she first came to public notice. During this brief span she published eight short stories, several reviews and essays, and two novels—*The Street* (1946) and *Country Place* (1947). Immediately after the appearance of *The Street*, critics celebrated the arrival of a powerful new author of black protest fiction, a categorization that Petry openly rejected for its reductive and constricting connotations. The popular and critical success of *The Street* cast her other works from this moment into a shadow from which they have only just begun to emerge.[1] Contributing to the neglect of her stories is the privileged place that the novel, as genre, holds in African American literary history. Her second novel's primary focus on the lives of white characters and such seemingly "apolitical" subjects as "man" and "his" moral and psychological conflicts, has for most critics made the novel seem irrelevant to an assessment of her early career, and to the study of African American novel more generally.[2]

If we suspend these critical habits, however, and look at her early career in the round, we can begin to better appreciate not only the range of her interests and accomplishments, but also her remarkable insights on the racialized politics of domesticity in mid-twentieth-century America. The first phase of Petry's career offers a brilliant and under-investigated set of counter-narratives to mid-century investments in "containing" radicals, women, minorities, and workers (none of these terms being mutually exclusive). Petry refigures the idea of "public" politics to include the interrelated notions of privacy, intimacy, and domesticity. In Petry's analysis, family and the home, historically considered a refuge from politics, were among the most sensitive registers of social conflicts and indices of power relations. What unites these otherwise highly varied works are aspirations for "racial privacy," a concept that I will discuss in detail below.

Due to limitations of space (and the ample attention already given to *The Street*), the first section of my essay will focus primarily on two short stories that appeared the same year as *Country Place*, "The Bones of Louella Brown" and "In Darkness and Confusion." I will argue that each of these works attempts to achieve a kind of provisional racial privacy by symbolically resolving African Americans' over-determined and exploitative relationship with publicity. Each text in its own way reclaims the public—scene and source of denigration and de-legitimation—as a way of projecting a space of private dignity. In *Country Place*, I argue that Petry's emphasis on white characters enacts a form of racial privacy for both the character Neola, a black maid, and the author herself; this shift in focus allows Petry an identificational mobility and creative freedom that was radically circumscribed for black novelists in mid-twentieth-century America. My reading elucidates the degree to which she engages contemporary moral and psychological discourses (especially the debates around "mother-blaming") in order to facilitate a momentary switch from "The Negro Problem" (and its reliance on depictions of black subjection) to "white problems"—in this case white moral and psychological deficits. Over the course of the novel she proffers a powerful refiguring of white male domestic privilege—the very thing that symbolically and materially determines the (im)possibility of black privacy—and in the process imagines an alternative notion of American progress.

My thinking on racial privacy draws principally on the treatments of the subject by Philip Brian Harper, Lauren Berlant, and Alex Lubin, although none of these authors use the phrase "racial privacy." My use of the expression "racial privacy" is intended to highlight how one's capacity for social agency and self-mastery, particularly in the private sphere, is fundamentally determined by public meanings of race. By private sphere I am referring principally to the domestic sphere, intimate relations, and forms of labor, both paid and unpaid. Although most paid labor takes place in public, in the United States the market economy is "private" insofar as it is nominally extrapolitical—operating largely independently of the state, and structured around individuals acting as private economic agents and owners of property (Taylor 101).

A central concern in Petry's early fiction is how America's racialized and sexualized division of labor has had particularly adverse affects on black women's struggle for privacy. Overwhelmingly excluded from white collar jobs, black women in the 1940s found themselves commodified as either domestics or, at least in terms of dominant culture attitudes, prostitutes.[3] White male sexual exploitation of black women demonstrates forcefully the degree to which the latter historically have been rendered private objects of white male concern—black women are, in the words of Philip Brian Harper, "not private subjects who can themselves lay claim to and govern their own private domains" (19). Harper explains that these conditions function to solidify the subjectivity of white men "precisely because it emphasizes the degree to which he is master over his own private realm, king in his own castle, while simultaneously voiding the black woman's subjectivity by depriving her of a private realm over which she can hold sovereign sway."[4] More recently, Alex Lubin has demonstrated how the postwar "domestic imperative" (i.e., the national demand for women to give up their war time participation in public life and devote their energies to the private sphere, e.g., family and home) was rendered largely inoperable to black women, both because of antimiscegenation laws and because of the racialized economy that incorporated black women into the private spaces of white families as domestics.[5] These conditions were powerfully dramatized in *The Street*, and Lubin has shown how "for Lutie Johnson, that which ought to be private (her home and family life) is made public, while that which ought to receive recognition in the public sphere (her labor as mother, civil service worker, and blues singer) is rendered invisible" (129). Lutie is on the one hand unable to care for her own home and family because her labor is devoted to reproducing the private life of the Chandlers, while on the other the white man who owns her apartment building, Junto, operates a brothel in this same building, and attempts to incorporate her as an object of sexual commerce (128–33). Petry's fiction from this era repeatedly exposes the extent to which the nation's valorization and protection of the domestic sphere (as a locus of private subject formation and a quasi-sanctified zone of non-interference) is, in practice, an index of white hetero-patriarchal privilege underwritten by the construction of whiteness as "usable property, the subject of the law's regard and protection" (Harris 1737). Racial privacy necessitated the public authority and social agency that allows for the maintenance of the family in the private sphere, which includes access to adequate employment, housing, education, health services, reliable police protection, and freedom from unwanted exposure to certain behaviors (e.g., drugs, prostitution, and violent crime). "In Darkness and Confusion" and "The Bones of Louella Brown" in particular narrate incursions into the public sphere on behalf of racial privacy.

"In Darkness and Confusion" provides a fictionalized and highly subjective rendering of one family's participation in the devastating 1943 Harlem riots. The riot was triggered when a black soldier assaulted a white police officer who was arresting a black woman for "disorderly conduct"; the soldier hit the officer with his nightstick, who then shot the fleeing soldier in the shoulder. Reports of the shooting quickly spread, including rumors that the police officer had killed the soldier in front of his mother, who was with him at the time. As Petry's narrative describes in vivid detail, large, angry crowds formed, walking first to the hospital where the solider and police officer were taken, and then to the police station, before turning again toward 125th street where the destruction of the businesses and looting began and continued until dawn the next morning. The riot caused an estimated five million dollars of property damage, and directly led to six deaths and several hundred injuries and arrests; all those killed were African American, as were nearly all of the injured and arrested.

The explosion in Harlem was of course accompanied by an explosion in publicity. The mainstream press repeatedly insisted that it was not a race riot, but rather the work of gangs of hoodlums. Some white critics argued that it was the result of racial "agitators," and others argued it was the result of police laxity in law enforcement, especially Mayor La Guardia's "irresponsible" policy of police *restraint*. One *Washington Post* editorial denied not only that it was a race riot, but that it was even a riot at all. Rather, "what seems to have occurred was a complete breakdown of all law and order followed by an outrageous carnival of looting. Certainly it takes something of a *tour de force* of reasoning to translate such an episode into a subtle protest against social injustices" ("Harlem Post-Mortem" 8 Aug 1943). Petry's narrative constitutes just such a "*tour de force* of reasoning." It is at once an intervention in majoritarian public discourses about the riots, as well as an analysis of how the circulation of race in the public sphere destroys black privacy. Although based on a specific historical event, "In Darkness and Confusion" dramatizes a recurring theme in Petry's work: the extent to which African Americans experience their relation to the nation and the state as deprivation, violation, and evacuation of agency. In this story Petry imagines violent protest in the streets not as lawlessness and immorality, but rather as a momentarily galvanizing, therapeutic, and public act of resistance to the immorality of state violence and its role in protecting white supremacy, specifically in the form of "white" property and a white intimate sphere. The narrative levels a powerful critique of how the state's active role in maintaining white privilege and property systematically structures and disrupts the African American intimate sphere, and the possibility for privacy for black citizens.

Petry's reading of the event is aligned with other contemporary commentators and more recent historians for whom there is no question that it was in fact a race riot, and specifically a community wide assault on the immorality of racist state violence.[6] Some mainstream leaders of good will, black and white, wanted to avoid criminalizing the entire community, and thus the entire race, by confining the rioters to the "criminal" element in Harlem. Petry, however, stresses the fact that the riot was conducted by people from every aspect of the community. As the riot takes off, the protagonist, William Jones, looks around him and exclaims, "'Great God in the morning . . . everybody's out here.' There were girls in thin summer dresses, boys in long coats and tight-legged pants, old women dragging kids along by the hand. A man on crutches jerked himself past to the rhythm of the shuffling feet." William also sees in the crowd bag ladies, numbers runners, and "three sisters of the Heavenly Rest for All movement" (285).[7]

Absent from her depiction of the community are "agitators" and radicals. Rather, two of the figures responsible for touching off different phases of the riot are the central characters in the story, William and Pink Jones, both of whom appear to be largely apolitical figures. Petry gives no indication that their actions are influenced by involvement with local or national political campaigns and organizations, or even a heightened racial consciousness or resentment due to the outbreaks of white supremacist mob violence in Detroit and Los Angeles that had captured the nation's attention earlier in the summer. The story (utilizing free indirect discourse) is filtered almost entirely through William's consciousness, and thus the reader learns that William's primary preoccupation is his private, domestic life—specifically, his family's well being. The story makes it painfully clear that it is the state's recent attack on his son, in particular, and the long term destruction of his private life, more generally, that propels him into public action. Once he has "gone public" by taking to the streets, however, he has new insights, about himself, his family, and the state.

The story opens with William sitting alone on a stifling July morning, unable to enjoy his breakfast because "there were too many nagging worries that kept drifting through his mind" (252). The worries all have to do with his family. He hasn't heard from his son, Sam, who was drafted and stationed in Georgia; his wife is morbidly obese and has a heart condition, which means that continuing to live on the top floor of his rundown, dark, overcrowded apartment building is jeopardizing her life; and his eighteen year old niece seems clearly on the threshold of serious trouble. Although the story seems to revolve around the absent "good" son, the niece Annie May (who at first is presented as the "bad" or "difficult" child) plays a crucial role in the narrative's development. The first thing we learn about her is that she regularly stays out late and misses work; when William confronts her about her behavior she dismisses him flippantly, barely containing her rage: "he saw a deep smoldering sullenness in her face that startled him. . . . Lately every time Annie May looked at him there was open, jeering laughter in her eyes, as though she dared him to say anything to her" (256). Her late nights, lack of a steady job, and "cheap, bright-colored dresses she was forever buying" leads William to suspect her of engaging in prostitution.

All of these worries coalesce around a longstanding, overarching frustration—his desire to move: "The rooms weren't big enough for a man to move around in without bumping into something. Sometimes he thought that was why Annie May spent so much time away from home. Even at thirteen she couldn't stand being cooped up like that in such a small amount of space" (261). He suspects that their living conditions push his children into the streets, which are populated by prostitutes, and full of shadowy, lurking dangers, "disembodied figures" with "stealth[y]" movements "that revealed a dishonest intent . . ." (260).

In certain respects Petry reproduces commonplace images of poor black neighborhoods as zones of immorality. The dominant culture, abetted by conservative social scientists and reformers, attributed the alleged immorality of African Americans to a deep-seated racial nonheteronormativity—black neighborhoods, conflated with black bodies, were inherently pathologized and "broken," as evidenced by high rates of divorce, out of wedlock births, female headed households, etc.[8] This "immorality" however is exactly what William yearns to protect his family from. He fears it will destroy his children, especially Annie May, if it hasn't already. After Annie May derides him early in the story, "he groped in his mind for words to describe what he thought Annie May had become. A Jezebel, he decided grimly" (257). As the story unfolds, Petry goes on to complicate simplistic and erroneous notions of innate black immorality by situating these black neighborhoods and domestic spaces in relation to larger social forces and asymmetries of power.

Two years earlier William had gone to see Annie May's principal about persuading his niece to stay in school. After making him wait two hours to see her, the principal proceeds to "bur[y] [him] under a flow of words, a mountain of words" until he "lost all sense of what she was saying." The only phrase that he fully grasps is her repeated assertion that Annie May is "a slow learner," which he knows is not true. "Confused and embarrassed . . . before he knew it he was out in the street, conscious only that he'd lost a whole afternoon's pay and he never got to say what he'd come for" (265). Instead of locating an ally in his effort to steer Annie May in the right direction, he finds himself unexpectedly enduring Annie May's experiences in this institution— he is silenced, humiliated, and, before he knows it, forced "out on the street." William is silenced and humiliated by "white" public authority another time after he and Pink's child dies in childbirth. Pink's "loud grieving" prompts the nurse to say with "cold contempt. . . . 'You people have too many children anyway'" (284). William is stunned "speechless" by the cruelty of her remark. The nurse's comments express the dominant culture and the state's attitude toward black domesticity—it is inherently pathological and in need of regulation and intervention. Black reproduction is implicitly a threat to the state.

The state's crowning assault on William and his family takes place after Sam is drafted into the army. Sam is shot by a white military police officer "because he wouldn't go to the nigger end of the bus." Sam still manages to shoot the MP in the shoulder with his own gun, an act of resistance which gets him court-martialed and "twenty years at hard labor" (268). After learning about this from another black soldier who has been stationed at the same base, William feels, once again, incapable of speaking about this injury and avoids telling his wife. The next day, however, when he witnesses a white police officer shoot a young black soldier, he is so outraged that he ends up leading the crowd into the street.

William unintentionally becomes caught up in a spontaneous but collective act of public resistance. By taking to the streets in protest against police brutality he feels an unprecedented sense of agency and connection with the larger community.

"he got the feeling that he had lost his identity as a person with a free will of his own. It frightened him at first. Then he began to feel powerful. He was surrounded by hundreds of people like himself. They were all together, they could do anything. . . . It was as though, standing so close together, so many of them like this—as though they knew each other's thoughts. It was a wonderful thing." (282)

For the first time William is able to speak against racist authority, and when he does his words are automatically caught up and circulated through crowd. When he comments that "they moved the black cops out" of the area, "he heard it go back and back through the crowd until it was only a whisper of hate on the still hot air" (283). He senses the fear of the police, and when the crowd marches to the hospital where the soldier was taken (the same hospital where he encountered the racist nurse), "he saw with satisfaction that frightened faces were appearing at the windows" (284). This time the white state is afraid of him, and "He began to feel that this night was the first time he'd ever really been alive. Tonight everything was going to be changed. There was a growing, swelling sense of power in him. He felt the same thing in the people around him" (284).

Prior to this moment the street has been a symptom of his family's unchanging and oppressive relation to the dominant culture. He stopped going to church after the minister sermonized about "the streets of gold up in heaven." The minister's spatial metaphor for salvation in the next life is especially galling, because "This street where he and Pink lived was like the one where his mother had lived. It looked like he and Pink ought to have gotten further than his mother had. She had scrubbed floors, washed and ironed in the white folks' kitchens. They were doing practically the same thing" (273). The preacher's suggestion that the righteous will find a redeemed agency in the next life exacerbates his sense of impotency in secular time. William and Pink resigned themselves to the fact that it was "too late for them" (270) to change their lives, but had held out hope that Sam could have a future with different possibilities. He had largely given up hope on Annie May, but for the wrong reasons. During the riot he sees Annie May emerge from a store front and throw a "pinkish" "naked model" into the crowd; she then "stood in the empty window and laughed with the crowd when someone kicked the torso into the street." This act is a revelation for William, as

he felt that now for the first time he understood her. She had never had anything but badly paying jobs—working for young white women who probably despised her. She was like Sam on that bus in Georgia. She didn't want just the nigger end of things, and here in Harlem there wasn't anything else for her. All along she'd been trying the only way she knew how to squeeze out of life a little something for herself. (289–90)

Prior to this moment he perceived her signs of "wildness" exclusively as sexual transgression and moral failure. Now he recognizes that her refusal to go to work *on time* and to keep a "steady" or "regular" job, is not laziness, but her means of resisting the deadening regulation of her life, her humiliating incorporation into routines of labor that sustain the domestic sphere and private life of the white family she works for at the expense of her own. Her labor in their private sphere enables them to "progress" while locking her into performing the same tedious acts as countless generations of black women before her. Even so, Petry implies that Annie May's mode of rebellion of "staying out all night" (beyond domesticity and heteronormativity) is not "freedom"; rather, it will likely imprison her within an equally long standing history of sexual exploitation on the streets. The bleakness of her future is punctuated by the fact that the last time William sees her during the riot she is being arrested with a group of other looters with "a yellow fox jacket dangling from one hand" (291), being punished by the state for taking "a little something for herself."

In the final scene of the story, his wife, Pink—who joined the riot after it began, but was the first to smash a store front window—has collapsed in front of William, dying from a heart attack. William screams into the night, no longer "strangled by the words that rose in his throat" (295). Rather than representing a moment of redemption and triumph, his curses are an expression of agony in the face of the almost total destruction of his private life. However empowering it felt to publicly share his rage and grief with other members of the community, and however satisfying it was to know that the "white folks [who] owned these stores ... [would] lose and lose and lose" (288), while on the streets he also comes face to face with the fact that "There ain't no room for us anywhere. There wasn't no room for Sam in a bus in Georgia. There ain't no room for us here in New York. There ain't no place but top floors. The top-floor black people" (291). This passage elegantly encapsulates the role of the state, especially through state violence, in the destruction of black privacy. William's inability to control and safeguard his domestic space and intimate sphere—his family's confinement to the top floors of run down tenements in Harlem—clearly signifies the nation-state's refusal to create "room" for African Americans, a spatial metaphor that expresses a total lack of political agency and self-possession. The pathos of "In Darkness and Confusion" emerges not only through its recurrence to dead children and dead parents, but also its emphasis on the "surviving" children who are now, like William, *socially dead* subjects of state discipline who must remain trapped in the nation's racist past. Hence we see that the destruction of black privacy derives from a dominant culture mastery of space *and* time.

"The Bones of Louella Brown" deals with many of the same subjects—death, white supremacy, the quest for a home, and an engagement with the majoritarian public sphere—though in this case a poor black woman magically speaks truth to power and ends up the master of space and time. It has been almost entirely overlooked by critics, most likely because of its comedic tone and fantastic plotting.[9] It is a farcical tale about a dead black woman who becomes an international celebrity while haunting her way into the house of racial-national privilege. After being wrongfully exhumed from her grave, the spirit of Louella Brown, a poor black washer-woman, returns to dominate the body and mind of powerful white men in order to reclaim her privacy and dignity. It is also a story in which the entire nation, and most of the world, waits in rapt attention to see the resolution of her fate. It is, in short, absurd. Petry's turn to the supernatural and hyper-publicity, however, enable her to express a longing that the world could be otherwise—in particular, to imagine a world where black women have empowered publicity and racial privacy.

At the level of plot, "The Bones of Louella Brown" describes how Louella Brown, a deceased black laundress, secures a place for herself in Bedford Abbey, a newly constructed "private chapel" reserved for the "most distinguished family in Massachusetts" (163). A public scandal ensues after a reporter breaks a story revealing that the exhumed bones of Louella Brown have been mixed up with the remains of an aristocratic Bostonian (the Countess of Castro, "nee Elizabeth Bedford") who was in the process of being re-interred in Bedford Abbey. The problem occurs because an impetuous employee of the undertaking firm, Whiffle and Peabody Incorporated, calls a reporter to document what he believes is "the biggest story of the year"—that the bones of two women occupying such profoundly different social circumstances in life are "indistinguishable" (168). Although the employee is thrilled by the challenge his discovery poses to biological racism, the reporter is more interested in an opportunity for a sensational headline; he poses the employee and the two sets of bones in countless arrangements until the employee finally exclaims in dismay, "you've moved them around so many times I can't tell which is which—nobody could tell—m" (170). The story becomes front page news, featuring a photo of the abbey and a caption posing the question that "*seize[s] the imagination of the whole country*: 'Who will be buried under the marble floor of Bedford Abbey on the twenty-first of June—the white countess or the black laundress?'" (emphasis added 170). Given that Bedford Abbey radiates with national power and prestige, which I will discuss at more length below, both of the women become, almost overnight, "*famous as movie stars.* Crowds gathered outside the mansion in which Governor Bedford lived; still larger and noisier crowds milled in the street in front of the offices of Whiffle and Peabody" (emphasis added 171). The Associated Press picks up the story and wires it not only around the country, but throughout the world ("New York and London, and Paris and Moscow" 171). The entire western world (including its new Cold War antagonist) is transfixed for a moment on Louella Brown and the Countess of Castro, excitedly speculating about how America will resolve this symbolic crisis. The hyper-publicity surrounding the mix up is richly suggestive, particularly in relation to the issue of Louella Brown's privacy.

The original catalyst for the crisis occurs when Louella Brown's privacy was violated by the racist white cemetery owners (referred to in the story as Old Peabody—aged 79—and Young Whiffle—aged 75); they exhumed her from her grave in an all-white cemetery in order to remedy the "truly terrible error in judgment" (165) that allowed her to be buried there 45 years earlier. "It had taken the carefully discriminatory practices of generations of Peabodys, undertakers like himself, to make Yew Tree Cemetery what it was today—*the final home* of Boston's wealthiest and most aristocratic families" (emphasis added 166). Peabody's father had "grudgingly consented" to his wife's wishes that Louella Brown, their laundress, be buried there. The son decides to rectify this decades-old breach in racist practices after noticing "with dismay, that due to the enlargement of the cemetery, over the years, [Louella, whose grave 'had been at the very tip edge of the cemetery in 1902, in a very undesirable place'] now lay in one of the choicest spots—in the exact center." When Peabody announces his decision to put her "where she should have been put in the first place" on "the outskirts of the city" (165) he is disconcerted, "for he suddenly saw Louella Brown with an amazing sharpness. It was just as though she had entered the room—a quick moving little woman, brown of skin and black of hair, and with very erect posture" (166). Her spirit continues to confront Peabody, day and night: "In [a] dream, she came quite close to him, a small brown woman with merry eyes. After one quick look at him, she put her hands on her hips, threw her head back and laughed and laughed" (177–78). After these visitations "he could not forget the smallest detail of her appearance: how her shoulders shook as she laughed, and that her teeth were very white and evenly spaced" (178).

When Louella was living, Peabody considered her nothing more than "our laundress. Nobody of importance" (165). Consequently he feels free to desecrate the sanctity of her grave, or rather, her "final home," as the narrator refers to Yew Tree Cemetery earlier in the story; both the grave and the home are almost universally considered intensely private, even sacred, spaces that are entitled to protection from the ravages of the marketplace and racial politics. Of course the history of American race relations demonstrates that the opposite is true—at least for African Americans and other minority populations; the segregation of black neighborhoods and graveyards are the manifest subject of Petry's satire. She highlights this point when Whiffle chastises the careless employee, Stuart Reynolds, by lamenting that "The house . . . the honor of this house, years of working, of building a reputation, all destroyed" (170).

The "honor" of "this house"—the firm of Whiffle and Peabody, Incorporated (163)—is predicated explicitly on the preservation of white racial privacy via the exclusion of black bodies.

Petry undermines this commonplace denigration of black bodies by giving Louella Brown a visibility and mobility she conspicuously lacked in life. Louella enters Peabody's mind in harrowing vividness at the moment he decides to "bereave" her (in the term's archaic sense of forcible dispossession[10]) of her home in Yew Tree Cemetery. Instead of granting her the respect and dignity intended by her original burial, Peabody acts entirely in accordance with his interests as a private agent in the racially structured marketplace—the body of Louella Brown is a valueless object in his possession that threatens the value of his other possessions; it must be stored elsewhere so that he may both protect his investments and extract greater profit from her gravesite, "one of the choicest spots—in the exact center" of his property.[11] Louella's spirit refuses to suffer the invisibility, silence, and immobility that was her former lot, socially and politically. She is now "quick," "very erect," and "merry," with an aristocratic comportment and an irreverent, powerfully unsettling laugh. She commands unfettered access to his mind (arguably the most private place imaginable) and reverses the interrogating, dominating gaze which is the historical privilege of the wealthy white man. Peabody's privileged status makes him "quite unaccustomed to being laughed at, even in a dream" (177–78); nevertheless, he is powerless to return or refuse her gaze, much less punish her for her impudence. Rather, he develops a sort of respect for her. When Young Whiffle continually bemoans that they are "ruined— ruined—ruined" for their role in this fiasco, Old Peabody shouts: "Will you stop that caterwauling? One would think the Loch Ness monster lay in the crypt at Bedford Abbey" (178). As he faces her laughing spirit once again, he observes, "Louella Brown was a neatly built little woman, a fine woman, full of laughter. I remember her well. She was a gentlewoman. Her bones will do no injury to the Governor's damned funeral chapel" (178).

The deluge of publicity surrounding the "Governor's damned funeral chapel" is at the heart of Louella Brown's fight for racial privacy. The story opens as Peabody and Whiffle read story after story in the Boston newspapers about "this fabulous project," Bedford Abbey, a "private chapel . . . which would be used solely for the weddings and funerals of the Bedford family" (163). Whiffle and Peabody stand to profit enormously, as the "long-dead Bedfords were to be exhumed [from Yew Tree Cemetery] and reburied" under the abbey chapel floor, and afterwards "Bedford Abbey would be officially opened with the most costly and the most elaborate funeral service ever held in Boston" (164).

The abbey and the "stupendous funeral service" are both the "brain-child" of Governor Bedford, an aging former governor of Massachusetts (164). The construction of this extravagant "sacred" space intended for the exclusive, private use of the governor and his family—including the deceased "Countess of Castro," who is notably "the nearest approach to royalty in the Bedford family" (167)—demonstrates both the profoundly in-egalitarian interpenetration of racial, church, and state power, as well as the pathetic attempt of a vain and frightened man to "buy immortality" (176). But the excessiveness of Governor Bedford's actions, including his attempts to generate public attention, may also derive from a more obscure, racialized source of insecurity.

After the newspaper's scandalous revelation about the confused identity of the women's remains, Peabody momentarily tries to minimize the damage done to their reputation:

"She might have been Irish," said Old Peabody coldly. . . . "And a Catholic. That would have been equally bad. No, it would have been worse. Because the Catholics would have insisted on a mass, in Bedford Abbey, of all places! Or she might have been a foreigner—a—a—Russian. Or, God forbid, a Jew!"

"Nonsense," said Young Whiffle pettishly. "A black washerwoman is infinitely worse than anything you've mentioned. People are saying it's some kind of trick, that we're proving there's no difference between the races." (172)

Hilary Holladay observes that this passage serves to convey a recurring theme in Petry's works, that "blacks are not the only ones who bear the brunt of prejudice" (127). While this may be true, I would add that it also illustrates Petry's awareness of the historically contingent nature of the color line, and whiteness in particular—Roediger reminds us that all of these "ethnic" groups were still only "situationally" white in 1947, and remained subject to forms of exclusion, depending on the context. Although during WWII the government celebrated American ethnic pluralism as part of its antifascist mobilization, the process of racial inclusion in the U.S. occurred in "crazy-quilt patterns" and varied widely across America depending on such localized factors as the "demographics of particular workplaces and industries, patterns of strikebreaking management strategies, language acquisition, and labor markets" (8). The significance of these ongoing debates around the exact parameters of whiteness in local, national, and international politics becomes clear when the bones of Louella Brown again disrupt the Governor's racial-national theatrics. When he concocted the idea of building a private abbey, he did so believing that he could use his privileged access to the public sphere (especially as an embodiment of state power and prestige) to further enhance his already con-siderable public stature. The symbolic potency of the abbey would emanate not merely from his private wealth, but especially from his association with the state.[12] Instead, his efforts to exploit publicity end up backfiring. After the ini-tial story about Louella and the Countess, Whiffle and Peabody decide to "call in ... the press" and have their embalmer publicly identity the remains; this gamble at first seems to resolve the question, and the funeral takes place, with the world looking on: "Because of all the stories about Louella Brown and the Countess of Castro, most of the residents of Boston turned out to watch the funeral cortege of the Bedfords on the twenty-first of June. The ceremony that took place at Bedford Abbey was broadcast over a national hook-up, and the news services wired it around the world, complete with pictures" (174).

The next day, however, the same reporter who broke the scandal in the first place runs another story proving that the embalmer's testimony is fraudu-lent, thereby raising the racial controversy again. The Governor "hastily called a press conference [declaring] that he would personally, publicly (in front of the press), identify the countess, if it was the countess" (175). Two days later he returns to "that marble gem," Bedford Abbey, "followed by a veritable hive of newsmen and photographers" (175). He "forgot the eager-eared newsmen" after he opens the casket, however, and

when he spoke he reverted to the simple speech of his early ancestors.
   "Why they be nothing but bones here!" he said. "Nothing but bones! Nobody could tell who this be." (176)

The Governor is undone by the site of the bones, and tries to assure himself "I'm alive. I can't die." But at this moment Louella's voice enters his mind, "saying over and over ... It will. It can. It will. It can. It will" (176).

It is striking that when faced with the bones of his ancestors, and his own imminent death, he loses control of his public, authoritative, and unmarked "white" voice, and speaks instead with an Irish brogue, "the simple speech of his early ancestors." This linguistic reversion brings to light a racial-national subtext that might otherwise be overlooked. The purpose of the press con-ference is to establish, in front of the nation and the world, absolute differ-ence between the two women—one white and one black—in order to try to manage the crisis that has emerged—the possibility that he has installed a black woman in his family home, making her a permanent part of his public family lineage. When faced with the impossibility of conclusively identifying one woman as white, and the other as black, he becomes *Irish* again, which, depending on your perspective, either undermines the idea of absolute racial difference or significantly qualifies his whiteness and public status authority— that is, if you are sympathetic to Whiffle's and Peabody's attitudes towards the Irish. It seems clear that Governor Bedford's original objective, consciously or not, was to manage the latter possibility: the construction of the abbey can be seen as an elaborate publicity stunt intended to bring all of the "long dead Bedfords," but most especially the quasi-aristocratic Countess of Castro, into his "home"; it is as though he is trying, through his privileged public status and association with the state, to make his dead Irish relatives, and himself, "white" for all time by appealing to national culture and eliminating the historical contingency of race, an act that would whiten his Irish past and future in one great synchronic, de-historicizing public ritual. To borrow from Lauren Berlant, we could say that his efforts at memorialization were an attempt to make his family's whiteness "dead"—i.e., fixed, frozen, and outside history.[13]

He fails spectacularly, though; instead of Irish becoming white, Irish, black, and white become "indistinguishable." As with Peabody's original attempt to remove Louella Brown from Yew Tree Cemetery, Governor Bedford's attempt to solidify the color line ends up directly undermining it. Even more importantly, though, because of the publicity that he summoned, and because of his intentional identification with state power, he, on behalf of the state, unwillingly becomes a powerful anti-racist spokesperson. "The Governor's statement ["Nobody could tell who this be"] went around the world, in direct quotes. So did the photographs of him, peering inside the casket, his mouth open, his eyes staring" (176). This statement, the most controversial of all because it comes from the Governor and directly implicates the state, ignites a firestorm in the public sphere:

Sermons were preached about the Governor's statement, editorials were written about it, and Congressmen made long winded speeches over the radio. The Mississippi legislature threatened to declare war on the sovereign state of Massachusetts because Governor Bedford's remarks were an unforgivable insult to believers in white supremacy. (177)

Paradoxically, even as the nation edges toward "civil war" over this apparent assault on America's enduring history of racial nationalism, the half-century old remains of these women become celebrities: "many radio listeners became completely confused and, believing that both ladies were still alive, sent presents, to them . . ." (177). Louella Brown is at least in one sense "alive" in a way she never was before her death. Not only in the confused mind of the public, but also, crucially, in the minds of these powerful white men. Moreover, her contribution to the Governor's loss of self-possession at the very moment that he tried to "deaden" his racial identity, actually makes it erupt into the realm of the living, or history, once again. In the end, Peabody, in a last ditch effort to "propitiate" Louella's spirit, is compelled to approach the Governor, and recommend that her name be inscribed alongside the Countess's name in the abbey, although with the new title of "gentlewoman" supplanting her former public identity of "black laundress." The Governor acquiesces "reluctantly" and only because he "had the uneasy feeling that he could already hear Louella's laughter" (180).

The use of the supernatural and hyper publicity allows Petry to symbolically resolve the exploitative and determinative relation of the majoritarian public sphere and nationality to the violated racial privacy of black women. As a ghost, Louella Brown has total control of her movements, and her bones, while exposed to the world, are immune to exploitation and denigration in the public sphere. It seems impossible to imagine a *realist* narrative in mid-twentieth century-America in which a living—that is, embodied—Louella Brown could successfully persuade a nation to act ethically on behalf of black women. Instead, Petry taps into a fantasy structure that is readily recognizable to those who experience nationality as private violation—the desire to violate the nationally sanctioned privacy of powerful white men, so much so that they speak publicly against their own racial national privilege.[14]

Country Place has proven difficult to align with Petry's other work in this period, as it appears to mark a dramatic departure in setting, characterization, theme, and even writing style. It takes place in a small, nearly all white New England resort town, has only one black character—who has a fairly minor role—and overall seems relatively unconcerned with racial conflict. The story's critical gaze is trained primarily on private white spaces: white homes, white families, white "hearts" and minds. Moreover, it appears curiously invested in traditional gender roles, given that the crises in the narrative seem to emerge from bad mothers, promiscuous wives, and weak, perverse men.

Country Place has also frustrated more contemporary readerly expectations by providing, with only a few exceptions, fairly *sympathetic* depictions of its white characters, thereby deviating from the unspoken critical dictum that black literature register a fundamentally dissident relation to the dominant culture. Claudia Tate explains that "we require [black novels] and especially those of canonical status to foreground the injustice of black protagonists' persistent and contested encounters with the material and psychological effects of a racially exploitative distribution of social goods, services, and power" (4). Accordingly, *Country Place* has appeared either irrelevant, or worse, as a kind of racial false-consciousness—seeming to evince what Langston Hughes famously termed "the urge to whiteness" within the race.[15]

Both *The Street* and *The Narrows*, unlike *Country Place*, are clearly consonant with these established "protocols of black textuality" (Tate 3), and have garnered the overwhelming majority of critical attention granted to Petry's novels. But it may be that the issues which have deterred critics actually provide the most productive points of entry for its reconsideration. My discussion thus far has attended to Petry's enduring interest in the domestic space as a register of power relations and the possibility of racial privacy. In my analysis of *Country Place* I will highlight how Petry's use of moral and psychological discourses in her depiction of privileged white domestic space facilitates a two pronged project; it enables her to simultaneously scrutinize a powerful emblem of American innocence, virtue, and normativity—middle class, small town America, which was, notably, often juxtaposed against the supposed immorality of black urban neighborhoods—while also protecting both her, and her character Neola's racial privacy.

Petry's shift in racial community and discursive strategy allows for several overlapping objectives. In particular, her emphasis on the psychological dynamics of white family life avoids the re-inscription of black suffering that the traditional "protest" narrative typically requires. Petry was well aware that this was a twice told tale, and one that constrained her choices for imagining the complexity of black experience. Throughout her career, Petry resisted efforts by critics and publishers to label or, we might say, "name" her, because this naming amounted to a form of racialized or gendered proscription. She was especially sensitive to being categorized as belonging to a particular school, or espousing a particular political position. This discomfort may have been due partly to the fact that critics incessantly compared her work to Richard Wright's, comparisons in which she was often cast as his protégé or, as one recent critic put it, as having been "fathered" by Wright.[16]

Petry was herself a very private person, and during her lifetime granted few interviews—when she did, she often resisted her interviewers' efforts to get her to interpret or categorize her work in line with other black writers, or to label herself politically or aesthetically.[17] Despite the racialized strictures around black literary production, Petry claims her right to a "free," autonomous, and self-directing imagination. The right to draw on one's personal experiences and to experiment with new subject matter and themes is the prerogative of all writers, though at the time it was a right seldom fully available to black authors.[18]

Petry's cultivation of her privacy as a writer can be seen at least partly as an attempt to manage her circulation in the majoritarian, always-already racialized public sphere. This self-positioning can also help shed light on the racial structure of *Country Place*, especially in relation to her other work of this moment. We've already seen that "protest" fiction demands black suffering, and we've also seen how, in realist works such as *The Street* and "In Darkness and Confusion," black women in particular experience publicity as exposure and violation. Lauren Berlant captures this dynamic in another context when she observes that "in twentieth-century America, anyone coded as 'low,' embodied, or subculturally 'specific' continues to experience, with banal regularity, the corporeal sensation of nationality as a sensation over which she/he has no control" (239). Consequently, when black women want to publicly engage the nation, these conditions often necessitate the "*evacuation* of erotic or sexual or even sensational life itself as a possible ground of personal dignity. . . ." Petry wants to critically engage the often unseen forms of violence that structure small town America—a commonplace symbol of national innocence—but without being compelled to narrate black female injury. In *Country Place*, Petry protects the personal dignity of her black female character, Neola, by making her a highly private and asexual character, which allows her to avoid subjecting Neola to the explicit forms of racial and sexual degradation that destroy Lutie Johnson's life, and have historically delimited the life chances of black women in America. Instead, via the suffering of her moral white characters, she re-imagines white male patriarchal authority and in the process transforms the white home from an archetypal site of racial exploitation into a scene of redemption and social justice. As we will see, Petry grants Neola, to paraphrase Virginia Woolf, a "house of her own"; but Neola's private, domestic triumph also transforms the town's (and, symbolically, the nation's) racial structure.

Neola's employer, Mrs. Gramby, is the grand dame of the community, an arrogant and aloof old widow who functions as something of a traditional moral barometer. Because she is dying, she spends a good deal of time reflecting on the changes she detects in the town, all of them bad. The most visible change is the apparent moral decline of the town's women. After she sees her son's stepdaughter, Gloria, on a tryst with the town rake, she thinks that "It was a changed world. . . . During the course of the years—not all at once, but slowly and surely—the line between good and evil had been rubbed out" (85). She wonders if "Gloria was not to be condemned. Instead of a sharp line of demarcation between right and wrong, Gloria and her generation had found only the vague blur made by erasures—it was all that remained of a moral code after the impact of two world wars" (86). She is especially disturbed by the moral character of Glory and her mother, Lil, because they will inherit Gramby House when she dies. Mrs. Gramby worries about this possibility "as though it were a *world* which Lillian would inherit" (220 emphasis added). Gramby House represents nothing less to Glory and Lil. They are both eager for Mrs. Gramby to die so that they can move into the house and, in Glory's words, "be somebody here in Lenox" (66).

The one character flaw all three women share, however, is their "failure" as mothers. We learn that Glory refuses motherhood for fear of losing her figure, while Lil seems almost pathological in her total self-absorption and hostility to mothering. She is an anxious and occasionally vicious woman obsessed with leaving behind her former life of penury and becoming "Mrs. Gramby." In contrast to Glory and Lil's evasion of mothering, Mrs. Gramby represents a classic case of the dominating mother. She considers the one "enormous crime" (84) in her life to be her overly-intense love for Mearns, which she believes "had made it impossible for him to leave, binding him closer and closer to [me]" (83). She effectively dominated his love life as well, bullying and harassing the women he brought home to her as possible mates. She acts this way because she "had been terrified lest he marry some cheap impossible young girl" and so naturally Mearns ends up with Lil, a woman more threatening and dangerous than she ever imagined. Mrs. Gramby reflects that "nothing worse could have happened to him. The name would die out. Lillian was too old to have children" (83). Mearns's experience of mother domination leads him to marry Lil, who is hard, shallow, barren, and even potentially homicidal; these qualities mark Lil as a monstrous woman, where the "ideal" woman would presumably be "soft," "deep," and fertile. Lil's barrenness means that there will be no male heir to carry on the Gramby patronym. In short, the Gramby house—a resonant symbol of traditional patriarchal authority—is in a sorry state; it is dominated by women with "excessive desires" and there's not a (white) man in sight capable of bringing them in line.

Petry seems to be fully participating in the mid-century discourse of "Momism." A term coined by journalist Philip Wylie, author of the enormously popular misogynist diatribe, *Generation of Vipers* (1942). Wylie proclaimed with alarm and disgust that "The mealy look of men today is the result of 'momism.'" "Moms," according to Wylie, were (implicitly) white women whose apparent maternal love masked their narcissism and desire for power. Their "policy of protection" led to a "possession of the spirit of a man" akin to "slavery" (Feldstein 41). Many critics associate the proliferation of "Momism" with a postwar conservative backlash—white male anxiety about the need to force women back into the home after the relative freedom of World War II.

But Ruth Feldstein has demonstrated that this discourse had been around at least since the Depression, and that it was deployed for liberal as well as conservative agendas. Feldstein shows how by the 1930s a consensus across social science disciplines emerged that mothers "were not only responsible for the physical, educational, and religious well-being of future citizens, but also were responsible for their children's *psychological* well-being" (6 emphasis in original). Psychology became increasingly important among progressive thinkers for assessing social, political, and personal issues. "After World War II, psychological and political analyses increasingly overlapped. Categories like repression, neurosis, paranoia, insecurity, and frustration became vehicles for analyzing both personal and political problems, and for determining who and what was a healthy American citizen" (6).[19] By the 1930s, "bad" women were not just those who wielded power in the public sphere, but also those who "failed" in the private sphere as wives, and especially as mothers.

Feldstein explains that "most liberal narratives equated healthy and strong citizens with healthy and strong men, hence their primary concern was with sons, black and white. In maternal ideologies, women who failed as mothers were objects of concern because they raised men who (for different reasons at different moments) failed to meet the criteria of healthy citizenship" (5). Accordingly, Feldstein argues, the mid-century liberal social scientists' fixation on psychological health of families, and especially the role of mothering in the production of fit or unfit citizens, despite consistently relying on normative, conservative gender roles, was intended to do progressive political work. Social scientists believed that racism and other anti-democratic socio-political ills (such as personal tendencies toward fascism and communism) were frequently caused by "unhealthy" family dynamics, especially bad mothering. For example, it was believed that many racists had failed to adequately resolve their oedipal conflicts with their mothers. The mothers were to blame, because they had either been too dominating, or too "rejecting." Despite the inherent misogyny of this supposition, this approach was in fact a hopeful one—if "the problem" is properly diagnosed and addressed early enough, it might be changed, and thus American families could instead produce psychologically healthy, anti-racist (as well as anti-fascist and anti-communist) democracy-loving citizens.

Mearns seems to be a case study in the deleterious effects of mother-domination, as bad mothering was alleged to produce "sons who were either insufficiently aggressive, inhibited, and sexually passive and repressed; or sons who were too aggressive, insufficiently cooperative, and violent" (Feldman 60). Doc Fraser comments disdainfully that Mearns has been a "walking medicine cabinet ever since he was born. [He has a] fussy, old-maid concern about the state of his internal organs" (134). His mother worries that "The name of Gramby had once stood for something. . . . It was almost gone now, for the name meant nothing—just an old, diabetic woman and a house made of pink brick and a middle-aged man who was addicted to vitamin pills and mouth washes" (83–84). Mrs. Gramby's maternal domination has produced not only a womanish, finicky man, but also something of a sexual deviant. Doc "tattles" on Mearns when he reveals that Mearns has long been an avid reader of "The Tattler," "a weekly newspaper which specializes in unpleasant stories of sexual perversion and promiscuity. It is the only paper I have ever seen that prints the detailed verbatim testimony in divorce cases" (231). Based on this evidence, Doc asserts that "I am certain that he expected Lil's lean shanks would offer him the same hot excitement he had found recorded in The Tattler's shabby pages" (231).[20]

By the end of the narrative, though, Mearns does in fact become "a man." Notably, this transformation takes place after his mother dies. Mearn's manhood emerges during the reading of the will. At this time it is revealed that Gramby Pasture has been willed to the Catholic Church, and that Gramby House has been left to Neola and the other servants, both of whom are first generation southern European new immigrants whose accents and swarthy skin seem intended to mark them, in accordance with contemporary racial attitudes, as non-white minorities. When the will is read by the Jewish lawyer Mrs. Gramby has hired to make the changes that exclude Lil, she loses all composure, and launches into a tirade of racist epithets, shouting "I won't have niggers living here—this is my house . . . pigpen Irish . . . everybody in the will but me" (263). Eventually, Mearns slaps her, covers her mouth, and shouts, "keep quiet!" Doc remarks, "The sound startled me, for it was so like his father's voice, and it was the first time I had ever heard Mearns speak in that fashion" (264).

Once released from his mother's dominating yoke, Mearns's voice, finally, changes, and he becomes his father. But Mearns is not simply Mr. Gramby reincarnated. By participating in the decision to will the house to the servants, he has chosen *not* to perpetuate the tradition of inherited, unearned white male privilege, but rather first to symbolically divest himself of his possessive investment in whiteness by giving up the house, as the house symbolizes white heteropatriarchal authority in the town, just as it does in the nation more generally.[21] In other words, rather than consolidating his patriarchal privilege by becoming "master" of Gramby House, he refuses his "white man's estate" by transferring one of the most powerful symbols of his authority to his non-white servants. He has in fact become Mr. Gramby, but he is

Mr. Gramby with a difference. Once he succeeds in overcoming his mother's domination (and implicitly becomes psychically healed) he symbolically puts the meaning of white heteropatriarchy into play—he brings his status as a white man to "life" so to speak, in contrast to Governor Bedford, and Lil and Glory, who were using the ancestral home to deaden and fix whiteness.

For Mrs. Gramby, willing the house to the servants is a method of addressing her anxiety about the family "name," which is linked in her thoughts to the nation's future. She remedies her life long elitism and self absorption by integrating her town and, symbolically, the nation. Although she is certainly motivated partly by her selfish desire to thwart Glory and Lil, she also wishes to prevent them (and people like them) from controlling "the world." Early in the narrative Glory fantasizes that when "Mrs. Gramby dies you [Neola] or someone very like you will bring me my breakfast in the morning" (57). Thus the danger of Lil and Glory inheriting the house is precisely that they *won't* change things—they will perpetuate, even worsen, the town's racial and ethnic stratification. They will intentionally stand in the way of progress and make a point of firing Neola and then hiring, say, a Lutie Johnson, an Annie May Jones, or a Louella Brown precisely as a symbol of their ascent to white supremacist authority. Mrs. Gramby had worried that the patronym "Gramby" now "meant nothing." It does in fact still signify, but now it signifies the change that William Jones so desperately longed for. It is the new American house of progress, with a harmonious, multi-ethnic domestic arrangement (Neola and Portulacca are engaged by the novel's end). It signifies hope for an integrated national future. Myrdal believed that white America was "*free to choose whether the Negro shall remain her liability or become her opportunity*" (1022 Qtd in Feldstein 47 emphasis in original). Mearns and Mrs. Gramby in a sense solve their "American Dilemma"—by refusing to will the world to irrational and selfish white bigots who would perpetuate social oppression. Instead she makes the "Negro" her "opportunity" to change the "world" symbolically by changing the racist social structure of the Lennox. This has the effect of restoring moral order in town, even as it reconfigures its social structure. Thus we see that Neola, much like Louella, moves from the margins to the very center of privilege.

Although Petry insisted that she never wanted to write the same story twice (and I believe she succeeded) there are, nevertheless, striking continuities in her work from this phase of her career. She repeatedly foregrounds the manner in which the circulation of race in the majoritarian public sphere underwrites white male domestic privilege and destroys the possibility of African American privacy in general, and domesticity in particular. Moreover, we can also see that the loss or achievement of racial privacy revolves around property, which again underscores the fact that, historically, whiteness has instantiated itself through an investment in and mastery over property, symbolic as well as material. Petry's deployment of the domestic space also exceeds normative contemporary understandings of the home as radically separated from the public sphere; on the contrary, the home is precisely a publicly determined site of racial and gender contestation. Given Petry's sense that black women in particular experience publicity as violation, she represents the achievement of private, domestic space in these narratives as enclosing and protecting the black female body while also publicly destabilizing, however provisionally, the meaning of white male authority. While the future is doomed to be an oppressive and traumatic repetition of the past in *The Street* and "In Darkness and Confusion," in "The Bones of Louella Brown" and *Country Place* the future is tantalizingly unscripted. The dramatic re-configuration of the racial structure and authority of Bedford Abbey and Gramby House (and Gramby Pasture, which was willed to the Irish Catholic Church) simultaneously rewrites and puts into play the future and the past of Lennox and the Bedford family—and, implicitly, the nation.

COUNTER-MODERNITY, BLACK MASCULINITY, AND FEMALE SILENCE IN ANN PETRY'S FICTION

Melina Vizcaíno-Alemán

Criticism surrounding Ann Petry's *The Narrows* since its 1953 publication is conflicted at best. In her introduction to the novel's 1988 republication, Nellie Y. McKay positions the book within a tradition of African American women's literature and celebrates Petry's "unique black female vision" (xvii); others have explored what Keith Clark calls the "unequivocally female context" in Petry's work and its proto-feminist features (Clark 1992 495).[1] Yet, critics were initially ambivalent about *The Narrows*, a sentiment that some scholars, like Mary Helen Washington, still retain. One 1953 reviewer, for instance, maintained that the novel "has depth and complexity, but the surface drama central to the tragedy is like a tissue of tabloid day-dreams, projected by the characters" (Morris 27). Another critic appreciated Petry's underlying message with its illicit interracial love story but concluded, "Ann Petry will write better" (Redding 26). In a more recent assessment, Washington calls Petry's fiction disturbing because of "its lack of subtlety and flexibility, its manipulation of characters to serve an ideological function, its refusal to give women a voice" (299–300). As Washington has it, Petry's novels do not narrate entirely from a female perspective, so they lack the kind of feminist politics that make revolutionary change.

Still, Washington acknowledges how *The Narrows* circumvents its female domestic space, and she argues that *Miss Muriel and Other Stories*, a 1971 collection of short stories, presents a "strong, first-person female voice [that] indicates an important change in Petry's presentation of women" (304). While Petry's fiction does not call for radical feminist change, it does reveal the limitations of feminist consciousness within and across black and white communities. Petry's focus on women's experiences, of both the middle and working classes, demonstrates how the black middle-class home mirrors and repels what Kimberly Drake calls "white domestic ideology" (69). Drake argues that Petry breaks with the asexual heroine in African American women's literature with her use of "sexualized minor female characters who act as foils to female protagonists with bourgeois values" (66). The "liminal blues woman" that Drake celebrates, like Mamie in *The Narrows*, is the character type that so disturbs Washington in Petry's fiction. Petry's juxtaposition of asexual and hypersexual women creates a dualistic domestic setting that generates ambivalent criticism because it embodies W. E. B. Du Bois's notion of double consciousness. As Petry's fiction demonstrates, the double consciousness of the black middle-class home serves as a barrier to radical feminist politics while it provides an inroad to interracial female solidarity.

The black middle-class home is a literary setting in Petry's fiction that embodies the sense of two-ness that Du Bois described as "this sense of always looking at one's self through the eyes of the others" (11). Du Bois used the term double consciousness in *The Souls of Black Folk* (1903) at a time when double-ness and dual personalities were dominant ideas in Anglo-European literature and medicine. As Dickson D. Bruce, Jr. argues, Du Bois used psychological knowledge "to talk about an African mode of thought and what we would now call a cultural conflict between the African and the American in a way very like that made possible by a notion of relativism" (243). Du Bois proposed that the resolution to black America's double consciousness was the merging of their African and American selves, an approach that "drew with special clarity on the medical background" of his Harvard mentor (Bruce 243–44). Merging the two selves would create a synthesis, or a third, new Self that, according to Henry Louis Gates, Jr. and Terri Oliver, inspires a Hegelian tripleness: a tripartite structure of thesis, antithesis and synthesis (Gates xxxi). Indeed, the Harvard medical world of Du Bois's time supported his rhetorical resolution to the problem of the color line—synthesis would resolve the dilemmas of black America's dual worlds—but as Petry's fiction demonstrates, double consciousness divides the black middle-class home and generates the contradictory fissures that enable and simultaneously disable interracial and feminist coalitions.

Du Bois's double consciousness has evolved into a scholarly apparatus that forms the basis of what Paul Gilroy calls counter-modernity and the black Atlantic. Slavery and black masculinity are central tropes in the black Atlantic's politics of counter-modernity and black America's double consciousness. Indeed, as Gilroy argues, black masculinity is counter-modern in the U.S.'s public sphere, but as Petry's fiction demonstrates, black masculinity is also complicit with the nation's imperialist policies abroad and with its gender performances within the home. Ships constitute a trans-historical symbol for Gilroy's epistemology of routes, not roots, to make connections among black men across the Atlantic and across historical settings. Petry's fiction anchors Gilroy's floating signifier and phallocentric symbol to the home and the street to suggest that black men are torn between white domesticity and black international politics. *The Narrows*, for instance, written at the height of the McCarthy era and during the U.S.'s Cold War when domestic policies of containment dovetailed into widespread paranoia against foreign peoples and ideologies, tells the tragic story of an interracial romance between a black man and a white woman. On the surface, *The Narrows* appeals to white America's sensational stereotypes about black men and white women, but the romance is a vehicle that unveils the U.S.'s fictions of white domesticity and black masculinity. Set against World War II and during the Korean War, Petry deploys the black middle-class home as a literary site that challenges both white domestic ideology and the politics of counter-modernity. Women, both black and white, are central to the formations of double consciousness in the home and on the street, thus Petry's home space is a counter-space to the politics of counter-modernity and the black intelligentsia's imaginary solutions to slavery and diaspora.

Petry begins *The Narrows* with an epigraph from *The Life of Henry V*, a reference that "creates an ironic context for Petry's story" because while "Shakespeare's Monmouth is the birthplace of an English king who triumphs in battle, hers is the hometown of Link Williams, a young black man who served as a Navy censor during World War II" (Holladay 77). Petry radically revises Shakespeare's *Henry V* through the story of an interracial romance between Link and Camilo Treadway Scheffield, a married woman and white heiress to the Treadway Munitions Company; the romance concludes with Link's murder after the affair goes public. Set in Monmouth, Connecticut, or the Narrows, as it is so called since "Negroes had replaced those other earlier immigrants, the Irish, the Italians, and the Poles" (Petry 1988 5), the Narrows is an offshoot of King Henry's birthplace and the ironic setting that frames the novel's double consciousness, or its two-ness in Du Boisian terminology. Indeed, the Crunch home embodies the double consciousness that shapes all of Monmouth. *The Narrows* opens with Abbie Crunch's memories of eight year-old Link as she walks home, reading the signs that say to her, "Dumble Street had changed. The signs tell the story of the change" (5). Abbie's walk maps out Monmouth from the river to the Crunch home where she meets up with Malcolm Powther, the butler for the Treadway mansion, who is interested in renting out Abbie's top floor. Mistaken by Powther's aristocratic appearance, Abbie discovers that she binds herself to an unpleasant living arrangement when she meets Mamie Powther and the three Powther sons. From the beginning, the Crunch home is split between the top and bottom floors; between the front and back doors; between Mamie Powther, a public woman, and Abbie Crunch, a proper lady.[2] Mamie and Abbie thus define the contours of female sexuality in the Crunch home.

The Abbie-Mamie arrangement of the Crunch home sustains and collapses the boundaries of white domestic ideology. Abbie's fancies herself "the Englishman dressing for dinner even in the jungle" (38), a reflection she sees in Malcolm but repulses in Mamie. The Crunch home provides Abbie a limited space of creativity in which she chants self-composed jingles that mimic Mother Goose nursery rhymes in her head, but she feels silenced by the street and her memories of Link. Mamie epitomizes Dumble Street and all of its vices for Abbie, thus the blues woman living above Abbie collapses the self-contained boundaries of Abbie's middle-class world. But Mamie simply gives body and voice to the ghosts that haunt Abbie's middle-class home and that pull Link in (at least) two different directions, between the Crunch home and the Last Chance Bar, between Abbie Crunch and Bill Hod, owner of the Last Chance. Hod and Abbie's relationship is a historical one that reaches back to Major Crunch's death when Link was six years old and only a few years after the Crunches adopted him. Abbie blames Hod for the Major's death because he suffers a stroke at Bill Hod's Last Chance Bar one afternoon. When the two men appear at Abbie's front door step, she assumes the Major is just drunk and orders Bill Hod to put him in the parlor while she "hurriedly spread newspapers all around the chair, thinking, My carpet, my beautiful carpet" (29). The Major's death confounds public and private spaces, as the presence of the newspaper "symbolizes the power of the press and the power of the community sentiment that the press both mirrors and molds" (Holladay 36). The very presence of Hod in Abbie's home signals this collapse of the home and the street; this upsets Abbie more than anything else. Hod tells Abbie to get a doctor, but she orders him out of her house with a metal poker in hand. "'You fool—you goddamn fool—get a doctor,'" an angry Hod tells Abbie while she thinks to herself, "Eyes of a hangman. Face of hangman" (30).

Abbie falls into a deep depression after the Major's death and she begins to neglect Link, so Hod becomes the boy's surrogate father, boss, teacher, and warden. Abbie's home and Bill's bar pull link in two different directions, between white domesticity and black masculinity, thus Dumble Street reproduces locally the double consciousness of the black Atlantic and the black middle-class home. Petry breathes life into the narrative landscape to suggest that it shapes the home and the street, but not through natural forces; rather, the unspeakable history of slavery contaminates the very soil of the Narrows. An old maple tree, aptly named The Hangman, is a metonymic reminder of slavery that evades and intrigues Abbie's bourgeois mind:

She had tried, years ago, to find out why the tree was called The Hangman and couldn't. There would always be something of the schoolteacher's tiresome insistence on accuracy left in her, so she had searched through all the books on horticulture in the Monmouth Library, but she could not find any mention of a hangman's maple. She decided that some one may once have said that the big maple was the kind of tree a hangman would choose to swing his victim from— tall, straight, with mighty branches; that whoever heard this statement changed it when he repeated it and called the tree a hangman's maple; that, finally, some imaginative Negro, probably from South Carolina, gave the tree its name. These days she, too, called the maple The Hangman, as easily, and as inaccurately, as the rest of The Narrows. (5–6)

Abbie has no language with which to identify the Hangman, save for the oral lore that she ties to the South, perhaps a veiled recognition of the Major's southern background. Yet, like the Major's death and Link's alienation, Abbie represses her connection to the South and slavery. Instead, she distances herself from the hangman and its representative history by linking it to Hod, her adversary, whose very presence silences her on the street and in her own home.

The Crunch home and the Last Chance bar face each other from across Dumble Street and they pull Link in two different directions, between the home and the street, dividing his loyalties between Abbie, his adopted mother, and Bill Hod, his surrogate father. As an orphan and an adopted child, Link has no genealogical past—no roots—save for Link's imagination, a fact hardened by the secrecy of his affair with a married white woman. Ironically, as a "history major and would-be historian of slavery, Link is at a loss when it comes to his personal history" (Holladay 80). As a result, Link wanders from Abbie's home, to the Last Chance bar, to Harlem with Camilo, for acceptance; he attempts to resolve his two worlds, the home and the street, through his romance with Camilo and through his performative acts in Harlem that collapse white domesticity and black masculinity. The Hangman, like Link, forces Abbie to compromise her bourgeois knowledge as both are reminders of the history she wants to erase. Yet, as the Major's memory testifies, history is what haunts Abbie's sensibilities and her middle-class home.

Camilo's presence in the black middle-class home signals the break down of the home, the street, and the history of slavery. There is a violent confrontation when Abbie, Link, and Camilo co-habit the same space, and this confrontation spills out into the street as Mamie's laughter wafts from the top window. Abbie discovers Camilo in Link's bed, "yellow hair on [Abbie's] pillow cases, the bridal ones," and the aristocratic lady turns into a feisty alley cat as she throws Camilo out onto Dumble Street (250). Abbie's afterthoughts race in and out of the past as she rants, "A white girl. In my house. In bed with Link. Tramp of a white girl. Pale yellow hair on the bridal pillowcases. Sweet smell in the hall. In Link's room. He would bring a tramp into my house. I am a fool. Frances. 'Howard's a fool.' You fool. You goddam fool. Get a doctor" (253). Abbie's response to Camilo rehashes the Major's memory and Abbie's guilt, the very things that erase Link in the home and push him out into the street even before Camilo enters. Abbie also recalls her dear friend, Frances Jackson, Frank or F. K., the community undertaker who "becomes a kind of surrogate spouse for Abbie just as Bill Hod becomes a surrogate father to Link" (Holladay 83). Link resents the two women's relationship because their female intimacy excludes him, thus Link's forbidden affair conjures up Abbie's own hidden fear, guilt and (forbidden) desire that act as fissures in her bourgeois mind and home.[3]

The Last Chance Bar becomes a second home for Link after Abbie neglects him for three months, and Hod teaches Link to be proud of his blackness. Ironically, Hod's body conflates and confuses heteronormative gender and racial categories, just as his business collapses public and private spaces. Link's gaze aligns Hod's and Camilo's bodies and collapses his desire for Camilo, a white woman, with the figure of his racial pride, Hod. Looking at Bill Hod's body the first morning he awakens in Hod's bedroom at the back of the bar, Link thinks:

He supposed he ought not to look at this man who was walking about the room barefooted. But he couldn't help it. He had no corns on his feet, no bunions. His stomach didn't stick out, it was flat, absolutely flat; his waist was narrow and his shoulders were wide. The skin on his body was almost white, the forearms, and his face, tan by contrast. He made no sound as he walked, and Link thought, He's air-borne, light as air. (119)

While Abbie feminizes the Major in the hours before his death, Link likewise feminizes Hod in the days afterwards in Hod's bedroom, and he later connects Hod's body to Camilo's. "She sleeps like Bill Hod, like a cat, all of her relaxed, stretched out, remembered Hod walking barefooted, in a room full of sunlight, full of cold air, Hod, making no sound as he moved air-borne, creature from another planet, Mars, perhaps, looked at her and thought of Bill Hod" (264). Camilo rehashes Link's desire for Hod as she rehashes the Major's memory and F. K. Jackson for Abbie, suggesting that Link's fate was written long before Camilo came into the Narrows.

Camilo functions as an ideological fissure that collapses white domesticity and black masculinity, Abbie's black middle-class home and Hod's business establishments. Both Abbie and Hod police Link's sexuality, as Abbie's response to Camilo demonstrates, and as Link's ensuing memories of China's brothel make evident. At the age of sixteen, Link defies Hod's order to stay away from China's place, one of Hod's multiple business establishments on Dumble Street. When Link appears as a paying customer, the obedient madam reports to Hod before Link can get past the front entrance. Hod gives Link a good beating and forever taints China in Link's mind. "Buddha became in his mind a symbol of treachery, indelibly marked in his memory with the smell of incense" (275). As a WWII soldier, Link has a political history in the Pacific, and as a Monmouth resident, a personal one. China is a literal and symbolic figure whose marginality is central to the novel's critique of the Narrows public space, just as Camilo's centrality fissures the black middle-class home. But whereas Camilo's voice seals Link's tragic fate—she screams when he breaks up with her—China is forever silent and merely a figment of Link's fear of and desire for Hod.

Petry's China, like the home, is a dual figure that counters counter-modernity because it reveals black men's complicity with the U.S.'s global wars, particularly within the context of WWII and the Korean War, while Hod's sex trade points to black men's reproduction of foreign power relations in the domestic sphere.[4] Petry juxtaposes China and the black Atlantic to reveal the mutability of black masculinity both within and outside of the U.S.'s domestic borders. The Orient, or the Far East, haunts the Cold War U.S. as slavery haunts the North and as the Major's death haunts the Crunch home.[5] Camilo collapses and sustains the double consciousness of the black middle-class home, but China threatens to undo the black Atlantic's double consciousness by dismantling altogether white domesticity and black masculinity. At the end of the novel, immediately before his execution, Link recalls working for the Valkills on the edge of the river, and Mrs. Valkill has Link put on a kimono to serve her tea party one afternoon. Mr. Valkill comments that, "'Mrs. Valkill is a genius. I never would have noticed—never would have known how attractive a Japanese kimono could be'" (392). When Mr. Valkill puts his hand on Link's shoulder, "Mr. Valkill's hand reminded him of Bill Hod's hand, firm warm wellcaredfor clean hand, the nails filed, but the forearm was thickcovered with blond hair, like blond fur on the forearm, forearm of a blond ape, and revulsion made him move" (394). Link's confla-tion of Mr. Valkill and Hod represents a rupture in his racial consciousness, but this homoerotic moment rest on Link's performance in Oriental garb. The Valkill home turns Link's blackness into Japanese exoticism, silencing him as a boy and silently making a return of the repressed before his death as a young man.

Link attempts to synthesize his black middle-class worlds through his romance with Camilo, but his history with China serves as a counter-synthesis that dismantles his black and white worlds altogether. Link sits between and betwixt competing forces that shape the home, the street and the nation. His body turns toward (and into) the Pacific to counter counter-modernity and to queer black masculinity, but this countered counter-modernity also provides a potential base for interracial female solidarity. The novel concludes with Abbie's decision to visit the police station to protect Camilo from becoming Hod's next "Chinaman," a reference to Hod's trafficking of Chinese laborers across the U.S.-Canadian border. Abbie Crunch arrives at this decision as she contemplates the newspaper coverage of Link's murder and with F. K.'s rev-elation of Hod's illicit trafficking in the back of her head. The two sites, the media and the community, shape Abbie's coming to consciousness and her decision to assert herself in public (the police station); but Abbie's decision does not necessarily resolve the narrative conflict, nor does it "transcend" that conflict, as critics have argued in the past.[6] Instead, Abbie's decision affirms her white domestic ideology, the source of narrative conflict from the start, at the same time that it lays the groundwork for a tenuous, middle-class femi-nine (feminist?) consciousness that will continue the symbolic war she so far silently wages. The conclusion has all the trappings of a proto-feminist platform, but Abbie's decision rests on the dubious, patriarchal assertion that she will save Camilo from the historical forces of the Hangman. Petry's novel then does not so much lay groundwork for feminism as much as it demon-strates the complexity and contradictions of middle-class feminist coalitions, particularly in the context of the U.S.'s literal and symbolic wars that find muted and duplicitous expressions within the home.

Black America's double consciousness frames *The Narrows* and its critique of the U.S.'s foreign and domestic wars in the 1950s while the three selected short stories from Petry's 1971 collection critique the racial politics of the Black Power Movement and the limitations of female subjectivity within the black middle-class home. "Miss Muriel" (1963) is the collection's title story and introduces Petry's audience to Wheeling, New York, the rural setting for five of the thirteen stories in the collection, including "The New Mirror" (1967), while "Mother Africa" (1971) and the remaining stories take place in Harlem. As *Miss Muriel* moves from rural to urban New York, the collection suggests the interdependence of rural and urban spaces in the U.S.'s Northeastern center.[7] This spatial interdependence manifests itself in the black middle-class home and demonstrates how geo-social and racial dynamics shape the formation of women's voices and simultaneously demand their silence. The home and the street reflect and refract each other; they generate in the process an ambivalent feminist consciousness that enables female agency by appropriating and circumventing the patriarchal discourses that shape the home and the street.

The second story in Petry's collection, "The New Mirror," takes up the theme of reflection and uses it as a framing device for the racial and sexual formation of a fifteen year-old girl alongside the ambiguity of her father, Samuel Layen's, public and private personas. "The New Mirror" is as much a coming-of-age story for the young female narrator as it is a story of her father's mid-life crisis. The family's new mirror connects the two and establishes the contradiction that (un)makes her father's—and her own—identity. When Samuel goes missing for a day, the narrator must assume his role as manager of the family pharmacy, and she comes of age within an environment of racial terror, largely imagined but firmly made manifest by the reaction of her mother and aunt to her father's absence. The mirror serves as a reflective trope and points to the internalization and refraction of racial stereotypes within the narrator's black middle class family reinforced by the image of deviant black masculinity that local newspapers publicize and that her mother and aunt reproduce. She contemplates her father's identity—"Colored druggist. Negro pharmacist. Black man. My father?"—and learns to veil at the same time that she unveils her racial identity in her father's absence and with the mirror of her sexuality in the background.

As the title suggests, "The New Mirror" refers to "the new plate-glass mirror that had been hung over the basin just the day before" in the narrator's family bathroom (Petry 1971 59). The narrator explains that her mother had the mirror installed in the downstairs bathroom so that her father could shave downstairs, "because it placed him closer to the drugstore while he shaved. Our drugstore was in the front of the building where we lived" (59). From the very beginning the story establishes the boundaries that inform the narrator's middle-class identity, but her reflection suggests that those boundaries are fragile:

The bathroom walls were white, and under the brilliant, all-revealing light cast by the new fixture I looked like all dark creatures impaled on a flat white surface: too big, too dark. . . . I decided that the way I looked in the white-walled bathroom was the way our family looked in the town of Wheeling, New York. We were the only admittedly black family in an all-white community and we stood out; we looked strange, alien. There was another black family—the Granites—but they claimed to be Mohawk Indians. Whenever my father mentioned them, he laughed until tears came to his eyes, saying, "Mohawks? Ha, ha, ha. Well, five or six generations of Fanti tribesman must have caught five or six generations of those Mohawk females named Granite under a bush somewhere. Ha, ha, ha." (60)

For the narrator, her family's new bathroom mirror reflects three interrelated things: herself, the public image of her family's blackness, and her father's (privately sexual) racial humor. The narrator's reflection thus collapses the public and private spaces that structure her life, but ironically, it is in her father's absence that the narrator begins to see the other half—the reflection—of her father and herself in the drugstore and in her family's domestic space. "It might have been a conjurer's shop, except, of course, for the cigarettes and the candy and the soda fountain. The bottles gleaming darkly along the walls could have held wool of bat and nose of Turk, root of the mandrake and dust of toad. I went out in the back room and looked into the yard. It seemed to go on forever, reaching into a vast, mysterious distance, unexplored, silent—not even the twitter of a bird. It was pitch black" (82–83).

Samuel's absence compromises the Layen family's middle-class respectability, but what lurks beneath the surface of the Layen family history is the narrator's sexual flowering, the mystery she cannot identify (with) and the unspeakable event that Samuel's absence both reveals and conceals. When her father returns to the drugstore well into the night and explains that he went to Norwich to get his false teeth, the narrator connects the pearly whites to "the white porcelain fixtures in the downstairs bathroom," reminding the audience of her private misgivings about her identity at the start of the story (84). Samuel explains that the new mirror forced him to see "what all those white people saw when he sang a solo" at church on Sunday mornings (86): "the open mouth all red and moist inside, the naked gums with a tooth here and there" (85). The teeth make Samuel sound as though "he were speaking through or around a formidable obstruction that prevented his tongue and his lips from performing their normal function" (84), so the narrator must call the police before her mother reports her father missing. She discovers, however, that she has no voice and her father's teeth force her to become silent and to speak in code to avail the white policeman, "Officer O'Toole, who was undoubtedly listening" to the narrator speak to her mother (88).

The women in "The New Mirror" force the narrator to assume her father's role and, in the process, enforce her silence and double speak: it is her mother who installs the family mirror in the first place, and it is her aunt who leaves her to her own devices in the drugstore. The narrator comes of age within a matrix of racial terror that supercedes her sexuality, and she must conform to a white world through which she sees herself and her blackness—much like her father sees his reflection in the bathroom mirror. On the surface, "The New Mirror" narrates the internalization of racial terror for a fifteen year-old young woman, but a much deeper mystery resides within the opening of her father's mouth. Like her father's red and naked gums, the narrator must conceal her private misgivings, the mysterious blackness that collapses the Layen's public and private spheres even before her father goes missing. Samuel's mouth is an allegory for the narrator's sexual maturation because it is the orifice through which the narrator comes of age. The town's whiteness reflects the Layen's blackness, on the one hand, and Samuel's absence refracts the narrator's sexual awakening, on the other. Both forces coincide to swallow up the narrator's social and sexual agency.

Blackness and female silence link the narrator in Petry's title story, "Miss Muriel," to her counterpart in "The New Mirror," but reflection is not an issue for the twelve year-old narrator in "Miss Muriel," neither in its form nor its content. The narrator speaks from the perspective of a diarist, and, as Hilary Holladay explains, "[t]his format gives the story a compelling immediacy and accommodates the speaker's struggle to understand the nuances of her story" (95). At one point, the narrator explains that "It has taken me two months of practice in front of a mirror to master the art of lifting one eyebrow" (3). Unlike the teenager in "The New Mirror," the young narrator in "Miss Muriel" is not self-conscious, but her diary-like narration reveals the cultural conditions and social codes that generate the mystery of female sexuality in the Layen family. "Miss Muriel," then, provides the refractive lens through which the young narrator comes of age in "The New Mirror."

The narrator in "Miss Muriel" makes friends with Wheeling's white populace and she moves in and out of racially proscribed boundaries that divide the town. The story opens as she and her white friend, Ruth, walk home from school together, and as they sit on the front steps of the Layen's family pharmacy, Ruth says, "'I wish I lived here,' and pat[s] the steps though they are very splintery" (2). The narrator's friendships facilitate the transgression of the social sanctions that maintain her black middle-class world, and her interaction with the shoe repairman, Mr. Bemish, leads to his courtship of the narrator's Aunt Sophronia while it also raises the narrator's awareness of her own racial "training" as she contemplates her disapproval of Mr. Bemish pursuing her aunt:

I have thought a great deal about Mr. Bemish. I like him. He is truly a friend. But I do not think he should be interested in Aunt Sophronia—at least not in a loving kind of way. The thing that bothers me is that I honestly cannot decide whether I object to him as a suitor because he is white or because he is old. . . . I know how I was trained to be a Christian—Sunday school, prayers, etc. I do not know exactly how I've been trained on the subject of race. Then why do I feel this way about Mr. Bemish? (30)

While the narrator nonchalantly notices that skin color differentiates her from Ruth, her friendship with Mr. Bemish makes her conscious of her racial prescriptions. Yet, as the narrator is aware, this racial consciousness is linked to Mr. Bemish's romantic interest in her aunt, and though a child, the narrator links race and sex and begins to doubt the validity of her own racial awareness.

The simultaneous courtship of her Aunt Sophronia by three different men—Mr. Bemish, Chink Johnson and Dottle Smith—provides the setting for the narrator's racial awareness. Chink is "the quintessential blues player" from the South (G. Washington 23) while Dottle is a white-skinned black man who teaches literature at an all-black college in Atlanta. As Holladay points out, the three men represent three types of sexuality: Bemish is a-sexual; Chink is hyper hetero-sexual; and Dottle is homo-sexual. The narrator's father vehemently objects to all three. He is "prejudiced against Bemish's race and age, Chink's sexually suggestive music and lower-class status, and Dottle's homosexuality. . . . Although Sophronia is an adult capable of making her own choices, [Samuel] is extremely protective of her" (Holladay 96). What the narrator presents to the audience, as Keith Clark explains, is an "exploration of men's intraracial and interracial relationships and the conflicted dimensions of black male subjectivity" (2004 82). In Clark's assessment, Samuel represents patriarchal masculinity; Chink, liminal masculinity; and Dottle feminine masculinity. These different forms of black masculinity collapse in their responses to the lone white male in the text: Bemish. While the story's title seems to suggest that the narrative is about female consciousness, it is merely "the punch line to a 'joke' that involves white male privilege, black male psychic erasure, and racial and sexual taboos" (Clark 2004 81).

According to Paul Weibe, "Miss Muriel" employs both primary and counternarratives that come to the fore through Dottle and Chink and their struggle to define Miss Muriel. When the narrator repeats Dottle's story to Chink about a black man being commanded to ask for a Miss Muriel cigar by a white clerk because of the picture of a white woman on the box, Chink explains "'It ought to be told the other way around. A black man should be tellin' a white man, 'White man, you see this picture of this beautiful black woman? *White* man, you say *Miss* Muriel!'" (37). As Weibe explains, "Miss Muriel [explores] the counternarrative that has developed in the black characters in response to the racist narrative and that is activated by Bemish's attentions to Sophronia. The narrator senses the presence of this counternarrative when she reflects on why Bemish is not 'right' for Sophronia" (67). The narrator struggles with her racial ideology—the counternarrative, as Weibe puts it, or counter-modernity, to follow Gilroy—and she actively resists it when Dottle and Chink force Bemish to leave Wheeling. "'You both stink,'" she tells the two black men. "'You stink like dead bats. You and your goddamn Miss Muriel—'" (57). Yet, the narrator's anger is complex and ironic since Dottle and Chink do precisely what she desires when Bemish enters the Layen's backyard without permission earlier in the story: "I hoped someone would say: 'What are you doing in our back yard, our private place, our especially private place? You are in intruder, go back to your waxed thread and your awl, go back to your house and your cat.' Nobody said anything" (15). When Dottle and Chink threaten to sew up Bemish with his own waxed thread, they recall the narrator's own resistance to his presence; her reaction to the two black men is also a silencing of her own self.

The narrator's troubled identity spawns from the silence between her and the other black women in the story. Perhaps the only one with whom the narrator has a verbal relationship is Francis Jackson, or Aunt Frank, who "is always cross and usually drunk. She drinks gin. Mother says this is what has made Aunt Frank's lip look as though they were turned inside out and she says this is called 'gin lip.' . . . Because I am young, she tries to boss me and to order me around, and she calls me Miss in a very unpleasant, sarcastic way" (23). Neither the narrator nor Aunt Frank can keep their lips sealed. They are dialectical figures in which Aunt Frank represents the other side of youth, the experience that the narrator is yet to encounter but what the drunk woman predetermines by sarcastically referring to the child as "Miss," a phrase that interpellates the narrator in the likeness of Miss Muriel. The afternoon before Dottle and Chink force Bemish to leave Wheeling, Aunt Frank walks into the pharmacy and lets in a swarm of bats. Dottle hops around like a woman, Chink tries to kill the bats with a newspaper, and Bemish pulls Sophronia into his chest while Samuel walks in and lets the bats out the same way in which they entered the store. When the youngster compares Dottle and Chink to "dead bats," she remembers and repeats Aunt Frank's accusation that Chink, Dottle and Bemish are "'Worse than bats'" (51). By damning Miss Muriel the narrator also reflects Aunt Frank's irrational hostility as she turns the Miss Muriel story inside out to expose the black community's—and her own—hypocrisy.

The narrator damns Miss Muriel as a way to resist both the primary and counternarratives that shape her blackness and her sexuality, but she still cannot escape the discursive and symbolic modes of representation with which she identifies. As Weibe suggests, "Perhaps the most powerful story left untold in 'Miss Muriel' is Sophronia's" (73), for she is silent about her history but certainly imbued with a his-story. The narrator gazes at her aunt from a male-dominant vantage point:

Aunt Sophronia came and stood in the window. She had washed the glass globes that we keep filled with blue, red, and yellow liquid. She was wearing a dark skirt and a white blouse. Her hair was no longer skinned tight against her fore-head, perhaps because she had been working in the garden, bending over, and the hairpins that usually hold it so tightly in place had worked themselves loose. She didn't look real. The sun was shining in the window and it reflected lights from the jars of colored water back on her face and her figure, and she looked golden and rose-colored and lavender, and it was as though there were a rainbow mov-ing in the window. (25)

The narrator mimics the male gazes directed at Sophronia—the prism through which the narrator imagines her own identity—and her father's pharmacy frames Aunt Sophronia while the desires of Chink, Dottle and Bem-ish color Sophronia's face and figure. Yet, where Sophronia is the object that captures the sunlight in Samuel's pharmacy window, the narrator is the agent that refracts—bends and turns—the meaning of Miss Muriel and her Aunt Sophronia's silence when she repeats and affirms Aunt Frank's assessment of Sophronia's suitors.

The narrator's role as a speaking subject within the black community forces her to align herself with her worst enemy, Aunt Frank, while it also paradoxi-cally disassociates the youngster from her own self. Feminist consciousness

within the black community, following Petry's stories, is a complex and contradictory mobilization because *both* racial terror and counter-modernity
prescribe the silence that characterizes black women's relationships with each
other.[8] Perhaps the only moment of feminine, indeed, even feminist, consciousness is in the first scene as Ruth and the narrator walk and talk home
together. The first conclusion we can draw from this, suggests Weibe, is that
"there is an initial solidarity among women that transcends race. . . . The second conclusion that we can draw is that even though Ruth disappears from the
narrative, there is a strong suggestion that her experiences as an adolescent girl
will parallel the narrator's" (75). But perhaps a third conclusion suggests that
white women are a formative absence in the mobilization of a feminist movement within the black community, both in the form of a consumptive object
(Miss Muriel) and a speaking subject (Ruth). "Miss Muriel" and "The New
Mirror" together demonstrate how young black women internalize the double consciousness that structures the black community and reinforces (black)
women's silence, even as they develop the ability to speak and to resist.

Petry's "Mother Africa" strikes at the heart of women's silence and the
ideologies of race and gender within the black community. "Mother Africa"
centers on Emmanuel Turner, Man, the Harlem community junk trader
and the quintessential Black Nationalist: self-reliant, unattached and racially
conscious. Man walks the Harlem streets yelling in "a big baritone voice" "'I
B-u-y, b-u-y, b-u-y! Ole rags, ole bottles, ole sewin' machines!" (129), and he
caresses the sound of "machines," suggesting that he signifies the modern
man, his body an extension of the inanimate objects that support his business. "He was fond of pushing his cart; the handles were worn smooth, polished by his hands. They seemed almost like an extension of his hands and
arms. And the balance of it on the wheels was beautiful. The cart wheels
made a faint rumbling that he could hear despite the street noises, the roar
of traffic, the sound of car horns" (128). When Man assumes the ownership
of an oversized bronze statue of a naked woman, what he names "Mother
Africa," the statue disrupts his simple, uncomplicated life. Yet the statue also
appeals to Man's desire for metal. "Thus he reverses the courtly love tradition of treating an unattainable woman as if she were a goddess sculpted on a
pedestal," says Holladay. "The statue's color precipitates [Man's] reverence as
much as her voluptuous features do. He sees her as an emblem of both racial
pride and female beauty. As 'Mother Africa,' the statue becomes the motivat-
ing presence in Man's life" (124).

The statue's silence fosters Man's desire for an African homeland
untainted by white colonial power. However, its bronzed metal also appeals

to his modernity and suggests that Black Nationalism mirrors the colonial power that it attempts to evade. In fact, "Mother Africa" recalls in Man's mind the personal and political histories that he represses to facilitate his liberation from the forces of slavery, both physical and ideological. When the statue shows up at his place his thoughts race back to his school days in Mississippi when he was taught how to spell the state's name. "[I]n moments of stress the damn thing popped into his thoughts and he would find himself saying it over and over, in march time, just as he as doing now: "M-I-crooked letter-crooked letter-I-crooked letter-crooked letter-humpbacked letter-humpbacked letter-I" (134–35). Ironically, "Mother Africa" disassociates Man from the black community, and he "must protect himself against especially deleterious forces *within* the community" (Roberts 30) because it forces Man to see that his "Mother Africa" is just a white woman made out of dark metal. When Man clambers up a ladder to remove a red bandanna a member of the community puts on the statue's head, he steps back and falls ten feet to the ground when he comes face-to-face with his worst fears. "He got up slowly, painfully. He tried to run as he went toward the house and couldn't, could only limp. He had hurt his leg and his back and from the way it felt, he must have wrenched his shoulder" (161). The statue literally re-members Man's body as a vestige of the South's racial/spatial history and thus alters forever his sense of self and his ability to walk freely the streets of Harlem; he instead embodies the "crooked humpbacked state where there was a year-round open season on black folks, no bag limit, no rules. . . . And up North? Here in Harlem? Killum. Play tricks on um. Send um statues of big and buck-naked black women" (135).

The statue returns Man to a state of slavery, both physically and ideologically, and the story's ambivalent resolution refracts Man's role in the slave trade while at the same time it reflects the historical condition of black people in the U.S. Ruth Roberts argues, "The white community has poisoned [Man's] life as surely as the white girl in Petry's later novel *The Narrows* (1953) poisons the black community that is the focus of the novel. In retaliation, Man returns to his former ways, and sells the statue for scrap metal. The only artistic discourse he will countenance will be a reprise of his buy and sell song" (31). Yet, Petry suggests a more nuanced reading of Man and his former ways because he does not return to his former self the same person. Unlike his business with the community, he owns title to the statue by way of a piece of paper signed by Mrs. Treadway, the rich white woman who gave it to Man in the first place. "He called the Harlem Metalworks. He'd done business with them for years. He said he had a large bronze statue. About ten feet tall.

He was selling her for scrap. Yes, he had all the papers on her" (162). Man continues to personify the statue, referring to it as "her," and this business transaction with the Metalworks recalls the buying and selling of a female body much like at an auction block. His "return" to his old ways, then, suggests that Man metonymically becomes a slave trader, the very figure that he despises throughout the course of the story.

Man's transfiguration of the U.S.'s slave trade recalls Bill Hod's trafficking of Asian bodies across the U.S.-Canadian border. Thus, "Mother Africa" extends *The Narrows*' sub-textual critique of black masculinity and black men's participation in the colonial forces that alienate them. Petry suggests that the convergence of race, gender and sexuality in the ideologies of Black Nationalism facilitate black men's alienation, but the ambivalent resolution to "Mother Africa" also points to the absent presence of white women in these ideologies of blackness and to the silencing of black women. Mrs. Treadway in "Mother Africa" mirrors Mrs. Treadway in *The Narrows*, for they both give birth to the desirous body that ruptures the black community—one physically, the other ideologically. Man's object of desire collapses white women with the African homeland; both mirror the white domestic ideology Man attacks, if only in reverse, and when he finally discovers his (dis)identification the statue disfigures Man's body and transfigures the U.S.'s modes of slavery. Petry's fiction thus establishes a line of continuity between two literary genres and time periods: Mrs. Treadway of *The Narrows* reflects Mrs. Treadway in "Mother Africa"; Chink is a refraction of Link; Frances Jackson in "Miss Muriel" both reflects and refracts her namesake in the novel; and Man becomes synonymous with Hod in their modern-day slave trades. All the while, Mother Africa remains silent and on the auction block.

HUNTING COMMUNISTS AND NEGROES IN ANN PETRY'S *THE NARROWS*

Farah Jasmine Griffin

Before the Bottom, before Brewster Place, there was the Narrows (also called "Eye of the Needle, The Bottom, Little Harlem, Dark Town, Niggertown). Before China, one of the whores in Toni Morrison's *The Bluest Eye*, there was China the whore who lived in the Narrows. Before Alice Walker's sexy blues singer Sugg Avery, there was Mamie Powther the busty, sensual, blues-singing woman desired by all the men of the Narrows and beyond. And, before Milkman Dead, the middle-class protagonist of Morrison's *Song of Solomon*, there was Link Williams, the Robesonesque lead character of Ann Petry's third and final novel, *The Narrows*. Although each of the later works are better known than Petry's, her book anticipates many of their major themes. In fact, *The Narrows* foreshadows much of what would follow in all of African American Literature; if for this reason only, the book deserves far more critical attention than it has thus far received.

Published in 1953, *The Narrows*—Ann Petry's most ambitious novel—is her masterwork. In spite of this, for the most part, contemporary reviewers found it to be less successful than her first novel, *The Street*. Later critics have also ignored it in favor of the better-known first work. There are a number of reasons for this: Petry's novel was published in a cultural context that also produced Ralph Ellison's *Invisible Man* (1952) and James Baldwin's *Go Tell It on the Mountain* (1953) as well as the lesser-known small gem *Maud Martha* by Gwendolyn Brooks (1953). Although Brooks received the Pulitzer for her collection of poems, *Annie Allen*, her first and only novel made less of a splash. Following the publication of their first novels, Baldwin and Ellison emerged as leading new literary voices; both produced works focusing on the development of young black men and each novel was less overtly political and more experimental than the earlier work of Richard Wright, the dominant figure of African American letters. The form and content of their novels announced a shift from the social realism and naturalism of the 30s and 40s and proved to be more in line with the conservative political climate of the times. This is especially true of Ellison's *Invisible Man*, which was explicitly anti-Communist.

Following the emergence of Black feminist literary criticism in the 1970s and 80s, Petry's work began to receive a modicum of attention. With its focus on a working class black woman, Lutie Johnson, *The Street* became a vehicle for exploring the intersections of race, class and gender in black women's lives. Nonetheless, Petry's other two novels and her short stories have yet to receive the kind of attention devoted to *The Street*.[1] And, *The Street* has not yet gained the stature of Zora Neale Hurston's *Their Eyes Were Watching God*.[2] Although Gloria Naylor became an outspoken advocate of Petry's novel, she did not have the same impact as did Alice Walker in her advocacy of Hurston's work. It is possible that later Black Feminist critics may have been less interested in *The Narrows* because it does not center around a self-actualized black female character. Pioneering Black Feminist critic Nellie McKay did write an insightful introduction an edition of *The Narrows*; her essay focuses on the unconventional representations of Black women in the novel.

When other critics have turned their attention to *The Narrows*, they have focused on the volatile interracial relationship at its center. Rarely do they take note of the novel's politics. Vernon E. Latin, in his essay "Ann Petry and The American Dream" (1978) is one of the few critics to take focus on Petry's political critique of McCarthyism.

It is possible that both contemporary reviewers and literary critics who followed them have been put off by the novel's anti-McCarthy stance and its attention to class. Or, perhaps the sensationalism of the interracial romance overshadowed these other elements of the novel. In an important essay on Alice Childress, Lorraine Hansberry and Claudia Jones, Mary Helen Washington argues for the existence of a radical tradition of black women writers whose "largely unrecorded history" has fallen victim to "the Cold Warriors [who] tried to wipe the country clean of left-wing ideas" (Washington, 204). According to Washington, these efforts have been exacerbated by the failure of scholars of the American Left who have produced narratives devoid of African American women and especially by:

African American canonization practices [that] have always followed the lead of the Cold Warriors, excising the black Left [so that] we know African American literature of the 1950s through writers like Richard Wright (he tried to be a

Communist but publicly renounced the party in 1944), or more typically through
Ralph Ellison's conservative, and anticommunist, high modernist Invisible Man.
(Washington 185)

During her time in Harlem, Ann Petry traveled in circles of left intellectuals, artists and activists. She was the woman's editor of the radical newspaper *The People's Voice* and she participated in the early stagings of the radical American Negro Theater alongside Ruby Dee, Ossie Davis, Harry Belafonte, Sidney Poitier and Alice Childress. This essay seeks to redress the absence of critical writing on the politics of this important novel. For Petry the responsibility of the artist is to reveal injustice without sacrificing craft.

The Narrows, which is set in a small New England town, Monmouth, Connecticut, is ostensibly the story of the tragic love affair between the married Camilo Sheffield, a white socialite and heiress, daughter of the town's wealthiest family and heir to the Treadway Munitions fortune, and Link Williams, a black scholar/athlete, son of the town's black community, The Narrows. When Link tries to end their relationship Camilo falsely accuses him of rape. He is arrested and released on bail only to be kidnapped and murdered by Camilo's husband and mother. Here I note that Link is the son of the community because he is an orphan who was raised both by the upstanding model of respectability, Abbie Crunch and the town's powerful, influential and at times dangerous Bill Hod, "a gambler, operator of houses of ill fame, a numbers king ... [and] racketeer" (202). Abbie's well-kept brownstone sits opposite Hod's bar, The Last Chance. Abbie's best friend, the undertaker, Miss Frances K. Jackson (called F. K. Jackson) and Weak Knees the Last Chance's gifted chef, join Abbie and Bill respectively in rearing the magnificent Link. While the love affair forwards much of the narrative's action, the novel uses the relationship as a vehicle with which Petry forces a confrontation between opposing elements within the narrative: that between black and white, yes, but perhaps even more important, that between different classes of people. For while the novel offers an important critique of racism, it also offers a stinging critique of class especially the devastating impact of a market-driven society on the press, the police and an individual's conception of his or her self. In short, *The Narrows* (as with *The Street* before it) is an eloquent statement of Petry's anti-capitalist, anti-racist politics.

Furthermore, while the interracial relationship at the novel's center is indeed an exploration of taboo sexuality, *The Narrows* also presents us with other considerations of sexuality as well. Through the introduction of an explicitly homosexual character, Howard Thomas, as well as the sensual, sex-loving Mamie Powther and her white counterpart, Lola, the redheaded wife of the town's editor (both of whom use their sexual prowess to control their husbands) Petry explores a multi-dimensional sense of sexuality. Furthermore, by having Link reared by Abbie Crunch and F. K. Jackson on the one hand and Bill Hod and his cook Weak Knees on the other, Petry provides examples of alternative family formations as well. In fact, after the death of Abbie's husband, the Major, the masculine Jackson steps in as provider and protector. Of F. K. Jackson, Link thinks: "Impossible to think of [F. K. Jackson] hunting a mate, handsome or otherwise. She was too brusque, to self-sufficient. Perhaps she, in her own person, was the dark handsome lover, and to her Abbie had been [the woman] that the male hunts for and rarely ever finds" (142). It is quite possible that Petry's attention to sex and sexuality as well as the interracial romance landed *The Narrows* on the list of books banned by the National Organization for Decent Literature (NODL). In 1956 The American Civil Liberties Union's *Statement on Censorship Activity By Private Organizations and the National Organization for Decent Literature* notes that NODL was the most prominent, influential and successful of a number of organizations engaged in censorship activity. Over 160 prominent writers, including Ann Petry signed the statement.

Before further discussion of the novel, it is important to situate it in the repressive and highly conservative climate of the early 1950s and to provide a discussion of Petry's essay, "The Novel as Social Criticism," which lends insight into the aesthetic and political sensibility that produced the novel.

As noted above, Ann Petry spent much of the 1940s in Harlem, where she worked as a journalist and editor while honing her craft. She was also an active participant in a number of activist and cultural organizations that were overtly political. As a number of scholars have noted, for Black intellectuals and activists the Popular Front continued well into the middle of the 1940s.[3] This sensibility informed Petry throughout her life and is most explicitly stated in her essay "The Novel as Social Criticism."

Published four years after *The Street* and three before *The Narrows*, "The Novel as Social Criticism" (1950) (which appeared in *The Writers Book*) is Ann Petry's most sustained aesthetic statement. That it appears along side essays by W. H. Auden, Pearls S. Buck, Lionel Trilling, and her mentor Mabel Louise Robinson, the publication of the essay also suggest Petry's stature among other writers. In the essay, Petry defends the "sociological novel" which had come under great scrutiny and critique during the years following World War II. Just one year before "The Novel As Social Criticism," in 1949, a young James Baldwin published his scathing critique of Harriet Beecher Stowe's *Uncle Thomas Cabin* and his mentor, Richard Wright's *Native Son.*

Petry addresses these kinds of critiques head on:

Being a product of the twentieth century (Hitler, atomic energy, Hiroshima, Buchenwald, Mussolini, USSR) I find it difficult to subscribe to the idea that art exists for art's sake. It seems to me that all truly great art is propaganda, whether it be the Sistine Chapel, or La Giconda, Madame Bovary or War and Peace. (33)

Echoing W. E. B. Du Bois's famous essay "Art as Propaganda" Petry argues for the continuing significance of sociological fiction, identifies its deep roots in Western culture, and distances it from charges of Marxist propaganda without denying the significance of Marxism:

Not all of the concern about the shortcomings of society originated with Marx. Many a socially conscious novelist is merely a man or a woman with a conscience. Though part of the cultural heritage of all of us derives from Marx, whether we subscribe to Marxist theory or not, a larger portion of it stems from the Bible. (33)

Petry situates Marx in the context of Western thought; his thought has influenced Western society in much the way Freud has—one need not to have read either to have been to have experienced their influence. The same might be said of the Bible; although most Westerners are more familiar with the stories of the Bible, especially those that are meant to inform our behavior and our morality. And certainly, especially during the Cold War, even the most right wing of readers would not argue with the importance of Biblical injunctions.

From here, Petry accomplishes the task of arguing for the importance of sociological fiction in a number of ways: First, she grounds the tradition in the Bible, particularly the Old Testament story of Cain and Abel whereby Cain asks God "Am I my brother's keeper?" Petry writes:

In one way or another, the novelist who criticizes some undesirable phase of the status quo is saying that man is his brother's keeper and that unless a social evil (war or racial prejudice or ante-Semitism or political corruption) is destroyed man cannot survive but will become what Cain feared he would become—a wander and a vagabond on the face of the earth. (33)

Petry also argues against art for arts sake while insisting upon the importance of craft, especially in the development of full, complex characters. "When society is given the role of fate, made the evil in the age-old battle between good and evil, the burden of responsibility for their actions is shifted away from the characters" (36). According to Petry that which distinguishes success-ful novels from their more didadic cousins is craftsmanship and the author's development of characterization and theme: "Once the novelist begins to manipulate his characters to serve the interests of his theme they lose whatever vitality they had when their creator first thought about them" (36).

The Narrows is Petry's novelistic example of the theories she espouses in this little-known essay. Together, the essay and novel serve as a critical interven-tion in the midst of an era of censorship and witch-hunting. In the same year that Petry's essay was published Joseph McCarthy gave his first public speech against Communists, alleging "I have in my hand a list of 205 cases of individ-uals who appear to be either card-carrying members or certainly loyal to the Communist Party." Later that year, The McCarran Act, or the Internal Security Act of 1950 passed in spite of a veto by President Truman. Among other things, the Act required members of the U.S. Communist Party to register with the Attorney General and Communist organizations to provide lists of their mem-bers. The Act also established the Subversive Activities Control Board to select individuals and organizations that had to comply with its regulations.

In 1951, under the leadership of Senator McCarthy, the second set of HUAC hearings became his stage for accusing American citizens of betraying their country. Having been members in Communist organizations or having had friends and associates who were members was evidence enough for McCarthy.

Among the many artists and intellectuals whose lives and careers McCarthyism threatened were a number of African Americans. Mary Helen Washington notes: "Whether on the Left or the Right, African Americas were, by virtue of their blackness, subversives in the Cold War" (Washington, 184). The two most famous, Paul Robeson and W. E. B. Du Bois are especially sig-nificant for our purposes for just as both are undergoing assault Ann Petry chose to create a DuBoisian Robesonesque character in Link Williams. Inter-estingly, in 1946, Petry wrote to Shirley Graham upon the publication of her book about Paul Robeson that the book was "wonderful . . . I must confess to feeling very smug because I am able to say that I know you."[4] In 1951, Graham would marry W. E. B. Du Bois; in that same year he was indicted for failing to register as a foreign agent (the charges would later be dropped) and he ran for the United States Senate on the American Labor Party Ticket. The F.B.I., under J. Edgar Hoover, began their surveillance of Robeson in 1941. In 1952 the HUAC sought to cite him for his refusal to sign the non-Communist declara-tion and the United States Department denied him his passport.

As with Du Bois, Link Williams is a New England born, Ivy League (Dartmouth) educated intellectual. As with Du Bois he writes a thesis about slavery and he aspires to become a scholar of Black History. However, unlike the young Du Bois, Williams is no elitist. In fact he finds the DuBoisan elitism of Abbie and the black bourgeoisie repressive and stifling, preferring the more egalitarian environs of the Last Chance, The Dock, Dumble Street. The struggle between Abbie Crunch's racial politics and those of Bill Hod represent the distinction between an uplift ideology of respectability and one that found value in Black vernacular culture. Link recalls Abbie's assertions about his responsibility to "The Race":

She said colored people (sometimes she just said The Race) had to be cleaner, smarter, thriftier, more ambitious than white people, so that white people would like colored people. The way she explained it made him feel as though he were carrying The Race around with him all the time. (138)

Bill Hod and Weak Knees "re-educated him on the subject of race" (144). Through conversations about contemporary events and black history Link loses his fear of laughing at white people and learns to appreciate the color Black: "After a month of living with Bill and Weak Knees he felt fine. He felt safe. He was no longer ashamed of the color of his skin" (145).

Link's connection to Robeson is a bit more explicit. In fact, Robeson is the object of conversation between Link and Weak Knees who articulates a signifying defense of Robeson and critique of the United States. Weak Knees explains to Link:

You know, Sonny, I get sick of all these whafolks askin' me first thing, first drop of a hat, what do I think about Paul Robeson. The meat man he come in here thismornin', a brokedown dogass white man if I ever see one, all bandylegged from carryin' carcasses, and he come inhere with my order, and before he gets the meat put down on the table good he wants to know what do I think about Paul Robeson. So I made him happy, I said I thought he oughtta hightail it back to Russia where he come from, and that softened him up, and I waited awhile and I give him a cup of coffee, and then I says, The reason he oughtta have stayed in Russia, mister, is because over there if he went around talkin' about the changes he wanted made, why'd he get hisself shot full of holes, but nobody over there would be goin' around about to piss in their pants because he was a black man talkin' the wrong kind of politics. . . . And if his boy went and married hisself a little white chickadee over there in Russia, the whafolks woudn't wasted their time runnin' to tell all the colored folks they see askin' 'em what they thought about it. I says over there they wouldn't give a damn mister, and I don't give a damn over here. Any country where the folks can't marry each other when they got a heat on for each other why. . . . (265–66)

Significantly, Weak Knees doesn't claim to share Robeson's politics; in fact, he seems to disagree with him. Nonetheless, he defends Robeson's right to freely express his political opinions, and Weak Knees offers a critique of the United States for its obsession with miscegenation and laws against interracial marriage. Consequently, here we have an argument against the racial politics of the United States as well as a defense of Civil Liberties but no explicit statement about capitalism. Furthermore Weak Knees foreshadows the exact taboo over which Link will lose his life—the fact that he and a white woman fall passionately in love with each other. Petry reserves expressions of critiques of capitalism for the photographer Jubine.

As with Robeson, Link Williams is a charismatic scholar athlete whose voice is "a deep resonant musical voice. A perfect speaking voice." His Aunt Abbie looks at "the line of his throat, at the slight thrust of his chin, at the smoothness of his skin, the perfection of his nose and mouth, the straightness of his hair and thought 'Sometimes, just sometimes, I wish he weren't so very good looking.'" Indeed it is his dignity, his nobility and his beauty that help incite the fury of racists, the envy of most men and the lust of women black and white. Following Camilo's accusation of rape and her car accident where she runs down a poor child of the Narrows, the photographer, Jubine, himself a Communist, who has "the unkempt look of a Bolshevist" sells a photograph of Link to a New York tabloid. The photograph is an effort to counter any possible attempts to portray him as a dangerous animalistic rapist. The editor of the Monmouth newspaper, Bullock, who has refused Jubine's photograph and chosen not to run a story critical of Camilo under threat of losing her family's advertising money, looks at the photograph and thinks:

So here was this Negro standing on the dock, lordlylooking bastard, leaning against the railing, head slightly turned, profile like Barrymore's, sunlight concentrated on his left side, so that the head, the shoulders, the whole length of him had the solidity of sculpture, the picture damn near had the three-dimensional quality of fine sculpture. There was an easy carelessness about the leaning position of his body, controlled carelessness, and the striped T-shirt, the slacks; the moccasins on the feet suited his posture.

Every woman who saw this nigger's picture would cut it out, clip it out, tear it out, and drool over it. Every white man who saw it would do a slow burn. (365)

The photograph could very well be one of the many that portray Robeson as a Black Adonis, especially those of him as Shakespearian actor or the nudes taken by Van Vechten that show him in the classic poses of the athlete. In fact, Bullock describes the photograph as a work of art. The Link of this photograph is the construction of Jubine, the artist. That the photograph is published in a New York tabloid is a demonstration of art in the service of social justice. In "The Novel As Social Criticism" Petry writes, "The novel like all other forms of art, will always reflect the political, economic and social structure of the period in which it was produced" (33). Jubine's photographs possess both beauty and devastating honesty.

Although Petry stresses the artistic nature of Bullock's photographs, she has him publish them in fashion magazines and newspapers. For Petry, the press is an arena of conflict. As a former reporter for the Black Press she understood the power of the media in shaping public consciousness about race. In both *The Narrows* and *The Street*, she demonstrates the way the mainstream press feeds racial hatred and fear by exaggerating the size and potential danger of black people, by painting portraits of black neighborhoods as jungles. And yet, through Jubine the photographer who sells his photographs to fashion magazines and newspapers, she also demonstrates the possibility of an alternative use of the Press. Jubine prefers that his photographs be printed as a series and not out of context so that they create a narrative. He uses photography as a means of indicting the wealthy while portraying the dignity of the poor without romanticizing their poverty. When Bullock does publish Jubine's photographs in the Monmouth Chronicle they are part of an important series on housing and poverty. When he chooses to ignore him, he allows his paper to be used in the service of capital and racial violence. Jubine is a minor but important character for as the narrative's artist, he is the vehicle through which Petry speaks. Interestingly in both *Country Place* and *The Narrows*, Petry chooses to have the author's perspective articulated by white men, the pharmacist in *Country Place* and Jubine here. When Bullock accuses him of setting up his photographs, Jubine responds, "Jubine watches. Jubine waits. Jubine records but Jubine never, never interferes." Through Jubine and the novel's other white characters we gain even further insight into the novel's critique of American capitalism.

If Link is a Robesonesque character, his lover, the beautiful blond Camilo is a forerunner to Sophia, Malcolm X's married white lover in *The*

Autobiography of Malcolm X. Even as she falls in love with Link she continues to maintain a sense of entitlement, paternalism and condescension. She uses her wealth to pay off hotel staff, maitre d's and others in order to create a cocoon for herself and her black lover. She often speaks to Link as if her were her servant. When he expresses his resentment and chooses to end their relationship, she accuses him of rape. She represents an elite class in the midst of transition. In the novel this transition is, "the passing of aristocrats" (49) to "millionaires" from "aristocratic" people like Abbie Crunch who possesses "an air of quiet elegance … attributed to aristocratic old colored women and a handful of aristocratic old white women" (378) and her late husband's former employer, "The Governer" to "common" people like Mamie Powther who "is Dumble Street." Throughout the novel there is a sense of flux about class matters and it is characterized by a kind of vulgarity amongst both the wealthy and the poor. On the one hand, the houses of The Narrows are being torn down and replaced by high-rise projects. On the other, it is not a white mob that kidnaps and murders Link, but instead educated, wealthy whites seeking to protect their name and their wealth.

Malcolm Powther, butler to the Treadways and husband of Mamie, is representative of an old fashion, loyal servant, proud of his proximity to wealth and whiteness. He makes note of the confusion created by differences and changes in class. He oversees Mrs. Treadway's annual mid-winter tea for young women who work in her munitions plant. While he used to enjoy the tea because the young ladies wore their best dresses and were on their best behavior, he comes to despise them when they spread gossip about Camilo following her accusation of rape. He used to make distinctions between the young women and the rowdy workmen for whom Mrs. Treadway holds a summer picnic on her mansion's grounds. He observes:

These girls smelt of perfume, their hair curled, they were wearing their new Spring dresses, but they were exactly like the sweaty beer-drinking workers, who invaded the park in July. They too, resented the fact that the Madam belonged to the millionaire class. . . . The beer drinkers wrecked the grounds or tried to and the tea drinkers . . . were just as hostile. (352–53)

Yet Petry, like Jubine, recognizes the dignity of the poor Irish women who hold their families together, the honesty of the poor white farmer's wife who refuses to say a black escaped convict raped her, the generosity of Miz Doris, F. K. Jackson's housekeeper and Mamie Powther's lack hypocrisy. The novel's worst characters are the status hungry Bullock and Malcolm Powther. Each of them worship wealth and are easily bought and controlled by it. Furthermore each is also fully aware of their complicity and wrestle with their cowardice. The cuckold Powther, who looks in his wife's closets and bureau drawers for evidence of her infidelity, identifies with Camilo's husband. Consequently, when Mrs. Treadway requests that he accompany them to Dumble Street and "point out" (name names) Link, he agrees to do so. While waiting in the car with Mrs. Treadway, Capitan Sheffield and two of his college classmates, Powther hears a sermon broadcasts from the loudspeaker of a local storefront church:

And the Lord said unto Cain
Where is Abel thy brother?
What hast thou done?
The voice of thy brother's blood
crieth to me from the ground. (385)

Powther is counterpart to slaves who hid their mistresses' silver from the Union Army or those who informed their masters of planned rebellions. He represents the worst extreme of a politics of respectability. Hearing the sermon, he thinks: "He wasn't my brother. I have to prove he wasn't my brother. Prove to these people . . . that all Negroes are not criminal, some of them are good, some of them are first-class butlers named Powther" (386). With this conviction, he identifies Link and delivers him to his murderers.

Powther and Bullock are linked by their cowardice, their willingness to be pawns to wealth, their inability to confront their wives for fear the women will deny them access to their bodies. As with Powther, Bullock also "points out" Link by using his paper to paint the Black community as violent, depraved and dangerous. It is through Bullock that Petry articulates the connection between anti-Red and anti-Black ideologies and practices. In a moment of self-reflection about his complicity he thinks:

Even the State Department was acting like a harried housewife, searching out the
hiding place of mice and cockroaches and bedbugs, any vermin that from time to
time invade a house, searching carefully under beds and bureau drawers and or
closet shelves, in cellars and in attics, peering inside ovens and sugar bowls looking
in every likely and unlikely place for Communist and heretics and unbelievers.

So what difference does it make, he thought, whether we here in Monmouth
hunt down Negroes or whether we hunt down Communists? . . . There is a differ-
ence but at the moment it escapes me. (378)

Black and white disapproved of Link and Camilo not because they were involved in an adulterous affair, but because of race. What ought to have been a private, personal relationship between lovers is the object of great concern to people who follow, pursue and observe them. A society obsessed with weeding out Communist nourishes an anti-black racism, nourishes those who police the color line. A society that tolerates surveillance, and censorship is dangerous for anyone considered marginal or capable of threatening the status quo.

In *The Narrows*, Petry realizes the aesthetic vision she forwards in "The Novel As Social Criticism." She creates characters who are challenged to wrestle with themselves, who must confront their own demons and cowardice. This is especially true of Bullock and Powther who make possible Link's murder, who name names by pointing him out and paint a climate of fear by telling dangerous lies about entire groups of people. The novel closes on a note of hope, when Abbie, following her own self-critical self-reflection acknowledges her complicity in the downfall of Link and Camilo. Concerned that Bill Hod will seek revenge on Camilo, Abbie decides, at novel's end, to try and prevent further violence. Hand in hand with Mamie Powther's unkempt, "urchin" J. C. Powther, she goes to the police to request protection for Camilo. So Petry gives us a vision where the black bourgeoisie, along with a child of the urban poor (who is sure to benefit from his association with her), together take the moral high ground by seeking to ensure peace, security and forgiveness.

In the past twenty years a number of historians have produced a body of work documenting a history of Black Radicalism. A number of cultural and literary historians have also started to include African American thinkers in broader histories of the left. However, literary critics and theorists (of African American literature) have sacrificed attention to politics and literary history in favor of more formalist and theoretical concerns. Following the lead of Ralph Ellison, the emergence of contemporary African American literary criticism sought to ensure more "literary" and less "sociological" readings of black fiction in order to acknowledge the sophistication and artistry of these works. Ann Petry's *The Narrows* has fallen between the cracks of all of these efforts. Petry's work does not sacrifice artistry for politics and yet it cannot be properly read or appreciated without attention to the political. There is little evidence that Petry actively participated in the left leaning literary circles of Harlem during the years she lived in Connecticut; consequently she does not emerge as part of groups of writers such as those gathered around Robeson's publication Freedom Ways or organizations such as the Harlem Writers Guild. Given her intensely private nature it is difficult to place her. However a close reading of her fiction reveals a great deal about her understanding of the relationship between political and aesthetic concerns.

Attending to Petry's fiction of the 50s (and that of a number of other underappreciated black authors) gives us a fuller view of that period. It also provides a bridge from the fiction of the 1940s to the work of the Black Arts Movement in the late 1960s and 70s. As such, most histories leap from Ellison and Baldwin to a group of young militants who rediscover Richard Wright during the Black Power Movement. This gives an appearance of a black radicalism that has lain dormant for over twenty years. Ann Petry should be a central figure in a revisionist history of African American literature; her novel, *The Narrows* helps to demonstrate the aesthetic and political complexity of African American literary culture during the Cold War years. Additionally, *The Narrows* should join Zora Neale Hurston's *Their Eyes Were Watching God* as an important forerunner to the later emergence of black women's literature with which it shares a great deal. While critics and writers alike have claimed that black male writers have been most concerned about relationships between black men and white men while black women writers have focused on intra-racial matters, *The Narrows* attempts to do both by attending mutually to intimate familial and communal issues while also turning its attention to issues of race and most importantly, class.

NOTES

INTRODUCTION

1. Petry notebook. Undated, Ann Petry Manuscript Collection. Howard Gottlieb Archival Research Center, Boston University.
2. This is a subject I cover in *Romance and Rights: The Politics of Interracial Intimacy, 1945–1954*. Jackson: University Press of Mississippi, 2005.
3. Michael Denning, *The Cultural Front: The Laboring of American Culture in the Twentieth Century*. New York: Verso, 1998.
4. Richard Wright, "Blueprint for Negro Writing," in *The Portable Harlem Renaissance Reader*, edited by David Levering Lewis. New York: Penguin, 1995.
5. There are many excellent analysis of the "literary left." See for example, Mullin and Smethurst, eds. *Left of the Color Line: Race, Radicalism, and Twentieth-Century Literature of the United States*. Chapel Hill: University of North Carolina Press, 2006, Bill Mullen, *Popular Fronts: Chicago and African American Cultural Politics, 1936–1946*. Urbana: University of Illinois Press, 1999, Alan Wald, *Exiles From a Future Time: The Forging of the Mid-Twentieth-Century Literary Left*. Chapel Hill: University of North Carolina Press, 2001, James Smethurst, *The Black Arts Movement: Literary Nationalism in the 1960s and 1970s*. Chapel Hill: University of North Carolina Press, 2006, Stacy Morgan, *Rethinking Social Realism: African American Art and Literature, 1930–1953*. Athens: University of Georgia Press, 2004, and Michael Denning, *The Cultural Front*.
6. Chester Himes, *Lonely Crusade*. New York: Thunder's Mouth Press, 1997.
7. Stacey Morgan, *Rethinking Social Realism*, Paula Rabinowitz, *Black & White & Noir*. New York: Columbia University Press, 2002, and Rebecca Schreiber, *The Cold War Culture of Political Exile: U.S. Artists, Writers and Filmmakers in Mexico, 1946–1966* forthcoming from University of Minnesota Press.
8. Himes, *Plan B*. Jackson: University Press of Mississippi, 1993.
9. See Rebecca Schreiber's account of Motley's travel narrative in *The Cold War Culture of Political Exile*.
10. Petry letter to Edward G. Guinier, June 10, 1942. Ann Petry Manuscript Collection. Howard Gottlieb Archival Research Center, Boston University.
11. Petry letter to Samual Thompson, July 1, 1958. Ann Petry Manuscript Collection. Howard Gottlieb Archival Research Center, Boston University.
12. Ann Petry to Kenneth Reeves, March 8, 1969. Ann Petry Manuscript Collection. Howard Gottlieb Archival Research Center, Boston University.
13. Ann Petry, "The Novel and Social Criticism," in Helen Hull, ed., *The Writer's Book*. New York: Barnes and Noble, Inc., 1950: 33.

"ANN PETRY'S 'NEW MIRROR' "
Rachel Rubin and James Smethurst

1. W. E. B. Du Bois, *The Souls of Black Folk*, 1903, edited by David Blight and Robert Gooding-Williams. Boston: Bedford, 1997: 38.
2. For scholarly treatments of the Harlem Renaissance and the Left, see Anthony Dawahare, *Nationalism, Marxism, and African American Literature Between the Wars: A New Pandora's Box.* Jackson: University of Mississippi Press, 2003; Barbara Foley, *Spectres of 1919: Class and Nation in the Making of the New Negro.* Urbana: University of Illinois Press, 2003; William J. Maxwell, *New Negro, Old Left: African American Writing and Communism Between the Wars.* New York: Columbia University Press, 1999.
3. Barbara Foley, "From Communism to Brotherhood: The Drafts of Invisible Man." In *Left of the Color Line: Race, Radicalism and Twentieth-Century Literature of the United States,* edited by Bill V. Mullen and James Smethurst. Chapel Hill: University of North Carolina Press, 2003.
4. Interview with Marvel Cooke by Kathleen Currie, New York City, November 1, 1989, Women in Journalism Oral History Project of the Washington Press Club Foundation: 92.
5. "Editorial Policy of the Voice," *People's Voice* (August 22, 1942): 4.
6. For an example of the work of Negro Women, Inc., see Ann Petry, "Negro Women Wax Indignant Over Latest Crime Campaign," *People's Voice* (August 15, 1942): 3.
7. Interestingly, Petry's essay is broken up by the printing of two Harlem poems by Langston Hughes: "Ballad of a Landlord" and "College Formal: Renaissance Casino."
8. With rather striking reversal of cause and effect, Marjorie Pryse writes, "Perhaps if Ann Petry had been able to read recent novels by Paule Marshall, Alice Walker, Toni Morrison, and Toni Cade Bambara, she might have been more aware of the fictional potential of Granny . . ." (124). Ironically for this particular context, Pryse makes this comment in a book called *Conjuring.* ("'Pattern Against the Sky: Deism and Motherhood in Ann Petry's *The Street*, in Marjorie Pryse and Hortense J. Spillers, eds., *Conjuring: Black Women, Fiction, and Literary Tradition.* Bloomington: Indiana University Press, 1985: 116–31.
9. Frederic Jameson, *The Political Unconscious.* Ithaca: Cornell University Press, 1981: 9.

"OBJECT LESSONS: FETISHIZATION AND CLASS CONSCIOUSNESS IN ANN PETRY'S *THE STREET*"
Bill V. Mullen

1. See for example the following books: Martha Biondi, *The Struggle for Civil Rights in Postwar New York City* (Cambridge, London: Harvard University Press, 2003); Barbara Foley, *Spectres of 1919: Class and Nation in the Making of the New Negro* (Champaign-Urbana: University of Illinois Press, 2003); Robin D. G. Kelley, *Hammer and Home: Communists in Alabama During the Great Depression* (Chapel Hill: University of North Carolina Press, 1993); William J. Maxwell, *African-American Writing and Communism Between the Wars* (New York: Columbia University Press, 1999); Bill V. Mullen, *Popular*

Fronts: Chicago and African American Cultural Politics, 1935–1946 (Champaign-Urbana: University of Illinois Press, 1999); James Edward Smethurst, *The New Red Negro: The Literary Left and African American Poetry, 1930–1946* (New York, Oxford: Oxford University Press, 1999).

2. In "Modernism and the Aesthetics of Management, or, T. S. Eliot's Labor Literature," Erick Shocket powerfully reads Eliot's "objective correlative" as a managerial trope, meant to signify and contain Eliot's relationship to working-class life and culture. He argues persuasively that Eliot's description of literature as an affect-producing mechanism echoes the language of industrial capitalism and Fordism in particular. My reading of objective correlative differs here, but I would also underscore that Eliot's (and Petry's) use of "symbol" drives us closer to consideration of the object world not as metaphor but as materiality. See Eric Shocket in Bill V. Mullen and James Smethurst, editors, *Left of the Color Line: Race, Radicalism, and Twentieth-Century Literature of the United States* (Chapel Hill: University of North Carolina Press, 2003), pp. 13–38. See especially pp. 25–35.

"PULPING ANN PETRY: THE CASE OF *COUNTRY PLACE*"
Paula Rabinowitz

1. While there are many references to *Country Place* in interviews and reviews, only one scholarly article deals with it directly. More typical is Barrett which despite two significant chapters in his recent book on Petry's novels doesn't mention it.

2. See Rabinowitz ch. 6, especially, pp. 160–62.

3. Holding's 1947 novel was also set on coastal Connecticut; it, too, registers a changed racial and gender dynamic as white middle-class mother, Lucia Holley maintains her household while her husband is stationed in the Pacific by conspiring with her black maid and a blackmailer to protect her daughter's reputation. Its location was changed to Balboa Island and its post-war reason for absenting Tom was his work as an engineer in Germany repairing bridges under the Marshall Plan. Despite the patriotic reasons for the father's absence, both versions hint at the failure of heterosexual married men as the more engaged criminal offers a deeper intimacy to Lucia. Holding also registers how "queer" this wartime family arrangement had become (Holding 206). Fluet argues that middle-class housewives actually have more in common with gangsters than with their absent husbands as each must "negotiate" multiple invisible tasks.

4. Notebook. Ann Petry Papers. Box 19. Howard Gotlieb Research Center. Boston University.

5. Mixed in with this notebook in Box 4, are manuscript pages for both *The Narrows* and *Country Place*.

6. Dove's "Not Welcome Here," a long section from her new poetry collection touches on a similar experience for black GIs returning from WWI.

7. Wee Gee worked for the same newspapers as Petry; their tenure at *PM* overlapped. His two books—*Naked City* and *WeeGee's People*—featuring his photos of crime scenes and automobile accidents were reviewed on the verso of the same *Saturday Review of Literature* in which Martha Foley's *Best Stories of 1946*, featuring Petry's story "Like a Winding Sheet" got a favorable notice.

8. On George Petry: With the exception of a mention by Mangione of a George Petry being a member of the writer's union and a WPA employee and repeated tales about him as a mystery writer, I cannot actually ascertain that he published anything, though Ann Petry notes his work on *People's Voice* in her journals and in an interview says he used to write copy for an advertising agency—which she did, too. This was clearly a touchy subject for her; the dedication page mock-up for NAL's *Country Place* needed to be revised from George W. Petry to George D, possibly suggesting that there were two George Petrys or else hinting at some unconscious wish to alter his identity, or most likely, just a mistake [NAL Collection].

   LOWRIE: Is your husband a writer also?
   PETRY: Well, yes, in a way. He used to write copy for an advertising agency. . . . One of the first questions that people used to ask me was, "What does your husband do?" and I would look them right in the eye and say, "If I were a man, would you ask me what my wife did?" ("Visit" 88).

   Moreover, in 1947, Petry had published a proto-feminist essay: "What's Wrong with Negro Men?" the same year she published *CP*.
   On the story of Arnold Petri's and the "pulp" facsimile and text of "Marie of the Cabin Club," see Jarrett.

9. The sense that pulp fiction led to social depravities of its readers, of course, had a much longer history. In Lois Weber's 1916 film *Shoes*, for instance, the daughter Emmy resorts to prostitution to pay for a new pair of shoes in order to keep her job as a shopgirl at a Five and Dime store. She must turn all her earnings over to her mother for housekeeping because her father spends his time and carfare buying and reading cheap paperbacks instead of holding down a job. In this morality tale by a former crusader for the Salvation Army, it's not liquor but literature that dooms the working class.

10. Jenemann and Knighton argue that all Fearing's novels dissect Taylorism and the forces of capitalism pushing to reduce the time of transmission—of information of money, of labor and of capital. As such, they also describe the limits of autonomy, even for authors and especially for popular authors, working within industrial enterprises, which, by the 1940s, included all magazine, (and because it relied on magazine distribution) all paperback, publishing.

11. "I am a fiction factory," Erle Stanley Gardner wrote to the new editor of *Black Mask*, Joseph Thompson Shaw, in 1926, quoted in (Smith 21).

12. Notebooks Box 14, Folder 12.

13. For more on Petry's children's biographies and their connection to mid-century left-wing women's publishing history see Mickenberg, 259–71.

14. Her feminist anger at social constraints on motherhood and men's desire for feminine demureness seems to develop into crankiness when she ends up writing letters to newspapers complaining to the *New York Times* about Bonwit Teller advertisements and fashion articles displaying women in short skirts in the 1970s (Notebooks).

15. Stephanie Rothman, Post-screening discussion of THE WORKING GIRLS (1974). "Women with Vision." Walker Art Center. Minneapolis, MN. May 19, 2005.

"INVISIBLE HANDS AT WORK: DOMESTIC SERVICE AND MERITOCRACY IN ANN PETRY'S NOVELS"
Rachel Peterson

1. Claudia Jones, "300 Years of an Uphill Fight," *The Worker*, February 11, 1951: 5. In this essay, Jones specifically refers to the exploitation of "over a million [African American women] still confined to domestic service." See also Jones, "An End to the Neglect of the Problems of the Negro Women," *Political Affairs*, June 1949: 51–67.

2. McHenry, Beth, "Ann Petry Says 'The Street' Is First of Series on Negro Life," *Daily Worker*, March 29, 1946: 13.

3. Frederick Engels (ed.), *Capital, Volume 1: A Critical Analysis of Capitalist Production* (New York: International Publishers, 1992): 715.

4. Elsewhere in the essay, Petry insists that the Old Testament's notion of the brother's keeper (though this idea, in Petry's opinion, has been "corrupted in a thousand ways— sometimes it is offered to the world as socialism, socialism as communism") has had a greater impact than Marx on the social novel. Petry further advocates a "sociological" (36) approach that is independent of religious, political, and literary conventions in a logic that establishes her as an unaffiliated radical. Rideout's observation that proletarian authors produced "laboratory experiments, so to speak, [through which] the radical novelists helped other writers to create literature that was sociological but was not just sociology [explains] the achievements of the radical writers, mostly those of the independent left, in the 1940s" (288) is critical to recall here, despite Petry's seeming disavowal of leftist literature, her own work may have roots therein that she is reluctant to acknowledge.

5. See Paula Rabinowitz, "Domestic Labor: Film Noir, Proletarian Literature and Black Women's Fiction," in *MFS Modern Fiction Studies*, 47:1 (2001): 229–54 for a discussion of Brooks and Petry, and for a more general discussion, Trudier Harris, *From Mammies to Militants: Domestics in Black American Literature*. Philadelphia: Temple University Press, 1982.

6. The exploitation and dislocation of domestics in Petry's era was particularly vivid given the failure of the New Deal's initiatives to provide for this special labor category. Thus "the vast majority of African-American domestics struggle with the same assaults to their dignity that their great-grandmothers had contended with generations before" (Jones 342).

7. Michael Gold, *New Masses*, July 7, 1928: 2.

8. Petry's s depictions of domestics reveal another fundamental feature of reportage outlined by William Stott, the recounting of "the lives of specific individuals who represent people generally overlooked in the society." In *Documentary Expression And Thirties America*. Chicago: University of Chicago Press, 1986 (originally 1973).

9. Roi Ottley points out the attention of white and African American newspapers like *People's Voice* to the "Bronx Slave Market," where day domestics "waited for bidders." This exploitation led to the Bronx Citizens' Committee for the Improvement of Domestic Employees and other organizations geared toward reforming the "attitudes and habits" of domestic employers. Other organizations like the Domestic Workers Union were apparently a central venue for the organization of generally

unrepresented domestic workers (126–27). One Chicago based organization, the Domestic Workers Association, had about 150 members in 1938 and worked with the support of the NNC, the TUL, the Associated Negro Press, and the Chicago Urban League (Jones 367).

10. Mullen, "Popular Fronts: Negro Story Magazine and the African American Literary Response to World War II," *African American Review*, 30:1 (Spring 1996): 5–15.

11. Cooke, Wilkerson, Yergan and perhaps others were called before the committee. A former *People's Voice* secretary had been employed by the Navy, and her previous work at *People's Voice* led McCarthy to believe that she may have been an infiltrator for the Communist Party, because of the newspaper's connections to the CPUSA (Cooke interview, Yergan Papers). Thus members of the staff during the secretary's tenure were asked to testify as to the political perspective and contacts of the paper.

12. (May 27, 1947, folder 4, Box 3, Max Yergan Papers).

13. Petry, "The Lighter Side," *People's Voice*, July 11, 1942: 20.

14. In describing Petry's return to Old Saybrook, the *Daily Worker*'s Beth McHenry found it necessary to declare Petry's plan to take part in "full-time community activity for at least three months of every year" in an effort tot validate Petry's position as a radical (March 29, 1946: 13).

15. Wright argues that one strategy available to the African American writers is that of showing the absence of solutions like class or racial solidarity: "He may, with disgust and revulsion, say no and depict the horrors of capitalism encroaching upon the human being." In "Blueprint." 36.

16. As Trudier Harris's notes in *From Mammies to Militants*, Lutie absorbs of "the culture into which she moves, [and] concludes that white is indeed right and that is correct to oppress Blacks. She may seek to emulate the white world's pursuit of the American Dream and suffer an attendant corruption of her own values" (17).

17. "Lutie also notes that "[t]hey were so confident about what she must be like that didn't need to know her personally in order to verify their estimate" (46). The white supremacist assumptions of the Chandlers and their ilk erase Lutie's subjectivity, and her painful awareness of this objectification increases throughout her stay, yet does not negate her adoption of their meritocratic beliefs.

18. As Elizabeth Clark-Lewis notes, many domestics found laundry work as a step up from domestic service, granting more autonomy, greater contact with others, and a greater network for politicization (as is evident in Petry's own organizational work among laundry workers). For details on the transition from domestic to laundry worker, see Clark-Lewis's "'This Work Had an End': African-American Domestic Workers in Washington, D.C., 1910–1940." In *To Toil the Livelong Day: America's Women at Work, 1780–1980.* New York: Cornell University Press, 1987.

19. "Class and Color," *The Nation*, 162, March 9, 1946: 292. Bradford Smith, *Saturday Review of literature*, 30:17, October 18, 1947.

20. According to Kate Weigand, in 1949 the Party instituted a Domestic Workers' Union as part of a response to Claudia Jones accusation that there was "neglect" in the Party of black women and their "triple exploitation" (109–11).

21. As Marjorie Pryse states, "Min serves as Lutie's foil for Petry" (124). Carol E. Henderson also considers Min a "counter" to Lutie "'Pattern Against the Sky:' Deism and

Motherhood in Ann Petry's The Street," in *Conjuring: Black Women, Fiction and Literary Tradition* (Bloomington: Indiana University Press, 1985): 126.

22. Min's body itself is inscribed with the effects of her hard work: her slippers contain "a mute testimony to the size of the bunions on her feet," (111). These excruciating bunions are a recurrent concern for Min, and are significantly only relived in her approach to the Prophet's store: "she saw the sign in the window and forgot about the pain" (123).

23. That the Prophet is named David possibly references the biblical myth of David vs. the Goliath, in that the Prophet's power is diminutive compared to the monstrous street.

24. Min's unconventional method of changing her life reflects Robin D. G. Kelley's point in *Race Rebels*, that many "black working people struggled and survived without direct links to the kinds of organizations that dominate historical accounts of African-American and working class resistance" (4). Lutie, too, was once a domestic but, unlike Min, internalized her bosses' individualist, materialistic belief that hard work and ambition will result in success. As a foster mother, Lutie had also worked endlessly. Lutie, now a secretary, is depicted as committed to improving life for herself and her eight-year-old son, Bub, by investing in Ben Franklin's motto of self-help. The end results of her difficult labors disprove American maxims of individualism and industry. The character who does help herself, Min, relies instead on help from her neighbor, from a "root doctor," and through trusting in their advice, is able to leave her abusive relationship with Jones. Min's utilization of the available networks underscores Lutie's alienation.

25. Marjorie Pryse concurs that the street, rather than representing only suffering and poverty, continued within it the forces for collective work: it "does set up alternative forces which provide its denouement.... Petry presents Lutie as simply making the wrong choices, following the wrong models, but finally, the power she needs in order to counter the white world already exists, on the street itself" (123), presumably in the characters of Mrs. Hedges and the Prophet.

26. Margaret Just Wormley's review of *Country Place* cites Ann Petry as an example of "several Negro writers how have made notable departures in the direction of fiction divorced from the color theme" (in *the Journal of Negro Education*, Spring 1948, 169). More recent studies concur, for example Arthur P. Davis pronounces that "*Country Place* is an entertaining work. It is difficult to say more" (195) in *From the Dark Tower: Afro-American Writers from 1900 to 1960*, Washington, D.C.: Howard University Press, 1974. Nick Aaron Ford, in his 1950 condemnation of writers who "abandon racial material and launch out in the 'universal depths'" pronounces that *Country Place* is "greatly inferior" to Petry's first novel, Apparently unaware of Petry's experience growing up in white Old Saybrook, he asserts that her preoccupation with "conjuring up vicarious experiences of a white society with which she was not minutely familiar" resulted in an absence of "a naturalness of expression necessary to good art." However, Petry was perhaps more familiar with white small town life than other writers critiqued for "raceless" narratives.

The relative lack of attention *Country Place* has received is in part attributable to its apparent difference from Petry's other novels and stories that deal with African American characters primarily. Petry was frequently aligned with so-called "raceless" writers like Frank Yerby, Richard Wright, and Willard Motley in the pages of *Phylon* and in secondary scholarship.

Richard Wright himself observes in post-war African American writers, including Petry, a "sharp loss of lyricism, a drastic reduction of the racial content" that he, with reservation, attributes to an improvement in African American status as a result of early Cold War pressures in the United Sates to "put its racial house in order" (*White Man*, 107). Wright, however, appears to embrace the "universalism" in African American literature that others found troubling as an indication that "a humane attitude prevails in America towards us," whereas a return to subjects about racism would indicate "that we are suffering our old and ancient agonies" (108). Petry's *Country Place* and *The Narrows*, both featuring veteran protagonists, reveal the limits of post-World War II racial liberalism through the secondary narratives of domestics who contend with the "ancient agonies" typified by the servant/employer relationship.

27. (March 6, 1946, Boz 164, file 77, Alain Locke Papers, Moorland-Spingarn).

28. Beth McHenry, "Ann Petry Says 'The Street' Is First of Series on Negro Life," *Daily Worker*, March 29, 1946: 13.

29. Petry states that "Old Saybrook is mostly white, so the novel has mostly white characters in it. Besides, I have never wanted to write the same kind of book twice. Writing such a different book was a challenge, but one that I welcomed" (qtd. in Ervin 99). She also states that "I don't know what impelled other black writers to stop writing novels about blacks. . . . I decided to write about that violent, devastating storm and its effect on the town and the people who lived there." (Interview with John O'Brien, in Ervin 75). Such denouement has in part led to the dismissal of *Country Place* as a minor work.

30. Peter Lane was Old Saybrook's pharmacist, and was an important member of the community despite the racism he faced. Petry claimed that Doc "could have been based on my father, except my father was not white, and he was an infinitely kinder man than 'Doc'" (266). "Ann Petry" *Contemporary Authors Autobiography Series, Volume 6*, 253–69. Detroit: Gale Research Company, 1988.

31. Petry also admits that she is "in all of [her characters], I'm even part of the Weasel" ("A Visit" Ervin 83). Mrs. Gramby's compulsive proselytizing quotes presage Cesar's sidewalk writing in *The Narrows*. "The Lighter Side" column is full of such quotations, with a seeming preference for Enlightenment philosophers and nineteenth-century English poetry. For example, in her July 11, 1943 column, she quotes John Donne, and ends with an excerpt of a poem by Edwin Markham (20). She also quotes Henry A. Wallace's statement that "the revolution cannot stop until freedom from want has actually been attained."

32. Mark K. Wilson, "A MELUS Interview: Ann Petry: The New England Connection," in Ervin, *Ann Petry: A Bio-Bibliography*, 93.

33. Margaret Just Wormley noted in a contemporary review that Neola's "active role is small, but demands our attention and respect" (169).

34. Indeed, of all of Petry's domestics, Neola appears the most inscrutable, and the very lack of insight into her thoughts leaves open the possibility that she is as full of insights and angers as Petry's other domestics.

35. Generally, these observations appear to be made by the narrator pharamacist, Doc. Laura Dubrek notes that "[i]n stereotypical fashion, Doc presents [Neola] as the ever-faithful servant who would apparently do absolutely anything to please her employer,"

and chides him for being unable to "imagine even the possibility that Neola feels any-thing but love for Mrs. Gramby" (72). While we might conjecture that Neola, like so many African American domestics, resented her employer, Neola's doting care for Mrs. Gramby, in which she worries over keeping the house a the right temperature, dressing her appropriately for the weather, follows her eating habits, and keeps anxious vigil while Mrs. Gramby is dying, suggests otherwise. Mrs. Gramby conclusion that upon her death, her servant Neola would be the only person guaranteed to pray for her, is perhaps correct. In the context of anticommunism, with an emphasis on loyalty, the novel's conclusion perhaps suggests Petry's promotion of a loyalty to authority figures who ultimately rewards individual allegiance.

36. Lil goes on with a litany of the rebelliousness of the entire staff: "[Neola] never says ma'am to me? Never calls me Mrs. Gramby? Neither does the damn Portegee. He won't even touch his cap to me. And the cook—" (51).

37. However despicable Lil appears with her gold-digging and cruel inaccessibility to her daughter, Petry provides some motivation for these defects. Lil worked for years as a seamstress and resents her customers because of their contemptuous and exploit-ative treatment of her. After she marries the wealth Mearns Gramby, heir to his fam-ily's fortune, the town itself, particularly the Weasel, Doc and Mrs. Gramby, revel in reminding her of her past as a service worker, and Mearns, her husband provides only a small allowance while allowing his mother, Mrs. Gramby, to dominate the marriage. Lil's delusions of real class ascendancy are countered by the scorn of the household staff, who understandably vacillates between coldness, refusing of access to the kitchen, and targeted spitting at her daughter. Arguably, Lil relies on the "wages of whiteness" to psychologically elevate her own position, and becomes entangled in a hatred for those who she feels slight her and an obsession with the failure of those around her to recognize her rags-to-riches narrative. Thus Lil transfers these resentments onto those who she feels are below her because of her whiteness and new class position. Thelma Shinn notes that in *Country Place*, "the shoddiness, the inequities, and false illusions of society, and the inadequacies of the possibilities of women rob strong and weak alike of a chance for personal development and a sense of security." Bernard aptly notes that in fact "Lillian and Glory are the truly marginal characters in this commu-nity" (104).

38. Lil's abuse of the servants extends to "the Bates girl" who comes in on Neola's day off. On the day that Lil planned the murder, Mrs. Gramby marks the impact of Lil's cru-elty in the domestics' response: "The girl had resented the sounds of Lillian's nagging voice and had stared at her with a sullen expression" (155). Mrs. Gramby's concern for her domestics suggests her difference from other employers, and this more sym-pathetic rendering may be related to Mrs. Gramby's shared characteristics, however superficial, with Petry.

39. As Mrs. Gramby contemplates dying, she decides that a will "could cause certain changes in the town. But her reason would be vengeful. Could good come out of evil?" (154). As she realizes she may not survive to make out a will, Mrs. Gramby chastises her own materialist attachment to her mansion, thinking "even dying you think of this house as though it were a world which Lillian would inherit" (158). The Gramby mansion does, in some ways, function as a separate world. After Mrs. Gramby's death,

a Lennox citizen observes that "that big house and all that money set her apart from the rest of us" (184), suggesting that however benevolent Mrs. Gramby appears, her home demarcates class divisions. Weasel, on the other hand, having spent a great deal of time with Mrs. Gramby, says of the house's residents that "[t]hey were a bunch of stuck-up bastards . . . except, of course, the old lady" (77).

40. That Neola does not know how to drive a car indicates her economic position and possibly suggests that, like Lutie, she came to Connecticut as a servant from a city where cars were less necessary.

41. Her assessment of the town in the post-war moment, after the return of soldiers and the graphic revelations about the Holocaust, causes Mrs. Gramby to reflect Lennox's fears that Jewish inclusion in the town would "ruin it," she asks herself "Ruin it for what? For whom? The houses were of no great value" (64).

42. Mrs. Gramby's bequests to Neola, Portalucca, and the Cook recall "The Bones of Louella Brown," in which Mrs. Peabody insists that her African American laundress, Louella, be buried in a cemetery reserved for the most elite members of Boston society. As Amy Lee observes, Mrs. Peabody "challenges the issues of value and property in the public and political realm" (123), and similarly Mrs. Gramby disturbs Lennox's racial and class boundaries.

43. Roger Rosenblatt argues that Lennox "is not available to revenge or to any form of education" because of its racism (138–39).

44. This disruption recalls the attention to private and public space elaborated by Alex Lubin's *Romance and Rights*, which, applied to Neola and Portalucca, gives insight into the dynamics of interracial marriage in the World War II era.

45. Long after the event, Doc Fraser "often wondered why Mearns let her go on screaming her insults at us for so long" (188). This suggests Mearns either seeks to expose his wife's character, or, more likely, he shares some of her prejudices, perhaps informed by the sensationalistic magazines he regularly purchases from the pharmacy.

46. Petry's statement that she is "even a little part of the Weasel" begs the question of which part. Despite the Weasel's own grave defects, he uses his lowly position as cab driver to witness and expose the town's ills, and thus is aligned with Petry's own commitment to rendering social problems to facilitate change, and in this he also offers the sort of disclosures seen in Min and Lutie's accounts of their employers. While the Weasel reveals most of the salacious information, it is Neola who transforms the Weasel's malicious and intrusive meddling into a transformative agent.

47. Bradford Smith, "Glandular Imbalance." *Saturday Review of Literature*, October 18, 1947: 17. The *New York Times* also noted the "Gossip, malice, concoction, infidelity, adultery, attempted murder, sudden death" that occur in the novel, Richard Sullivan, *New York Times*, September 28, 1947: 12.

48. For example, Mary Ross notes, while "using a theme that might have been merely sensational [Petry] builds a novel that has depth and dignity." *New York Herald Tribune*, Book Review, August 16, 1953: 3. Similarly, Wright Morris praises Petry's character development which rescues the novel from the "tissues of tabloid day-dreams" to tell a compelling, intricate character driven narrative. *New York Times*, August 16, 1953: 4. Petry's publishers were well aware of the value in marketing "the explosive situation of a white woman entering a settled Negro world," suggesting that *The Narrows* would

do especially well in newsstands. "Editorial Dopesheet," January 16, 2953, Box 62, folder 1439, The Fales Collection, New York University Library.

49. While Mamie has garnered much of the attention deemed due her in *Time*'s review, most recent studies focus on Link, Camilo, and Abbie Crunch, with minimal attention to Powthers. "Color in Connecticut," *Time*, August 17, 1953: 94, 96.

50. Powther's previous employer, Old Copper, one of the wealthiest men in the nation, with Powther's assistance, purchases highly sexualized black female bodies. After Old Copper orders Powther on a debasing search for an African American nanny who can sing, Powther meets Mamie, whose roommate qualifies for the job. As Malcolm and Mamie take up residence in the Old Copper estate, however, the extent of Old Copper's prerogative eventually turns to Mamie, prompting Powther to find employment with a woman who could assure some protection to his marriage. Petry retreads this juxtaposition between the sexual exploitation of domestics and the power of white wealth and reputation to hide depravity in her account of Link's experience as a twelve-year-old boy employed by Mr. Valkill, a pedophile who attempts to molest Link.

51. Since her husband's death, when she took over active control of the plant, Mrs. Treadway expanded the length of the work day, minimized benefits, and sped-up production. This also coincides with the introduction of automaton and diminution of unions in the early Cold War, and thus reasserts Rabinowitz's point about reportage invoking both history and fiction.

52. The possibility of exposure and the ruin of the Treadway name intensify Powther's allegiance to his employer; indeed he seems to take the suggestion that Camilo was not raped as a personal affront.

53. Even so, Powther's identity rests on this employment, and he responds to the racism of his fellow workers "with a slightly contemptuous air because he had seen better, handled better, and the other servants knew it" (163). Powther copes with the racism of his fellow workers by recalling his history working for wealthier families than the Treadways. He concludes in a metaphor again evoking the military basis of Treadway wealth, that "a war of the kind that he was involved in had to be won quickly, and the ammunition consisted largely of a way of looking down one's nose, and a good stock of stories about the tremendously rich, famously rich, families he had worked for. . . . He won hands down" (163–64).

54. Reflecting on her discovery of Mr. Orwell passed out in a woman's coat, Miss Doris observes that there was nothing more terrible than "a multimillionaire who is far gone in drink" (239). Miss Doris further elaborates on Mr. Orwell's debauchery, describing a train ride where she was "ashamed to be with them, it was just like travelin' in a zoo" (240). The couple's dependence on Miss Doris and Sugar is further illustrated when Mr. Orwell mistakes a woodchuck for a buffalo in the train's lavatory, and cries out for Miss Doris to save him in such a state of hysteria Sugar is forced to physically restrain and silence him. At another point, Miss Doris describes Mr. Orwell as the "nearest thing to an ape I ever saw in human form," and is forced to waken him with the end of an umbrella (238).

55. The glimpse into Miss Doris's life presents one of the few happy marriages Petry presents, and that Sugar (based on the real Miss Doris's husband of the same name) works in the same home as his wife replicates the workplace romance of Portalucca and Neola, suggesting the blurring of one's private and public life that domestic service

requires. Lutie's divorce from Jim because of her absence underscores the degree to which domestic service determined the personal relationships of African American workers.

56. Domestic servant Laetitia Mackey recalls the frustrations and futility of such labor, commenting that "When you come to the point that you just can't go on with this no longer, that you're about to explode, you gotta just stop and catch yourself to keep from tellin these people what you really think" (Hamburger 98).

57. Miss Doris's employers' willingness to hear and act on her words indicates their dependence as well as the ways that alcoholism may have impaired their ability to maintain the absolute authority most employers exercised. The dangers of such open rebellion were recorded in the pages of *People's Voice*, as in the case of a maid who was jailed for three years for treason when she informed her employer that Hitler would "get [the employer] first." "Dixie Domestic Jailed On 'Treason' Charge," March 7, 1942: 3.

58. *The Narrows* contains Petry's most incisive critique of the sensationalistic, racist journalism the *People's Voice* and Petry herself protested in the 1940s. While this is beyond the purview of this essay, it is worth noting that Bullock, *Monmouth Chronicle*'s publisher, bemoans his wife's dependence on an extended household staff, and directly links the practices of cleaning house to that of McCarthyism, stating that "the State Department was acting like a harried housewife, ... searching carefully under beds and in bureau drawers, and on closet shelves, in cellars and attics, peering inside ovens, and sugar bowls, looking in every likely an unlikely place for communists and socialists, for heretics and unbelievers, and uncovering so much dust." He concludes, "What difference does it make ... whether we here in Monmouth hunt down Negroes or whether we hunt down Communists" (378).

"THE HOME AND THE STREET: THE DIALECTICS OF RACIAL PRIVACY IN ANN PETRY'S EARLY CAREER"
John Charles

1. Hazel Arnett Ervin and Hilary Holladay (eds.), *Ann Petry's Short Fiction: Critical Essays* (Westport, CT: Praeger, 2005). *The Critical Response to Ann Petry* (Westport, CT: Praeger, 2005).

2. In his influential study, *The Afro-American Novel and Its Tradition* (1987), Bernard Bell devotes only one brief paragraph to *Country Place* with the explanation that "Because the major characters are white, and because time and place are more important thematically than color and class, it is not as relevant ... to our theory of a distinctive Afro-American narrative tradition as *The Street* and *The Narrows*, her third and best-wrought novel" (180). For interesting recent reconsiderations of *Country Place*, see especially Emily Bernard, "Raceless Writing and Difference: Ann Petry's *Country Place* and the African American Canon," *Studies in American Fiction*, Vol. 33, Spring, no. 1, 2005: 87–117; Laura Dubek, "White Family Values in Ann Petry's *Country Place*," *MELUS: The Journal of the Society for the Study of the Multi-Ethnic Literature of the United States*, Vol. 29, Summer, no. 2, 2004: 55–76. Both Bernard and Dubek foreground Petry's subtle critique of white racial attitudes, though Bernard is more

focused on aligning Petry's novel with the history of black canonization and Dubek's analysis attends to Petry's engagement with contemporary gender constructions. Neither work compares *Country Place* to her other works in this period or addresses questions of privacy. Moreover, I depart from Dubek in her insistence that the entire novel must be read as a projection of Doc Fraser's consciousness. See also, Martin Japtok, "A Neglected Study in 'Whiteness'—Ann Petry's *Country Place*," in *The Critical Response to Ann Petry*, pp. 354–65.

3. In her classic study of black women's labor, *Labor of Love, Labor of Sorrow*, Jacqueline Jones writes that "by 1944 black women constituted 60 percent of all private household workers (up 13 percent over the figure for 1940), reflecting white women's hasty flight from service as soon as the Great Depression ended" (237). This statistic points to the fact that white women dominated the ranks of clerical positions, and that black women, far more than black men and white women, were excluded from nearly all war boom jobs. Moreover, Roderick Ferguson has shown that "with African American women dominating the ranks of prostitution in cities like New York and Chicago, and because of the already existent discourse of black women's sexual appetites, urban black womanhood became synonymous with prostitution" (42).

4. Lauren Berlant has analyzed how women from Harriet Jacobs to Anita Hill have felt compelled to publicly address the nation in the hopes of persuading the state to take an active interest in protecting the private lives of all black women, to remedy the fact that "coerced sexualization has been a constitutive relay between national experience and particular bodies," in this case, "the public history of African American women" (245). These women strive to expose how the nation's rhetoric of abstract formal equivalency obscures the degree to which the white male citizen's "domestic and erotic privilege" is underwritten by sexually denigrated black female (minority) embodiedness.

5. Lubin, along with David Roediger, George Lipsitz, and others, shows how these conditions were also underwritten by decades of national/federal intervention on behalf of whites, including racially structured access to housing, loans, forms of relief, and employment during and after the New Deal and World War II. Roediger has recently shown that these forms of exclusion and white supremacist privilege were even common practice in such overtly egalitarian, anti-racist organizations as the CIO. (See Roediger, *Working Toward Whiteness*, Lipsitz, *The Possessive Investment in Whiteness*.) The most influential discussions of the "domestic imperative" come from Elaine Tyler May, *Homeward Bound: American Families in the Cold War Era*. New York: Basic Books, 1988; Joanne Meyerowitz, ed. *Not June Cleaver: Women and Gender in Postwar America*, 1945–1960. Philadelphia: Temple University Press, 1994.

6. See, Cheryl Greenberg, *Or Does It Explode?: Black Harlem and the Great Depression*. New York: Oxford University Press, 1991; Nat Brandt, *Harlem at War: The Black Experience in World War II*. Syracuse, NY: Syracuse University Press, 1996.

7. Accounts of the riots from historians, sociologists, and writers, including Ellison and Baldwin point to the presence of people from all classes on the streets that night, not just hoodlums. Baldwin writes in his autobiographical essay, "Notes of a Native Son," "that summer I saw the strangest combinations . . . something heavy in their stance seemed to indicate that they had all, incredibly, seen a common vision, and on each face there seemed to be the same strange, bitter shadow" (*Notes of a Native Son* 100).

8. See Ferguson, *Aberrations in Black*; Kevin Mumford, *Interzones: Black/White Sex Districts in Chicago and New York in the Early Twentieth Century*. New York: Columbia University Press, 1997; Daryl Michael Scott, *Contempt and Pity: Social Policy and the Image of the Damaged Black Psyche, 1880–1996*. Chapel Hill: UNC Press, 1997.

9. For two brief considerations, see "Apartheid Among the Dead; Or, on Christian Laughter in Ann Petry's 'The Bones of Louella Brown,'" Gene Fendt; "The Narrator as Feminist Ally in Ann Petry's 'The Bones of Louella Brown,'" Amy Lee in *Ann Petry's Short Fiction: Critical Essays*.

10. *Bereave* derives etymologically from the Old English term, *bereafian*, which means "to rob."

11. The employee who causes the snafu, "Harvard medical student Stuart Reynolds," spends time comparing the bones of the two women because "he was making a private study of bone structure in the Caucasian female as against the bone structure in the female of the darker race, and Louella Brown was an unexpected research plum" (167). Reynolds, like Peabody, exploits Louella Brown's body, appropriating her as an object of racial science in his "private study." The political and "scientific" implications of his discovery are entirely ignored, however; she gains her final resting place in the center of white privilege because of her haunting, not because the public recognizes the bogusness of racial science.

    We might say that Peabody and Reynolds attempted to remand Louella to an absolute sense of privacy—at least in the ancient notion of the term, in which privacy indicated privation—a condition of total alienation from publicly guaranteed rights and agency (see Michael Warner, *Publics and Counterpublics*: ". . . in the classical conception [of privacy] as [Hannah Arendt] interprets it, the private is almost entirely without value, even without content. That, she emphasizes, is the point: the private is privative, a negative category, a state in which one is deprived of context for realizing oneself through action and in free interaction with others. *The most private person is the slave*. The life of the polis is opposed to all that is one's own [idion]—hence a merely private or idiosyncratic person would be an idiot," N. 66, p. 297).

12. The Governor is aware that the value of the "privacy" of his abbey is directly related to a maximal amount of (positive) circulation in the public sphere—the more people who know about the privileged privacy of the abbey (i.e., who know about their exclusion from his familial home), the more valuable it becomes—which makes the idea of the "official opening" of the abbey all the more ironic, given that it closes to the public the very moment that it opens.

13. Berlant argues that "in the fantasy world of national culture, citizens aspire to dead identities—constitutional personhood in its public sphere abstraction and supra historicity, reproductive heterosexuality in the zone of privacy. Identities not live, or in play, but dead, frozen, fixed, or at rest" (60).

14. See Berlant, "The Queen of America Goes to Washington City."

15. See Hughes, "The Negro Artist and the Racial Mountain," 23 June 1926, *The Nation*.

16. See Keith Clark, "A Distaff Dream Deferred? Ann Petry and the Art of Subversion," *African American Review*, Vol. 26, No. 3 (Autumn 1992): 495–505.

17. When asked whether she belongs to a Naturalistic school of writing, she replied: "No . . . it really doesn't interest me. I always want to do something different from what I have done before; I don't want to repeat myself. If I belong to a certain tradition,

I don't want to belong." When asked if she considered herself a feminist, she remarked: "I don't like labels like that. I'm just an individual who has a special way of looking at the world. But I am an ally of feminists, there's absolutely no question about that" (100). See Ervin, *Ann Petry: A Bio-Bibiography.*

18. The most well known contemporary articulation of these limits comes from Zora Neale Hurston, "What White Publishers Won't Print," *Negro Digest,* 8 (April 1950): 85–89; see also Richard Gibson, "A No to Nothing," *Kenyon Review,* XIII (1951): 252–55.

19. See especially Ellen Herman, *The Romance of American Psychology* (1995) for a discussion of the ascendance of psychological discourse into mainstream social and political commentary in the postwar period.

20. Mearns might take some consolation in the fact that he is not alone—the masculinity of nearly every man in the text is compromised in some fashion, either sexually, emotionally, physically, or some combination of all three. Due to limitations of space, I am focusing primarily on Mearns. Johnnie Rhone, however, despite being in many ways the most "healthy" of the men in the narrative, is also cast as having been somewhat smothered by his mother, and thus fairly passive in his relations with his wife, Glory, until the end of the narrative.

21. See George Lipsitz, *The Possessive Investment in Whiteness;* Roediger, *Working Towards Whiteness;* Ferguson, *Aberrations in Black.*

"COUNTER-MODERNITY, BLACK MASCULINITY, AND FEMALE SILENCE IN ANN PETRY'S FICTION"
Melina Vizcaíno-Alemán

1. For discussions of Petry's female characters and proto-feminist politics, see Keith Clark, Kimberly Drake, Joyce A. Joyce, Nellie Y. Mckay, Joyce Pettis, Guy Reynolds, Thelma J. Shinn, Sybil Weir. Nora Ruth Roberts suggests that "Petry was not a feminist in the way that term has come to be defined. Lutie, the heroine of *The Street,* is certainly a strong female protagonist, but clearly Petry was as interested in male characters as she was in female and she cannot rightly be taken up as a grandmother of African-American feminist revolution" (29). The current essay takes up Roberts's claim and analyzes Petry's constructions of masculinity. Petry's work unsettles feminism and blackness and suggests that we reconsider how we define these terms.

2. See Drake for a discussion of Mamie as a "cultural rebel." Also, see Johanna X. K. Garvey for a discussion of Mamie and the blues tradition in Petry's fiction. For a more critical look at Mamie, see Mary Helen Washington.

3. Pettis calls Frances an "androgynous" character who underscores the "supportive and nurturing friendship between women, the kind that has increasingly come to be valued for its role in one's psychological health, as, for example, in the work of Toni Morrison, Paule Marshall, and Gloria Naylor" (118). Pettis also points out that Bill Hod and his partner, Weak Knees, demonstrate androgynous characteristics as well. "Petry surprises readers with Bill Hod's androgynous qualities because she first presents him from Abbie's perspective as a symbol of criminal activity in the community" (18).

Yet, while Pettis makes a connection between Abbie and Camilla, she does not do so between Hod and Camilla.

4. Petry's representation of the Orient differs dramatically from W. E. B. Du Bois's in his 1928 romance novel, *Dark Princess*. Du Bois imagines an international solidarity among dark peoples across the globe through the marriage of a black man and an East Indian princess and their baby. Petry deploys the Orient not as a romantic category but as a symbolic reminder of black men's participation in the U.S.'s foreign and domestic wars. See Paul Gilroy's chapter four, "'Cheer the Weary Traveller': W. E. B. Du Bois, Germany, and the Politics of (Dis)placement," and Bill Mullen's chapter one, "W. E. B. Du Bois's Afro-Asian Fantasia" for discussions of *Dark Princess*.

5. Edward Said's foundational text makes this argument and other postcolonial critics have picked up where Said left off. See Homi K. Bhabha's work for a discussion of ambivalence and the colonized subject, as well as Henry Yu's work on Asian Americans in the twentieth-century U.S. See Bill Mullen for a different approach to the notion of orientalism and the African diaspora.

6. See McKay and Weir.

7. In contrast, Gladys J. Washington argues that "Petry's small-town world is a world that is placid and 'innocent' and appropriately viewed through the eyes of a child. It is a world of pleasant backyards, with lovely gardens, fragrant cherry trees, and 'talking honey bees'" (3). The urban and the rural settings, in Washington's summation, are worlds apart. On the surface, Petry's short fiction maintains this simple dichotomy but symbolically the short stories collapse the distinction between rural and urban spaces.

8. Petry's short stories throw bell hooks's notion of "homeplace" into question by demonstrating how black masculinity overdetermines the realm of feminine resistance within and outside of the home. In an interview with Mary Helen Washington, Petry says, "I think my view of myself was greatly affected by the women in my family. My mother was a chiropodist—one of my aunts was a pharmacist—she graduated from Brooklyn College of Pharmacy in 1908—the only woman in her class. Another aunt was a school teacher who created a very successful correspondence course. These women were role models for me. The left the world of the housewife in the early part of the 20th century—they became financially independent, successful women" (Washington 303). Indeed, what Petry emphasizes in her appraisal of the women in her family is their independence *outside* of the home. Petry tempers the female-centered homeplace that hooks identifies and suggests that women seek independence elsewhere. Her stories suggest that black men, not just white subjugation, restrict black female mobility within the home.

"HUNTING COMMUNISTS AND NEGROES IN ANN PETRY'S *THE NARROWS*"
Farah Jasmine Griffin

1. A few critics have long been devoted to Petry's corpus. These include Hazel Erving, whose tireless efforts have brought us comprehensive bibliographies, biographical information, and collections of critical essays, Diane Issacs, and Heather Hicks.

2. Hazel Carby argues that "In the search for a tradition of black women writers of fiction, a pattern has been established from Alice Walker back through Zora Neale Hurston which represents the rural folk as bearers of Afro-American history and preservers of Afro-American culture. This construction of a tradition of black women's writing has effectively marginalized the fictional urban confrontation of race, class, and sexuality that was to follow Quicksand: Ann Petry's *The Street* (1946); Dorothy West's *The Living Is Easy* (1948); Gwendolyn Brooks's *Maud Martha*. See, Carby, *Reconstructing Womanhood: The Emergence of the Afro-American Woman Novelist* (Oxford, 1997).

3. See Bill Mullen, *Popular Fronts: Chicago and African American Cultural Politics, 1935–1946* (University of Illinois Press); Mary Helen Washington, "Alice Childress, Lorraine Hansberry, and Claudia Jones: Black Women Write the Popular Front" in *Left of the Color Line: Race, Radicalism, and Twentieth-Century Literature of the United States.* Ed. Bill V. Mullen and James Smethurst. Chapel Hill: University of North Carolina Press, 2003: 183–205.

4. Quoted in Gerald Horne, p. 105. Ann Petry to Shirley Graham, 15 July 1946, Shirley Graham Du Bois Papers, Schlesinger Library.

BIBLIOGRAPHY

Anthony, David Henry, III. *Max Yergan: Race Man, Internationalist, Cold Warrior.* New York: New York University Press, 2006.

Barrett, Lindon. *Blackness and Value: Seeing Double.* Cambridge: Cambridge University Press, 1999.

Barry, Michael. "'Same Train Be Back Tomorrer': Ann Petry's *The Narrows* and the Repetition of History." *MELUS* 24:1 (Spring 1999): 141–59.

Bell, Bernard W. "Ann Petry's Demythologizing of American Culture and Afro-American Character." In *Conjuring: Black Women, Fiction and Literary Tradition*, edited by Marjorie Pryse and Hortense J. Spillers. Bloomington: Indiana University Press, 1985: 105–15.

Berlant, Lauren. "The Queen of America Goes to Washington City." In *The Queen of America Goes to Washington City: Essays on Sex and Citizenship*. Durham: Duke University Press, 1997.

Bhabha, Homi K. *Nation and Narration.* New York: Routledge, 1990.

———. *The Location of Culture.* New York: Routledge, 1994.

The Blue Dahlia. Dir. George Marshall. Perf. Alan Ladd, Veronica Lake, William Bendix. Paramount, 1946.

Biondi, Martha. *The Struggle for Civil Rights in Postwar New York City.* Cambridge, London: Harvard University Press, 2003.

Bone, Robert A. *The Negro Novel in America.* 1958. Rev. ed. New Haven, Conn.: Yale University Press, 1964.

Bonn, Thomas. *Heavy Traffic and High Culture: New American Library as Literary Gatekeeper in the Paperback Revolution.* Carbondale, Ill.: Southern Illinois University Press, 1989.

Bruce, Dickson D., Jr. "W. E. B. Du Bois and the Idea of Double Consciousness." In *The Souls of Black Folk: Authoritative Text, Contexts, Criticism*, edited by Henry Louis Gates, Jr., and Terri Hume Oliver. New York: W. W. Norton & Company, 1999.

Carby, Hazel. *Reconstructing Womanhood: The Emergence of the Afro-American Woman Novelist.* Oxford University Press, 1987.

Clark, Keith. "A Distaff Dream Deferred? Ann Petry and the Art of Subversion." *African American Review* 26:3 (1992): 495–505.

———. "'From a Thousand Different Points of View': The Multiple Masculinities of Ann Petry's 'Miss Muriel.'" In *Ann Petry's Short Fiction: Critical Essays*, edited by Hazel Arnett Ervin and Hilary Holladay. Westport: Praeger Publishers, 2004: 79–96.

Clark-Lewis, Elizabeth. "'This Work Had an End': African-American Domestic Workers in Washington, D.C., 1910–1940." In *To Toil the Livelong Day: America's Women at Work, 1780–1980.* New York: Cornell University Press, 1987.

Clippings. Ann Petry Papers. Box 14. Folder 10. Howard Gotlieb Research Center. Boston University.

Currie, Kathleen. Interview with Marvel Cooke, session 4, October 31, 1989. Women in Journalism Oral History Project of the Washington Press Club Foundation. http://npc.press.org/wpforal/cook.htm. April 16, 2006.

Davis, Arthur P. *From the Dark Tower: Afro-American Writers from 1900 to 1960*. Washington, D.C.: Howard University Press, 1974.

Dawahare, Anthony. *Nationalism, Marxism, and African American Literature Between the Wars: A New Pandora's Box*. Jackson: University Press of Mississippi, 2003.

Denning, Michael. *The Cultural Front: The Laboring of American Culture in the Twentieth Century*. New York: Verso, 1998.

Dove, Rita. *American Smooth*. New York: W. W. Norton, 2004.

Drake, Kimberly. "Women on the Go: Blues, Conjure, and Other Alternatives to Domesticity in Ann Petry's *The Street* and *The Narrows*." *Arizona Quarterly* 54:1 (Spring 1998): 65–95.

Dubrek, Laura. "White Family Values in Ann Petry's *Country Place*." *MELUS* 29:2 (Summer 2004): 55–76.

Du Bois, W. E. B. *The Souls of Black Folk*. Edited by David Blight and Robert Gooding-Williams. Boston: Bedford, 1997.

"Editorial Dopesheet." January 16, 1953, Box 62, folder 1439. The Fales Collection, New York University Library.

"Editorial Policy of the *Voice*." *People's Voice*, August 22, 1942.

Ellison, Ralph. *Invisible Man*. 1952. New York: Vintage Books, 1973.

Erickson, Alana J. "Draft: The Bronx Slave Market." http://www.columbia.edu/~aje4/bronx.html.

Ervin, Hazel Arnett. *Ann Petry: A Bio-Bibliography*. New York: G. K. Hall, 1993.

———. *The Critical Response to Ann Petry*. Praeger Publishers, 2005.

Fearing, Kenneth. *The Big Clock*. New York: Harcourt, Brace and Co., 1946.

Feldstein, Ruth. *Motherhood in Black and White: Race and Sex in American Liberalism, 1930–1965*. Ithaca: Cornell University Press, 2000.

Fellig, Arthur [Weegee]. *Naked City*. 1945. New York: Da Capo, nd. "First Novel." *Ebony*, April 1946: 35–39.

Ferguson, Roderick. *Aberrations in Black: Toward a Queer of Color Critique*. Minneapolis: University of Minnesota Press, 2004.

Fluet, Lisa. "Housewife Noir: Accidental Death, Time-Binds, and Negotiation." Negotiation as Theory/Theorizing Negotiation. MLA Convention Washington, D.C. 29 December 2006.

Foley, Barbara. *Spectres of 1919: Class and Nation in the Making of the New Negro*. Urbana: University of Illinois Press, 2003.

———. "From Communism to Brotherhood: The Drafts of Invisible Man." In *Left of the Color Line: Race, Radicalism and Twentieth-Century Literature of the United States*, edited by Bill V. Mullen and James Smethurst. Chapel Hill: University of North Carolina Press, 2003.

Ford, Nick Aaron. "Blueprint for Negro Authors." In *Black Expression: Essays by and about Black Americans in the Creative Arts*, edited by Addison Gayle, Jr. New York: Weybright and Talley, 1969.

Garrett, Lula Jones. *Afro-American* (Baltimore), 13 September 1958: 13. In *The Critical Response to Ann Petry*, edited by Hazel Arnett Ervin. Praeger Publishers, 2005: 32.

Garvey, Johanna X. K. "The Old Black Magic? Gender and Music in Ann Petry's Fiction." In *Black Orpheus: Music in African American Fiction from the Harlem Renaissance to Toni Morrison.* New York: Garland Publishing, Inc., 2000: 119–50.

Gilroy, Paul. *The Black Atlantic: Modernity and Double Consciousness.* Cambridge: Harvard University Press, 1993.

Girson, Rochelle. Rev. of *The Narrows. Hartford Times*, August 15, 1953.

Green, Marjorie. "Ann Petry Planned to Write." *Opportunity* 24 (April–June 1946): 78–79.

Greene, Graham. *The Third Man.* London: Faber and Faber, 1988.

Gwaltney, John Langston. *Drylongso: A Self-portrait of Black America.* New York: First Vintage Books Edition, 1981.

Hamburger, Robert. *A Stranger in the House.* New York: Macmillan, 1978.

Harris, Cheryl. "Whiteness as Property." *Harvard Law Review* 106 (June 1993): 1707–91.

Harris, Trudier. *From Mammies to Militants: Domestics in Black American Literature.* Philadelphia: Temple University Press, 1982.

Herbst, Josephine. *The Starched Blue Sky of Spain.* New York: HarperCollins, 1991.

Himes, Chester. *Lonely Crusade.* New York: Thunder's Mouth Press, 1997.

———. *Plan B.* Jackson: University Press of Mississippi, 1993.

Holding, Elisabeth Sanxay. *The Blank Wall.* 1947. Chicago: Academy Chicago Publishers, 1991.

Holladay, Hilary. *Ann Petry.* New York: Twayne, 1996.

hooks, bell. "Homeplace: A Site of Resistance." In *Yearning: Race, Gender, and Cultural Politics.* Boston: South End Press, 1990: 41–50.

Horne, Gerald. *Race Woman: The Lives of Shirley Graham DuBois.* New York: New York University Press, 2002.

Ivey, James. "Mrs. Petry's Harlem." *Crisis* 53 (May 1946): 154–55.

Jameson, Frederic. *The Political Unconscious.* Ithaca: Cornell University Press, 1981.

Jarrett, Gene. "Introduction: African American Noms de Plume." *PMLA* 121 (January 2006): 245–54.

Jenemann, David, and Andrew Knighton. "Time, Transmission, Autonomy: What Praxis Means in the Novels of Kenneth Fearing." In *The Novel and the American Left: Critical Essays on Depression-Era Fiction*, edited by Janet Galligan Casey. Iowa City: University of Iowa Press, 2004: 172–94.

Jones, Claudia. "An End to the Neglect of the Problems of Negro Women." *Political Affaires*, June 1949: 51–67.

———. "300 Years of an Uphill Struggle." *The Worker*, February 11, 1951: 5.

Jones, Jacqueline. *American Work: Four Centuries of Black and White Labor.* New York: W. W. Norton and Company, 1998.

Joyce, Joyce Ann. "Ann Petry: An Overview of Her Contribution to African-American Literature." *Warriors, Conjurers, and Priests: Defining African-Centered Literary Criticism.* Chicago: Third World Press, 1994: 91–110.

Lattin, Vernon E. "Ann Petry and the American Dream." *Black American Literature Forum* 12:2 (Summer 1978): 69–72.

Lee, Amy. "The Narrator as Feminist Ally in Ann Petry's 'The Bones of Miss Louella.'" In *Ann Petry's Short Fiction: Critical Essays*, edited by Hazel Arnet Ervin and Hilary Holladay. Westport, Conn.: Praeger, 2004: 119–25.

Littlejohn, David. *Black on White: A Critical Survey of Writing by American Negroes*. New York: Grossman Publishers, 1966.

Lubin, Alex. *Romance and Rights: The Politics of Interracial Intimacy, 1945–1954*. Jackson: University Press of Mississippi, 2005.

Marx, Karl. *The Portable Karl Marx*. Ed. Eugene Kamenka. New York: Viking, 1983.

———. *The Poverty of Philosophy*. Moscow: Foreign Languages Publishing House, Third imprint.

Maxwell, William J. *New Negro, Old Left: African American Writing and Communism Between the Wars*. New York: Columbia University Press, 1999.

McDowell, Margaret. "*The Narrows*: A Fuller View of Ann Petry." *Black American Literature Forum* 14 (1980): 135–41.

McHenry, Beth. "Ann Petry Says 'The Street' Is First of Series on Negro Life." *Daily Worker*, March 29, 1946: 13.

McKay, Nellie Y. "Ann Petry's *The Street* and *The Narrows*: A Study of the Influence of Class, Race, and Gender on Afro-American Women's Lives." In *Women and War: The Changing Status of American Women from the 1930s to the 1950s*, edited by Maria Diedrich and Dorothea Fischer-Hornug. New York: Berg, 1990: 127–40.

McKee, Julien. Letter to Victor Weybright. 11 May 1948. New American Library Collection. Series 2, Box 62, Folder 1438. Fales Library and Special Collections. New York University.

Meldon, John. "'The Street'—A Powerful Novel of Harlem Tragedy." *Daily Worker*, March 20, 1946: 11.

Mickenberg, Julia. *Learning from the Left: Children's Literature, the Cold War, and Radical Politics in the United States*. Oxford: Oxford University Press, 2006.

Morgan, Stacey. *Rethinking Social Realism: African American Art and Literature, 1930–1953*. Athens: University of Georgia Press, 2004.

Morris, Wright. "The Complexity of Evil (1953)." In *The Critical Response to Ann Petry*, edited by Hazel Arnett Ervin. Westport: Praeger Publishers, 2005: 27–28.

Mullen, Bill V. *Afro-Orientalism*. Minneapolis: University of Minnesota Press, 2004.

———. *Popular Fronts: Chicago and African American Cultural Politics, 1935–1946*. Chicago: University of Illinois Press, 1999.

Mullen, Bill, and James Smethurst, eds. *Left of the Color Line: Race, Radicalism, and Twentieth-Century Literature of the United States*. Chapel Hill: University of North Carolina Press, 2006.

New Statesman and Nation. Rev. of *The Narrows*. August 14, 1954. Clipping from Petry Papers. Gotlieb Cener: Box 14, Folder 10.

O'Brien, John. *Interviews with Black Writers*. New York: Liveright, 1973.

Ottely, Roi. *"A New World A-Coming": Inside Black America*. Cambridge: The Riverside Press, 1943.

Park, You-me, and Gayle Wald. "Native Daughters in the Promised Land: Gender, Race and the Question of Separate Spheres." *American Literature* 70:3 (September 1998): 607–33.

Petersen, Clarence. *The Bantam Story: Thirty Years of Paperback Publishing*. New York: Bantam Books, 1970.

Petry, Ann Lane. *Country Place*. 1947. New York: NAL, 1947, 1950.

———. *The Drugstore Cat* (illustrated by Susanne Suba). New York: Crowell, 1949.

———. "The Great Secret." *The Writer*, July 1948: 215–17.

———. *Harriet Tubman, Conductor on the Underground Railroad*. New York: Crowell, 1955.

———. *Miss Muriel and Other Stories*. Boston: Houghton Mifflin Company, 1971, 1999.

———. *The Narrows*. Ed. Nellie Y. McKay. Boston: Beacon Press, 1953, 1988. New York: NAL, 1955.

———. "Negro Women Wax Indignant Over Latest Crime Campaign." *People's Voice*, August 15, 1942.

———. Notebooks. Ms. Ann Petry Papers. Howard Gotlieb Archival Research Center. Boston University Library: Box 4, Folder 9 and Box 14, Folder 12.

———. "The Novel as Social Criticism." In *The Writer's Book*, edited by Helen Hull. New York: Harper and Brothers, 1950.

———. *The Street*. Boston: Houghton Mifflin, 1946, 1974.

———. *Tituba of Salem Village*. New York: Crowell, 1964.

———. "What's Wrong with Negro Men?" *Negro Digest* 5 (March 1947): 4–7.

Pettis, Joyce. "Reading Ann Petry's *The Narrows* into Black Literary Tradition." In *Recovered Writers/Recovered Texts: Race, Class, and Gender in Black Women's Literature*, edited by Dolan Hubbard. Knoxville: University of Tennessee Press, 1997: 116–28.

Pryse, Marjorie, and Hortense J. Spillers, eds. *Conjuring: Black Women, Fiction, and Literary Tradition*. Bloomington: Indiana University Press, 1985.

Rabinowitz, Paula. *Black & White & Noir: America's Pulp Modernism*. New York: Columbia University Press, 2002.

———. *Labor and Desire: Women's Revolutionary Fiction in Depression America*. Chapel Hill: The University of North Carolina Press, 1991.

———. "Domestic Labor: Film Noir, Proletarian Literature, and Black Women's Fiction." *MFS Modern Fiction Studies* 47:1 (2001): 229–54.

Redding, J. Saunders. "A Review of *The Narrows* (1953)." In *The Critical Response to Ann Petry*, edited by Hazel Arnett Ervin. Westport: Praeger Publishers, 2005: 25–26.

Reynolds, Guy. "Dysfunctional Realism: Ann Petry, Elizabeth Hardwick, Jean Stafford, Jane Bowles." In *Twentieth-Century American Women's Fiction: A Critical Introduction*. New York: St. Martin's Press, 1999: 146–67.

Roberts, Nora Ruth. "Artistic Discourse in Three Short Stories By Ann Petry." *Women and Language* 22:1 (Spring 1999): 29–36.

Roediger, David. *Working Towards Whiteness: How America's Immigrants Became White. The Strange Journey from Ellis Island to the Suburbs*. New York: Basic Books, 2005.

Rosenblatt, Roger. *Black Fiction*. Cambridge: Harvard University Press, 1974.

Rothman, Stephanie. Lecture. Working Girls Film Series. Walker Arts Center. Minneapolis. 21 May 2005.

———. Personal interview. 21 May 2005.

Ruhm, Herbert. "Raymond Chandler: From Bloomsbury to the Jungle—and Beyond." In *Tough-Guy Writers of the Thirties*, edited by David Madden. Carbondale: Southern Illinois University Press, 1968.

Said, Edward W. *Orientalism*. New York: Vintage Books, 1979.

Schreiber, Rebecca. *The Cold War Culture of Political Exile: U.S. Artists, Writers and Film-makers in Mexico, 1946–1966.* Forthcoming from University of Minnesota Press.

Schreuders, Piet. "The Paperback Art of James Avati." *Illustration* 1 (October 2001): 16–33.

Server, Lee. *Over My Dead Body: The Sensational Age of American Paperback, 1945–1955.* San Francisco: Chronicle Books, 1994.

Shinn, Thelma J. "Women in the Novels of Ann Petry." *Critique: Studies in Modern Fiction* 16:1 (1974): 110–20.

Smethurst, James. *The Black Arts Movement: Literary Nationalism in the 1960s and 1970s.* Chapel Hill: University of North Carolina Press, 2006.

Smith, Erin A. *Hard-Boiled: Working-class Readers and Pulp Magazines.* Philadelphia: Temple University Press, 2000.

Smith, Harrison. "Writers Are Unhappy." *Saturday Review of Literature,* December 28, 1946: 16.

Stein, Gertrude. *The Geographical History of America; or The Relation of Human Nature to the Human Mind.* 1936. Baltimore: Johns Hopkins University Press, 1973.

Stott, William. *Documentary Expression and Thirties America.* 1973. Chicago: University of Chicago Press, 1986.

Sullivan, Richard. "Injustice, Out of Focus." *New York Times Book Review* (28 September 1947): 12.

Tate, Claudia. *Psychoanalysis and Black Novels: Desire and the Protocols of Race.* Oxford: Oxford University Press, 1998.

Taylor, Charles. *Modern Social Imaginaries.* Durham: Duke University Press, 2004.

Taylor, Ivan E. "Review: *The Narrows.*" *The Journal of Negro Education* 23:1 (Winter 1954): 60–61.

Tettenborn, Eva. "Traumatic Reenactment and the Impossibility of African American Testimony in Ann Petry's 'Like a Winding Sheet' and 'The Witness.'" In *Ann Petry's Short Fiction: Critical Essays,* edited by Hazel Arnet Ervin and Hilary Holladay. Westport, Conn.: Praeger, 2004.

"A Visit with Ann Petry." Interview. College of Pharmacy. University of Illinois. Chicago. 16 May 1984. In *The Critical Response to Ann Petry,* edited by Hazel Arnett Ervin. Praeger Publishers, 2005: 77–88.

Wade-Gayles, Gloria. *No Crystal Stair: Visions of Race and Gender in Black Women's Fiction.* Revised and updated. Cleveland, Ohio: Pilgrim Press, 1997.

Wald, Alan. *Exiles from a Future Time: The Forging of the Mid-Twentieth-Century Literary Left.* Chapel Hill: University of North Carolina Press, 2001.

Warner, Michael. *Publics and Counterpublics.* Cambridge: MIT Press, 2002.

Washington, Gladys J. "A World Made Cunningly: A Closer Look at Ann Petry's Short Fiction." In *Ann Petry's Short Fiction: Critical Essays,* edited by Hazel Arnet Ervin and Hilary Holladay. Westport, Conn.: Praeger, 2004: 1–12.

———. "Folk Traditions in the Short Fiction of Ann Petry." In *Ann Petry's Short Fiction: Critical Essays,* edited by Hazel Arnet Ervin and Hilary Holladay. Westport, Conn.: Praeger, 2004: 18–29.

Washington, Mary Helen. "Alice Childress, Lorraine Hansberry, and Claudia Jones: Black Women Write the Popular Front." In *Left of the Color Line: Race, Radicalism, and*

Twentieth-Century Literature of the United States, edited by Bill V. Mullen and James Smethurst. Chapel Hill: University of North Carolina Press, 2003: 183–205.

———. "'Infidelity Becomes Her': The Ambivalent Woman in the Fiction of Ann Petry and Dorothy West." In *Invented Lives: Narratives of Black Women, 1860–1960*. New York: Anchor Press, 1987: 297–306.

Weibe, Paul. "'Miss Muriel': Rewriting Innocence into Experience." In *Ann Petry's Short Fiction: Critical Essays*, edited by Hazel Arnet Ervin and Hilary Holladay. Westport, Conn.: Praeger, 2004: 59–78.

Weir, Sybil. "*The Narrows*: A Black New England Novel." *Studies in American Fiction* 15:1 (Spring 1987): 81–93.

Weybright, Victor. *The Making of a Publisher: A Life in the 20th Century Book Revolution*. New York: Reynal and Co., 1967.

Wormley, Margaret Just. Review of *Country Place*. *Journal of Negro Education* (Spring 1948): 169.

Wright, Richard. (Edwin Rosskam, photo direction) *12 Million Black Voices*. 1941. New York: Thunder's Mouth Press, 1981.

———. *White Man Listen! Lectures in Europe 1950–6*. New York: Harper/Perennial Edition, 1995 (originally 1957).

———. "Blueprint for Negro Writing." In *The Portable Harlem Renaissance Reader*, edited by David Levering Lewis. New York: Penguin, 1995.

Ygelsias, José. "A Classy-Type People." *New Masses* (9 December 1947): 18.

Yu, Henry. *Thinking Orientals: Migration, Contact, and Exoticism in Modern America*. New York: Oxford University Press, 2001.

CONTRIBUTORS

John Charles is an assistant professor at North Carolina State University, where he teaches American literature, literary theory, and Africana studies. He has published essays on Alain Locke, the John Reed Clubs, and Zora Neale Hurston, among others, and is working on a study of the mid-twentieth-century African American novel.

Farah Jasmine Griffin is professor of English and comparative literature and African American studies at Columbia University. She is the author of *Who Set You Flowin': The African American Migration Narrative* (Oxford University Press, 1995) and *If You Can't Be Free, Be a Mystery: In Search of Billie Holiday* (Free Press, 2001) and co-author, with Salim Washington, of the forthcoming *Clawing at the Edges of Cool: Miles Davis and John Coltrane, 1955–1961* (St. Martin's Press).

Alex Lubin is assistant professor of American studies at the University of New Mexico. He is the author of *Romance and Rights: The Politics of Interracial Intimacy, 1945–1954* and is working on a new monograph tentatively titled "Promised Land: 'The Orient' in the African American Global Imaginary" that locates the Levant in the African American anti-colonial imaginary.

Bill V. Mullen is professor of English and director of American studies at Purdue University. He is author of *Popular Fronts: Chicago and African American Cultural Politics, 1935–1946* and *Afro-Orientalism*. He is at work on a book entitled "Unamerican: Reading the Global Du Bois."

Rachel Peterson is a doctoral candidate in the program in American culture at the University of Michigan. She has published essays on Richard Wright, John O. Killens, the radical presses of the Communist Party, the

Student Nonviolent Coordinating Committee, and the economics of anti-communism, among other topics. Her forthcoming dissertation is entitled "Marxist Culture: Race, Gender and History in the Early Cold War."

Paula Rabinowitz is professor of English and Samuel Russell Chair in the Humanities at the University of Minnesota where she teaches mid-twentieth-century cultural studies. She is the author of *Black & White & Noir: America's Pulp Modernism* and *They Must Be Represented: The Politics of Documentary* among other books. Her essay on Ann Petry is part of new project entitled: "The Demotic Ulysses: How Pulp Fiction Brought Modernism to the USA."

Rachel Rubin is associate professor of American studies at the University of Massachusetts Boston, where she is president of the faculty-staff union. She is author of *Jewish Gangsters of Modern Literature*, co-author of *Immigration and American Popular Culture*, and editor of the first scholarly edition of Polly Adler's autobiography, *A House Is Not a Home*.

James Smethurst is an associate professor of Afro-American studies at the University of Massachusetts-Amherst. He is the author of *The New Red Negro: The Literary Left and African American Poetry, 1930–1946* (Oxford University Press, 1999) and *The Black Arts Movement: Literary Nationalism in the 1960s and 1970s* (University of North Carolina Press, 2005). He is also the co-editor of *Left of the Color Line: Race, Radicalism and Twentieth-Century Literature of the United States* (University of North Carolina Press, 2003) and *Radicalism in the South Since Reconstruction* (Palgrave Macmillan, 2006).

Melina Vizcaíno-Alemán is a doctoral candidate in the American studies department at the University of New Mexico. She teaches courses in Southwest and Chicano/a studies, and her research is on the writings of Fray Angélico Chávez. The working title of her dissertation is "Southwestern Literary History and the Writings of Fray Angélico Chávez, 1939–1974."

INDEX

www.ingramcontent.com/pod-product-compliance
Lightning Source LLC
Chambersburg PA
CBHW020658030726
47498CB00002B/565